JSF 1.2 Components

Develop advanced Ajax-enabled JSF applications

Ian Hlavats

BIRMINGHAM - MUMBAI

JSF 1.2 Components

First published: November 2009

Production Reference: 2111209

Published by Packt Publishing Ltd.
32 Lincoln Road
Olton
Birmingham, B27 6PA, UK.

ISBN 978-1-847197-62-7

www.packtpub.com

Cover Image by Vinayak Chittar (vinayak.chittar@gmail.com)

Credits

Author
Ian Hlavats

Reviewers
Cagatay Civici

Ted Goddard

Daniel Hinojosa

Kito D. Mann

Eric Mulligan

Phil Stang

Ghazala Wahid

Matthias Wessendorf

Acquisition Editor
Rashmi Phadnis

Development Editor
Swapna Verlekar

Technical Editor
Namita Sahni

Editorial Team Leader
Akshara Aware

Project Team Leader
Priya Mukherji

Project Coordinator
Prasad Rai

Proofreaders
Chris Smith

Lesley Harrison

Andie Scothern

Indexers
Monica Ajmera

Rekha Nair

Graphics
Nilesh R. Mohite

Production Coordinator
Dolly Dasilva

Cover Work
Dolly Dasilva

Foreword

In the hyper-competitive and opinionated world of Java web frameworks, the strength of the community surrounding the framework is at least as important as the quality of the technology in framework. This statement is supported by the fact that no technology is perfect, there are always omissions and bugs, and the best remedy for these imperfections and flaws is a vibrant developer community from which everyone can pull ideas, workarounds, and help. I've long known of Ian Hlavats and his JSF Toolbox product but finally had the pleasure of meeting him in September 2008 at the first annual North American JavaServer Faces Developer conference. Ian's JSF Toolbox is the realization of one of the core ideas of JavaServer Faces: it takes a team of individuals with varying skills and expertise to build enterprise software, and not everyone on the team is an Object-oriented software developer. In fact, the great majority of the talented web designers practicing today use Adobe Dreamweaver as their workhorse tool. Bringing the power of JavaServer Faces to these users is very important to the success of JSF, and therefore, very important to me.

Just as Ian's tool builds on a core idea of JSF, so does his book: that of the power and centrality of UI components. In this book you'll find a detailed treatment of the most popular JSF component libraries in use as of this writing. Mastering the use of these components is just as important as mastery of the core JSF technology on which they are built. From his vantage point as the developer of JSF Toolbox, and the leader of the successful JSF consulting company Tarantula Consulting, Ian is very well placed to understand how JSF components are used in practice. Complementing this understanding is his sure skill in explaining their use in clear, easy-to-follow prose. I'm sure you'll find this book a valuable addition to your JSF toolbox.

Ed Burns
JavaServer Faces Specification Lead and Expert Group Member
Altamonte Springs 2009

About the Author

Ian Hlavats is an experienced Java developer, architect, consultant, and instructor specializing in JavaServer Faces (JSF). He has successfully designed, implemented, and released many JSF applications. One of his accomplishments is the creation of JSFToolbox for Dreamweaver, a suite of JSF UI development tools, which is now used by Fortune 500 companies and government agencies worldwide.

Ian has been teaching Java programming at the college level and in corporate training environments for several years. Ian was an invited speaker at the JSFOne conference in 2008 where he delivered a presentation on building JSF applications alongside a panel of other JSF industry experts. Ian was also invited to deliver presentations on hands-on JSF design and development using JSF tools such as Eclipse, NetBeans, and Adobe Dreamweaver at the JSF Summit conference in Orlando, Florida in December 2009.

Ian has been working professionally as a Java consultant and Java instructor since 2003. His first project was an internal audit project tracking system for the Government of Canada that was implemented using the Struts, Spring, and Hibernate frameworks, and a MySQL database.

After working extensively with Struts, Ian became very interested in JSF since it solved many issues that Struts did not address. Ian's involvement in the JSF community began around 2005 when he was active on JSF mailing lists, providing feedback and submitting bug reports to the JSF and Facelets development teams. While Ian was employed in the Government, he was also teaching Java courses at the Algonquin College in Ottawa.

Ian left his permanent job in the Government in 2006 to work for his own company, Tarantula Consulting Inc., and pursued Java development contracts with high tech startups and small businesses in the Ottawa area. He worked extensively with JSF and in the process he developed a suite of JSF extensions for Adobe Dreamweaver. JSFToolbox for Dreamweaver was released in 2006 and has since expanded its support for JSF to include new extensions for Facelets, Apache MyFaces Tomahawk, Apache MyFaces Trinidad, ICEfaces, JBoss Seam, and JBoss RichFaces/Ajax4jsf.

From 2007 to 2008, Ian worked as a Java instructor delivering Java training to software architects, engineers, and managers at Cognos/IBM. During this time, he also won a contract to consult on an enterprise Java application for the Government of Canada. Ian conducted an architectural assessment of an existing Java EE application, performed extensive code review, interviewed staff, coordinated with other consultants, prepared a report, implemented his recommendations to improve the Java application architecture, and trained Java development staff. Tarantula Consulting continues to work on JSF projects for high tech startup companies in Canada and the US.

In his spare time, Ian enjoys playing flamenco guitar and taking road trips on a Harley-Davidson motorcycle.

Ian is currently working on a second book on writing custom JSF components.

I would like to extend my sincere gratitude to all the technical reviewers who participated in this project. It means a great deal to me that so many experts and esteemed colleagues in the JSF community would take the time to help me improve this book. I would also like to thank my Java students for all their help over the past two years on my many Java projects. I would also like to thank my partner Helene for all her support and for the endless cups of coffee.

About the Reviewers

Cagatay Civici is the PMC member of open source JSF implementation Apache MyFaces and the project leader of popular PrimeFaces framework. In addition to being a recognized speaker in international conferences such as JSFSummit, JSFDays and local events, he's an author and technical reviewer of books regarding web application development with Java and JSF. Cagatay is currently working as a consultant and instructor in the UK.

Ted Goddard is the Chief Software Architect at ICEsoft Technologies and is the technical leader for the JavaServer Faces Ajax framework, ICEfaces. Following a PhD in Mathematics from Emory University that answered open problems in complexity theory and infinite colorings for ordered sets, he progressed to post-doctoral research in component and web-based collaborative technologies. He has held positions at Sun Microsystems, AudeSi Technologies, and Wind River Systems, and currently participates in the Servlet and JavaServer Faces expert groups.

Daniel ("Danno") Hinojosa is a self-employed consultant from Albuquerque, New Mexico who specializes in development, teaching, and speaking. Danno has been developing enterprise solutions for commercial and government entities since 1999. His primary consulting focus is the design of well-tested web and desktop applications using Java and Groovy. Danno teaches Java, Groovy, Ajax, Automated Testing, XML, and software testing at the University of New Mexico Continuing Education. He is also a co-founder of the Albuquerque Java Users Group. Danno has reviewed a number of books: Seam In Action, Hibernate Search In Action, and Programming Scala.

Kito D. Mann is editor-in-chief of JSF Central (www.jsfcentral.com) and the author of JavaServer Faces in Action (Manning). He is a member of several Java Community Process expert groups (including JSF and Portlets), and Principal Consultant at Virtua, Inc., specializing in enterprise application architecture, training, development, mentoring, and JSF product strategy. Kito has consulted with several Fortune 500 clients, including Prudential Financial and J.P. Morgan Chase & Company, and was recently the chief architect of an educational application service provider. He holds a BA in Computer Science from Johns Hopkins University.

Eric Mulligan is a certified Enterprise Java Developer who studied Java programming with Ian Hlavats. He was employed as a Java developer with Ian's company, Tarantula Consulting Inc., for almost a year on various projects including the JSFToolbox for Dreamweaver suite of extensions.

Phil Stang has been in software development for more than 20 years and has been working with Java since Java 1.01 release. He has developed and led software development teams in the financial, aerospace, and telecom sectors, as well as federal policing. He has been teaching Java since 1997. His hobbies include skiing, windsurfing, and flying model aircrafts competitively.

Ghazala Wahid has more than four years of experience as a Software and Reports Developer. She is a Sun Certified Java Programmer as well as a Sun Certified Web Component Developer.

Matthias Wessendorf is a principal software developer at Oracle. He currently works on server-side-push support for ADF Faces and Trinidad 2.0. Matthias also contributes to the OpenSource community, mainly Apache MyFaces and Apache MyFaces Trinidad. Follow Matthias on Twitter (@mwessendorf).

Table of Contents

Preface

Java developers and Web designers today need more powerful tools to deliver the richer, faster, and smoother web experience that users now demand. JavaServer Faces is an advanced web application framework that includes hundreds of powerful, feature-rich, Ajax-enabled UI components that provide all of the functionality needed to build web applications in a Web 2.0 world.

There has never been a better time to learn JSF. The JSF ecosystem is growing fast and the abundance of JSF components, development tools, industry conferences, and job opportunities is impressive. Learning JSF can be a challenge, but this book makes it easy by showing you the most important JSF technologies and concepts that you need to know to become a JSF professional.

What this book covers

Chapter 1: *Standard JSF Components* introduces you to the JavaServer Faces framework and the key concepts that you need to understand to build simple JSF applications. You will learn about Model-View-Controller, managed beans, the JSF expression language, converters, and validators. You will also discover how to use the standard JSF user interface components (such as text fields, radio buttons, selection lists, and checkboxes) to receive text, date/time, numeric, and other types of input from users as well as handle form submission, render messages, lay out components in a grid, and display a data table.

Chapter 2: *Facelets Components* introduces the Facelets view definition framework and compares it to JSP as the view technology for JSF. You will learn about working with valid XHTML documents and will see examples of how to use the Facelets framework to create simple and complex composite user interfaces based on Facelets templates. You will also learn how to use the Facelets component library to display debugging information, iterate data, include and remove UI components and markup, pass parameters between Facelets pages, create reusable view elements, and apply advanced Facelets templating concepts.

Chapter 3: *Apache MyFaces Tomahawk Components* covers the Apache MyFaces Tomahawk component library and looks at how to use Tomahawk components such as calendars, trees, a file upload component, and navigation menus to solve common web development tasks. You will learn how to use Tomahawk components to validate user input, accept date/time input, upload files, render tree components, create navigation menus, implement user interface security, display sortable data tables, and use newspaper layouts.

Chapter 4: *Apache MyFaces Trinidad Components* discusses the Apache MyFaces Trinidad framework and Ajax technology and will introduce you to many of the 100 plus rich user interface controls in this powerful component library. You will learn how to use color choosers, pop-up calendars, dynamic trees, data tables, a number spinbox, shuttle components, navigation menus, layout panels, and more, to implement typical web development use cases. You will also learn how to use the Apache MyFaces Trinidad dialog framework to add dialog windows to your application, how to enable Trinidad's client-side JavaScript validation, how to create dynamic navigation menus, how to design custom skins and icons for Trinidad's skinning framework, and how to use Trinidad's partial page rendering (PPR) Ajax feature to enhance your JSF pages.

Chapter 5: *ICEfaces Components* introduces the ICEfaces Ajax component library, and explains many of the important concepts that you need to know in order to develop JSF applications based on ICEfaces. You will learn how to use many of the more than 50 Ajax-enabled user interface components in the ICEfaces component library, such as how to add dynamic effects to your pages to enhance input validation, how to use navigation and context menus, how to work with tree components, how to render dynamic data tables that support sorting and paging, how to render pie charts and bar graphs, how to create a tabbed user interface, how to arrange elements using drag-and-drop, how to lay out components in a grid, and how to work with modal dialogs.

Chapter 6: *JBoss Seam Components* covers the JBoss Seam framework and introduces you to the fundamentals of building JSF applications that use the full Java Enterprise Edition (Java EE) technology stack. You will learn how to configure Seam, how to apply Seam annotations to Java classes, and how to use Seam JSF controls to bridge the gap between Enterprise JavaBeans (EJB3) components, the Java Persistence API (JPA), and the JSF framework. This chapter will show you how to validate user input efficiently using Seam, JPA, and the Hibernate Validator framework. You will also discover how to use the Seam tag library and Java API to display validation and success messages, render required field decorations, display debugging information, use Seam's conversation management feature to implement robust JSF workflows, and how to combine Seam with JBoss RichFaces and Ajax4jsf to build next generation JSF applications.

Chapter 7: *JBoss RichFaces and Ajax4jsf Components* covers the JBoss RichFaces and Ajax4jsf component libraries. You will learn how to use many advanced RichFaces components such as in-place editable text, a calendar, an Ajax-based auto-complete suggestion box, rich panel and menu components, a Google map component, a Microsoft Virtual Earth component, dynamic data tables with sorting and paging, data grids, a color picker, a slider component, a number spinner, a picklist control, a rich text editor, and more. You will also learn how to add Ajax support to non-Ajax JSF components with Ajax4jsf, and how to perform advanced Ajax tasks such as submitting forms asynchronously, submitting one component at a time, polling the server, and re-rendering parts of the page after an Ajax request.

Appendix: *Learning JSF: Next Steps* introduces JavaServer Faces 2.0 and provides a summary of the key features in the next generation of the JSF framework. You will discover how JSF 2.0 emphasizes convention over configuration by learning about the new JSF annotations to simplify managed bean configuration and reduce XML, the new JSF resource loading mechanism, the simplified navigation mapping convention, the integration of Facelets into the core JSF framework, the new "composite" JSF tag library for defining composite components, and the significantly improved support for Ajax that is now built-in to the framework. You will also learn about PrimeFaces, a promising new JSF component library.

What you need for this book

To run the example applications included with this book, you will need a Java Servlet/JSP container that supports JSF 1.2 such as Apache Tomcat 6.0 (http://tomcat.apache.org) and a Java EE container such as JBoss Application Server 4.2 (http://www.jboss.org).

The example applications were developed using Eclipse IDE for Java EE Developers (Galileo Release) (http://www.eclipse.org), Adobe Dreamweaver CS4 (http://www.adobe.com), and JSFToolbox for Dreamweaver 3.5 (http://www.jsftoolbox.com). You will also need the MySQL 5.1 database (http://www.mysql.org). The example applications can be downloaded from the publisher's website (http://www.packtpub.com).

Conventions

In this book, you will find a number of styles of text that distinguish between different kinds of information. Here are some examples of these styles, and an explanation of their meaning.

Code words in text are shown as follows: "The following example demonstrates some of the context parameters that we set in web.xml to enable the Facelets ViewHandler."

A block of code will be set as follows:

```
<application>
    <message-bundle>messages</message-bundle>
    <locale-config>
        <default-locale>en</default-locale>
        <supported-locale>fr</supported-locale>
        <supported-locale>es</supported-locale>
    </locale-config>
</application>
```

When we wish to draw your attention to a particular part of a code block, the relevant lines or items will be shown in bold:

```
<h:inputText id="emailAddress"
  value="#{customerBean.customer.emailAddress}"
  required="#{true}">
  <t:validateEmail message="The email address you have
    entered is not valid." />
</h:inputText>
```

New terms and **important words** are shown in bold. Words that you see on the screen, in menus or dialog boxes for example, appear in our text like this: "First let's examine the code for the **Cancel** button."

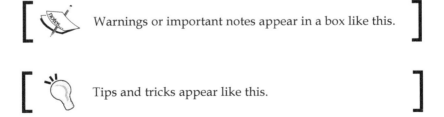

Warnings or important notes appear in a box like this.

Tips and tricks appear like this.

Feedback from our readers is always welcome. Let us know what you think about this book—what you liked or may have disliked. Reader feedback is important for us to develop titles that you really get the most out of.

To send us general feedback, simply drop an email to feedback@packtpub.com, and mention the book title in the subject of your message.

If there is a book that you need and would like to see us publish, please send us a note in the **SUGGEST A TITLE** form on www.packtpub.com or email suggest@packtpub.com.

If there is a topic that you have expertise in and you are interested in either writing or contributing to a book, see our author guide on www.packtpub.com/authors.

Customer support

Now that you are the proud owner of a Packt book, we have a number of things to help you to get the most from your purchase.

Downloading the example code for the book

 Visit http://www.packtpub.com/files/code/7627_Code.zip to directly download the example code.

Errata

Although we have taken every care to ensure the accuracy of our contents, mistakes do happen. If you find a mistake in one of our books—maybe a mistake in text or code—we would be grateful if you would report this to us. By doing so, you can save other readers from frustration, and help us to improve subsequent versions of this book. If you find any errata, please report them by visiting http://www.packtpub.com/support, selecting your book, clicking on the **let us know** link, and entering the details of your errata. Once your errata are verified, your submission will be accepted and the errata added to any list of existing errata. Any existing errata can be viewed by selecting your title from http://www.packtpub.com/support.

Piracy

Piracy of copyright material on the Internet is an ongoing problem across all media. At Packt, we take the protection of our copyright and licenses very seriously. If you come across any illegal copies of our works in any form on the Internet, please provide us with the location address or website name immediately so that we can pursue a remedy.

Please contact us at copyright@packtpub.com with a link to the suspected pirated material.

We appreciate your help in protecting our authors, and our ability to bring you valuable content.

Questions

You can contact us at questions@packtpub.com if you are having a problem with any aspect of the book, and we will do our best to address it.

1
Standard JSF Components

The components and examples covered in this chapter have been selected to introduce a number of important concepts for developing JSF user interfaces. It is necessary to understand the basic JSF components because they are the building blocks from which other components and component libraries are derived.

We will begin by looking at a number of common web application development tasks and how they can be implemented using standard JSF components. In the process, we will learn how to use other JSF artifacts, such as managed beans, converters, validators, and more.

An introduction to JSF

While the main focus of this book is learning how to use JSF UI components, and not to cover the JSF framework in complete detail, a basic understanding of fundamental JSF concepts is required before we can proceed. Therefore, by way of introduction, let's look at a few of the building blocks of JSF applications: the Model-View-Controller architecture, managed beans, EL expressions, converters, and validators.

The Model-View-Controller architecture

JSF is based on the **Model-View-Controller** (**MVC**) architecture. The *Model* in MVC represents the data of the application, and is typically implemented using **Plain Old Java Objects** (**POJOs**) based on the JavaBeans API. The *View* in MVC represents the user interface of the application and is responsible for rendering data and user interface controls to the user. The *Controller* in MVC represents an object that responds to user interface events and deals with querying or modifying the Model.

Managed beans

Managed beans are the Controllers of a JSF application, handling events in the user interface and updating the Model in response to user interaction. A **managed bean** is simply a Java class with instance variables and methods that are coupled to the application's domain model and to JSF's event handling API.

The JSF Expression Language (JSF EL)

The **JSF Expression Language** (**JSF EL**) is a simple, powerful, object-oriented, and typesafe scripting language used to bind UI components to managed bean properties and methods. The following example shows how to display a customized welcome message that references a backing bean property using the JSF EL:

```
<h:outputText value="Hello, #{backingBean.username}" />
```

Converters and validators

JSF includes standard converters for common data types such as numbers, Boolean values, and dates, and also supports custom converters for handling user-defined data types. Additionally, JSF includes standard validators for typical input validation scenarios such as checking required fields and numbers, and also supports custom validators. We will see a number of both, standard converters and validators and custom convertors and validators, throughout this book.

Next steps

Now that we have introduced the Model-View-Controller pattern, managed beans, the JSF Expression Language, and converters and validators, we are ready for a more in-depth discussion on how to use JSF UI components effectively to perform common web development tasks. Specifically, we will look at the following use cases:

- Getting input from the user
- Form submission
- Rendering text
- Making selections
- Laying out components
- Displaying tabular data

Getting input from the user

Accepting input from a user is one of the most common scenarios for web application developers. User input is typically character data that represents different types of information, such as dates, numbers, and text. JSF includes a number of standard components that represent HTML form elements that can be used to collect this information from users.

The HtmlInputText component, for example, is a good choice for accepting short textual input from the user. For use cases that require more text, such as a memo field or comment box, the HtmlInputTextarea component is a better choice as it can accommodate multiline text entry more easily.

Rendering a text field

The following example demonstrates how to accept text input from the user:

```
<f:view>
  <h:form>
    <div>
      <h:outputLabel for="name" value="Enter your name: " />
      <h:inputText id="name" value="#{backingBean.name}" />
      <h:commandButton value="Submit" />
    </div>
    <div>
      <h:outputText value="Hello, #{backingBean.name}"
        rendered="#{backingBean.name ne null and
        backingBean.name ne ''}" />
    </div>
  </h:form>
</f:view>
```

Notice the value attribute of the <h:inputText> tag. The text field is bound to a backing bean String property using the JSF Expression Language (JSF EL). When the form is submitted, the property is set to the value of the text entered by the user.

This example also demonstrates conditional rendering of JSF components. Most JSF tags support the `rendered` attribute. This attribute allows us to control when a JSF component should be displayed on the page. In this case, the `<h:outputText>` tag is conditionally rendered when the backing bean's `name` property is not null and is not equal to an empty string.

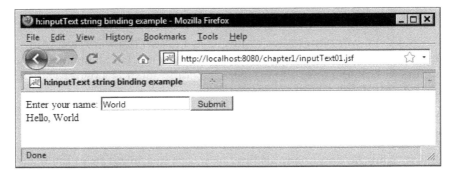

In the next example we will use a text field to receive a date value from the user. First we register the standard JSF date time converter on the UI component by nesting the `<f:convertDateTime>` tag inside the `<h:inputText>` tag. This converter will attempt to convert the text entered by the user to a date by using the conversion pattern specified in the `pattern` attribute. Next we register a custom date validator to make sure that the converted date value represents a valid birth date. The error message rendered below the text field was produced by our validator class.

```
<f:view>
<h:form>
   <div>
      <h:outputLabel for="name"
        value="Enter your birthdate (M/d/yyyy): " />
      <h:inputText id="name" value="#{backingBean.date}">
         <f:convertDateTime type="date" pattern="M/d/yyyy" />
         <f:validator validatorId="customDateValidator" />
      </h:inputText>
      <h:commandButton value="Submit" />
   </div>
   <h:message for="name" style="display:block"
     errorStyle="color:red" />
   <div>
      <h:outputText value="You were born on "
        rendered="#{backingBean.date ne null}" />
      <h:outputText value="#{backingBean.date}">
         <f:convertDateTime type="date" dateStyle="full" />
      </h:outputText>
   </div>
</h:form>
</f:view>
```

The following screenshots demonstrate a custom date validator class that determines if a date represents a valid birth date. The error message rendered below the text field was produced by our validator class.

When the validation is successful, our backing bean property is updated and the view is rendered again in the browser. This time, our conditionally rendered message is displayed to the user.

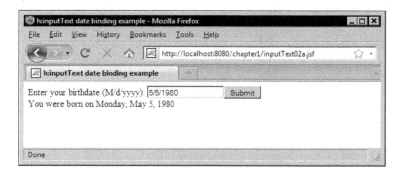

The next example shows how to accept numeric input from the user. JSF includes built-in converter classes that handle conversions between character data (strings) and Java data types, such as `Integer`, `Boolean`, `Float`, `Long`, and so on. In this example, we specify that the text field component can only accept a whole number between 20 and 50 by using the `<f:validateLongRange>` tag to register a standard validator on the component.

```
<h:inputText id="number" value="#{backingBean.number}">
  <f:validateLongRange minimum="20" maximum="50" />
</h:inputText>
```

Note that the error message below the text field was produced by the built-in JSF `NumberConverter` class and is the default text for this particular error. We can override the default JSF conversion and validation error messages by declaring messages with the same keys in our resource bundle.

If we enter a non-numeric value, we will receive an appropriate error message:

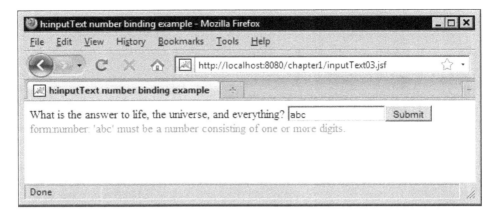

If the number is not in the specified range, we will also get an error:

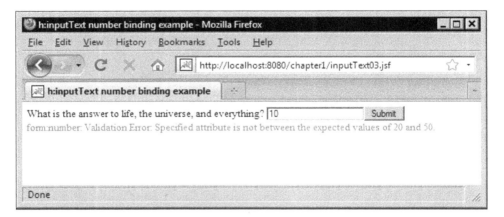

JSF validation messages

The JSF framework includes predefined validation messages for different validation scenarios. These messages are defined in a message bundle (properties file) including the JSF implementation JAR file. Many of these messages are parameterized, meaning that as of JSF 1.2, a UI component's `label` attribute value can be inserted into these messages; the default JSF validation messages can be overridden by specifying the same message bundle keys in the application's message bundle.

Finally, the value is accepted by the converter and our view is updated, displaying another conditionally rendered HtmlOutputText component.

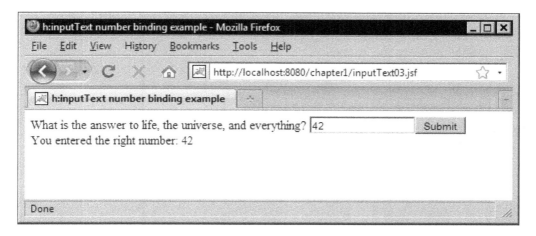

Rendering a text area

The HtmlInputTextarea component is identical to the HtmlInputText component, except that it can specify rows and cols attributes to control the width and height of the text area.

```
<h:inputTextarea rows="10" cols="80"
  value="#{backingBean.description}" />
```

Form submission

When the user clicks on a button or a link with JavaScript enabled, the browser collects the HTML form data and submits it to the web server for processing. It is important to note that web pages may contain multiple forms, provided that the forms are not nested. Also, typically the browser can only submit one form at a time. (We will look at how to use Ajax to submit multiple forms at the same time, later in this book.) Therefore, any UI components that should have their values included in the JSF lifecycle for a particular request should be contained within the same form. In this section, we will look at common ways to submit an HTML form using JSF components.

The standard JSF HTML component library includes components that can be used to render and submit an HTML form. Any components within the form are included in the form submission and will have their user input values sent to the server, converted, and validated during the JSF request processing lifecycle.

Rendering a form

To display a form on a JSF page, you can use the `<h:form>` tag. This tag renders a `UIForm` component as an HTML form using the default HTML RenderKit. This produces an HTML form tag at request time. In JSF, we should always use the `<h:form>` tag and not the actual HTML form tag to render a form because the JSF `<h:form>` tag renders additional hidden form fields containing important information about the UI component tree for the current view.

The `<h:form>` tag component is very common in JSF views, as almost all components need to be included in a form in order to be functional. A JSF view may contain several forms, and in general it is a good idea to divide your user interface into separate forms when it can accept different types of unrelated information from the user.

A good example is a JSF view that has a page header with a user sign-in form, and a content area with a user feedback form. The UI components and bindings involved in authentication have nothing to do with the components and bindings involved in gathering feedback from the user, so these two groups of components should be organized into separate forms. In JSF, all the components in a form are updated when that form is submitted. Therefore, we want to group related controls together and isolate them from groups of other, unrelated controls.

Before an HTML form can be submitted, the user must click on or invoke a user interface component that has been designated as a form submission component. Typically, this is an HTML input element of the type `submit` or `image` rendered as a button or an image in the browser, but using JavaScript it can also be a hyperlink, checkbox, radio button, select menu, or any other visible or non-visible element on the page.

To begin with a simple example, let's look at how to submit a form using a button or a link component. The standard JSF component library includes two components that are commonly used to submit a form. The `HtmlCommandButton` component is rendered as a submit button by the `<h:commandButton>` tag, and the `HtmlCommandLink` component is rendered as a hyperlink by the `<h:commandLink>` tag.

Rendering a button

The `<h:commandButton>` tag should have at least a label value. In this example, the component simply submits the form when it is invoked, and nothing else.

```
<h:commandButton value="Submit" />
```

The `HtmlCommandButton` component can also invoke our application logic when it is pressed. The component in this example now submits the form and, if conversion and validation are successful, it then calls a method in our backing bean. This is achieved by specifying a method expression for the button using the JSF EL. We can "wire" several `HtmlCommandButton` components to different methods in our backing bean.

```
<h:commandButton value="Add"
  actionListener="#{backingBean.addWord}" />
<h:commandButton value="Remove"
  actionListener="#{backingBean.removeWord}" />
```

The Java method in our `BackingBean` class would be implemented as follows:

```
public void removeWord(ActionEvent event) {
    words.remove(word);
}
```

In this example, we can add to or remove words from a collection of words that is stored in our backing bean using a simple JSF user interface.

Rendering a link

The `<h:commandLink>` tag is similar to the `<h:commandButton>` tag. The `value` attribute also specifies the label, and both the tags have an `actionListener` attribute that registers a backing bean method on the component using a JSF EL method expression.

```
<h:commandLink value="Add"
  actionListener="#{backingBean.addWord}" />
<h:outputText value=" | " />
<h:commandLink value="Remove"
  actionListener="#{backingBean.removeWord}" />
```

The same screen continues to function in exactly the same way after we replace our command buttons with command links.

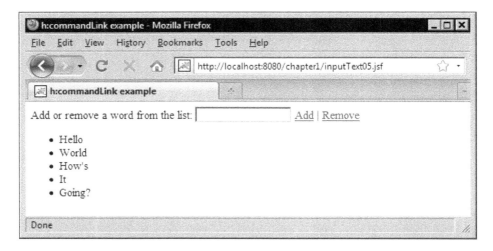

Rendering text

Another common task for web applications is to render text in the browser. The HTML markup language includes a number of elements that can be used to render text. JSF includes standard components that represent these HTML elements and extend their capabilities to include support for internationalization, conditional rendering, formatted text, validation messages, and more.

Many elements in HTML, such as `<p>`, `<div>`, `<span>`, and `<label>` for example, can be used to render text. The JSF `<h:outputText>` tag renders the `HtmlOutputText` component as an arbitrary text value or as a `<span>` element that contains text if CSS attributes on the tag are set. The `<h:outputText>` can be used to render plain text or HTML that originates from the backing bean.

The `value` attribute of the tag specifies the text to be rendered. If we are rendering HTML, we should make sure to set the `escape` attribute to false so that the HTML is rendered properly in the browser. The `<h:outputText>` tag can also be used to render arbitrary Java objects, such as `Date`, `Integer`, `Float`, and other types. When the `value` attribute contains an EL expression that evaluates to a Java type other than `String`, the component attempts to render the value as a string. If a converter is registered on the component, the converter is responsible for converting the object to a string.

One of the uses of the `HtmlOutputText` component is to display localized messages. Let's look at a few examples of how to use this component to internationalize our JSF pages. In the process, we will have the opportunity to look at the JSF framework's internationalization support in more detail.

Rendering localized text

One of the many benefits of the JSF framework is the ability to easily internationalize our applications. As the format of date and time, numbers, and currency values can change significantly from one locale to another, JSF conveniently extends Java's internationalization (I18N) support to our user interface.

For demonstration, our JSF application will support three locales: English (our default locale), French, and Spanish. Localized messages will be stored in three message bundles named "messages_en.properties", "messages_fr.properties", and "messages_es.properties".

Since JSF 1.2, there are two ways to make message bundles available to web pages in our JSF applications.

Registering a message bundle (JSF 1.1)

Registering a message bundle in JSF 1.1 requires adding the following XML to the `faces-config.xml` file:

```xml
<application>
    <message-bundle>messages</message-bundle>
    <locale-config>
       <default-locale>en</default-locale>
       <supported-locale>fr</supported-locale>
       <supported-locale>es</supported-locale>
    </locale-config>
</application>
```

Notice that we specify the name of the message bundle properties file (without the locale information and without the `.properties` file extension) for the `<message-bundle>` element. Next, we specify the locales supported by our JSF application in the `<locale-config>` element, indicating that English (en) is our default locale. To use our message bundles, we need to declare the `<f:loadBundle>` tag in our JSF pages:

```xml
<f:view>
  <f:loadBundle var="bundle" basename="messages" />
  <h:outputText value="#{bundle.welcomeMessage}" />
</f:view>
```

Registering a message bundle (JSF 1.2)

Since JSF 1.2, there is a more efficient way to use message bundles in our JSF pages. Instead of loading our message bundle on each page using the `<f:loadBundle>` tag, we can simply declare our message bundle once in `faces-config.xml` and use it from any page in our JSF application. The following XML must be added to `faces-config.xml` to enable this feature:

```
<application>
  <resource-bundle>
    <base-name>messages</base-name>
    <var>bundle</var>
  </resource-bundle>
</application>
```

The following example demonstrates how we can render our localized text in a JSF page using the `<h:outputText>` tag. In this example, the text is rendered from our default message bundle for the English locale.

```
<f:view>
  <f:loadBundle basename="messages" var="bundle" />
  <h:outputText value="#{bundle.welcomeMessage}
    (#{view.locale.displayName})" />
</f:view>
```

Developer tip: Message bundle keys and the JSF EL

Due to the syntax of the JSF expression language, if we use the "dot" notation as in the expression `#{bundle.welcomeMessage}`, then we must take care to choose valid key names for our message bundle. This means avoiding periods and spaces and using only letters and numbers for any message bundle keys we want to use in our JSF pages. Alternately, we can use the "map" notation as in the expression `#{bundle['another.message.key']}` to specify any arbitrary message bundle key containing any acceptable key characters supported by the Java properties file format.

Our message bundle contains the following key/value pair:

```
welcomeMessage=Welcome!
```

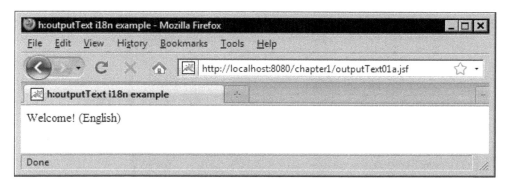

In the next example, we hardcoded the locale of our view by setting the `locale` attribute of the `<f:view>` tag to the French locale in a separate view, and the JSF framework loaded the messages from our French message bundle.

```
<f:view locale="fr">
  <f:loadBundle basename="messages" var="bundle" />
  <h:outputText value="#{bundle.welcomeMessage}
    (#{view.locale.displayName})" />
</f:view>
```

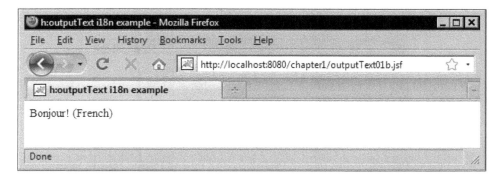

We created a third view for the Spanish locale. As we also configured a message bundle for this locale, JSF was able to render localized messages for this locale.

```
<f:view locale="es">
  <f:loadBundle basename="messages" var="bundle" />
  <h:outputText value="#{bundle.welcomeMessage}
    (#{view.locale.displayName})" />
</f:view>
```

Creating separate pages for each locale is one approach to implement internationalization in JSF. Another approach that we can use is to create a single view without specifying the locale and let the JSF framework determine the appropriate message bundle to use, based on the locale sent by the user's browser. As users can configure their browsers to specify their preferred languages, our JSF application can rely on this information to identify the user's locale.

Detecting the browser's locale in a single view can be a more efficient approach, as we no longer have to maintain a different copy of the view for each supported locale.

If the user's locale is not supported, they will see messages for our application's default locale.

Another use of the `<h:outputText>` tag is to render text conditionally. For example, we may want to display a message to the user only if he/she is currently logged into our web application. For this purpose, we can use the `rendered` attribute of the `<h:outputText>` tag. This attribute accepts a Boolean value, and we can use an EL expression to determine if the component should be visible or not.

Rendering date/time information

Web applications often have to display dates, currencies, numbers, and other types of information to the user in a variety of ways. For example, you may want to display the date January 1, 2009 in the short format "01/01/09", in the medium format "Jan 1, 2009", or in the long format (including time information) "Thursday, January 1, 2006 5:30:15 PM".

Conveniently, the JSF Core tag `<f:convertDateTime>` can be nested inside an `<h:outputText>` tag to control date/time formatting. The following example demonstrates date/time formatting using the `<f:convertDateTime>` tag. In this case, we display the date using the "full" date/time style.

```
<h:outputText value="You were born on "
  rendered="#{backingBean.date ne null}" />
<h:outputText value="#{backingBean.date}">
  <f:convertDateTime type="date" dateStyle="full" />
</h:outputText>
```

The <h:outputText> tag is also locale aware, so it renders the date according to the formatting conventions of the current locale.

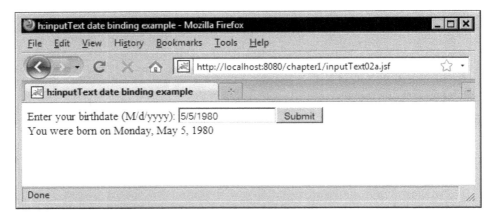

The <h:outputText> tag is a very flexible JSF component that supports a wide range of text rendering situations.

Rendering parameterized text

Sometimes we want to render formatted text that contains parameters to be specified later. JSF includes the <h:outputFormat> tag for this purpose. It is able to render messages that contain special placeholders that can be filled in at runtime. Let's look at how to render parameterized messages using the HtmlOutputFormat component.

In this example, we render a parameterized string from our message bundle and replace the parameters with values obtained from the query string, the current view, and our backing bean. The process of replacing parameters with values in a parameterized string is called **interpolation**. This example also demonstrates the flexibility of the JSF expression language. We are literally able to plug in values from just about any source of information available to our web page.

```
<h:outputFormat value="#{bundle.welcomeMessage2}">
  <f:param value="#{param.username}" />
  <f:param value="#{view.locale}" />
  <f:param value="#{backingBean.today}" />
</h:outputFormat>
```

The parameterized message is defined in our message bundle. We will have a similar definition for each locale.

```
welcomeMessage2=Welcome {0}, your locale is {1}. The current date is
{2}.
```

First, we configure our browser to use English as our preferred language.

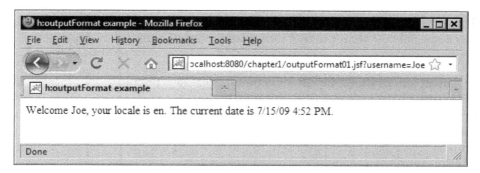

Next, we set French as our preferred language.

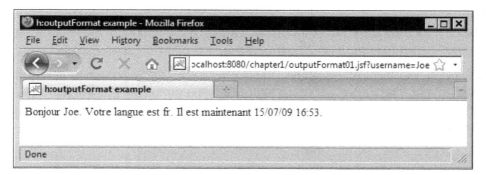

On our third try, we set Spanish as our preferred language.

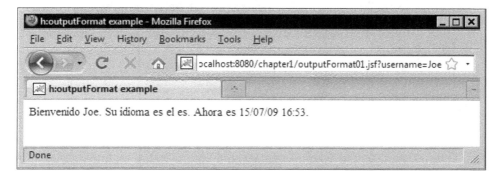

Rendering labels

When marking up our JSF pages, we should take care to provide proper labels for components to give them a clear purpose in our user interface. This way, users will have an easier time learning how to use our JSF applications.

When rendering labels, it is more appropriate to use the HTML `<label>` element than to use a `<span>` element. For this purpose, we can use the JSF `<h:outputLabel>` tag. This tag renders an `HtmlOutputLabel` component as an HTML `<label>` element and has a special `for` attribute that identifies the input component represented by the label.

A nice feature about this component is that it improves the usability of forms in web browsers by providing additional information about the relationship between text labels and form controls. One enhancement in particular is that users can now click on a radio button or checkbox label to change the selection state of the control. This makes a web page more intuitive to the user and also provides accessibility information for screen readers and assistive devices.

To set the text displayed by an `<h:outputLabel>` tag, you can specify a string literal or a JSF EL value expression for the `value` attribute of the tag. You can also nest an `<h:outputText>` tag inside an `<h:outputLabel>` tag, in which case the text will be provided by the child component. The `<h:outputLabel>` tag has the same internationalization support as the `<h:outputText>` tag.

This example shows how to use the `<h:outputLabel>` tag in conjunction with another JSF tag. The important thing to notice is the use of the `for` attribute. It expects the ID of another component on the page and informs the browser that the label is intended for that particular component.

```
<h:outputLabel value="Remember Me" for="remember" />
<h:selectBooleanCheckbox id="remember"
  value="#{backingBean.rememberMe}" onclick="submit()" />
```

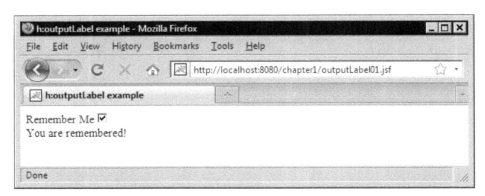

For our final example of text rendering JSF components, we can examine the <h:outputFormat> tag. This tag renders an HtmlOutputFormat component as formatted text within the JSF page. Formatted text can include a localized message from the application's message bundle for the current locale, or it can include a string pattern that is evaluated at request time. Interestingly, this string pattern can have placeholders that are substituted by any nested <f:param> tags.

So for example, if we wanted to render the message "Welcome, username", we could use an <h:outputFormat> tag that contains a parameter for the user's name. The value substituted for this parameter would be defined by a child <f:param> tag, so the actual name of the user could come from a database, an LDAP directory, or another source. The important point is that this tag simplifies a very common task for web applications, namely rendering localized, parameterized text messages conveniently and easily.

Rendering a validation message

The <h:message> tag renders an HtmlMessage component and is useful for displaying validation messages in a JSF page. It is important to include this tag on our JSF pages so that users will be informed when a JSF validation message occurs. Typically, the tag is placed immediately after a JSF component tag to display the validation messages for the associated component.

In this example, we render an HtmlInputText component and specify through the <h:inputText> tag's required attribute that the user is expected to enter a value into to the first name text field. If the user submits the form without entering a value, an error message will be rendered by the <h:message> tag beside the component. The for attribute is required and is used to associate the message with a particular UI component on the page. It expects the ID of the component that the message is for.

```
<h:inputText id="firstName"
  value="#{customerBean.customer.firstName}"
  required="true" />
<h:message for="firstName" errorClass="error"
  showSummary="true" showDetail="false" />
```

Rendering all validation messages

The `<h:messages>` tag is similar to the `<h:message>` tag except that it renders an `HtmlMessages` component that displays all validation messages for any components in the view in an unordered list. This is useful when our user interface requirements call for presenting all error messages in one place, for example, above any form fields on the page. The `globalOnly` attribute is false by default, but if we set it to true, then the component only displays messages generated by the application that are not associated with a particular component.

```
<h:messages errorClass="error" globalOnly="false" />
```

Making selections

Presenting the user with a choice from a list of available values is a common scenario for web-based applications. The HTML markup language includes a number of form elements that can be used to provide users with a list of options from which a selection can be made. Choosing the right HTML element or set of elements for a particular form depends on a number of criteria and is a common stumbling block for developers who are new to HTML. Fortunately, the standard set of JSF HTML components greatly simplifies the correct use of HTML selection elements. In later chapters, we will discover how other JSF component libraries introduce a rich and innovative set of user interface controls that can significantly extend the capabilities of HTML as a GUI toolkit.

Before we discuss JSF HTML selection components, let's consider the HTML elements that they represent. The HTML markup language includes a limited set of selection components such as checkboxes, radio buttons, and select menus. Both checkboxes and radio buttons are represented by the `<input>` element with different `type` attributes. A checkbox is rendered using the `<input>` element with the `type` attribute set to "checkbox", while a radio button is rendered using the `<input>` element with the `type` attribute set to "radio".

Both checkboxes and radio buttons can be grouped together to present the user with a range of inclusive or exclusive options. The HTML 4.01 specification explains that checkboxes are grouped together by users to represent several mutually inclusive options, while radio buttons are grouped together to represent mutually exclusive options.

For more details, refer W3C to Forms in
the W3C HTML 4.01 Specification: 13 July 2009
`http://www.w3.org/TR/html401/interact/forms.html`.

Checkboxes can also be rendered individually, representing a Boolean choice of true or false. A radio button should not be rendered individually because to the user that represents a mutually exclusive choice from a set of only one possible option! In addition, once the user selects a radio button it can only be deselected by choosing another radio button in the set, or by using JavaScript to override the default behavior of this control.

The standard JSF HTML component library includes several components for rendering radio buttons and checkboxes in our JSF pages. Depending on our needs, we might use the `<h:selectBooleanCheckbox>` tag, the `<h:selectManyCheckbox>` tag, or the `<h:selectOneRadio>` tag.

The `<h:selectBooleanCheckbox>` tag renders a single checkbox and is useful for presenting a Boolean option, such as a "remember me" checkbox in a login dialog. The `<h:selectManyCheckbox>` tag renders a set of checkboxes that can be used to display multiple of Boolean options to the user, for example, a list of interests for a newsletter subscription form. The `<h:selectOneRadio>` tag renders a set of radio buttons that can be used to present a set of mutually exclusive options such as a level of satisfaction on a scale from "very unsatisfied" to "very satisfied" in a customer feedback survey.

Rendering a checkbox

Recall from the `<h:outputLabel>` example that a label references another component's ID attribute in the label's `for` attribute. One of the benefits of the correct use of this component is that for certain components, browsers will recognize the label as an extension of the component itself and will allow users to click the label to toggle the component state. In this example, we use JavaScript to submit the form when the user clicks the checkbox.

```
<h:outputLabel value="Remember Me" for="remember" />
<h:selectBooleanCheckbox id="remember"
  value="#{backingBean.rememberMe}" onclick="submit()" />
```

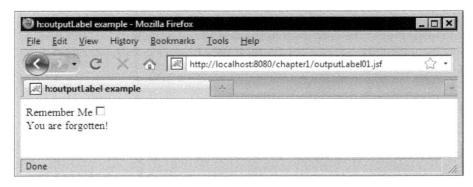

Rendering multiple checkboxes

This example demonstrates how to use the `<h:selectManyCheckbox>` tag. Notice that the options are defined using nested `<f:selectItem>` tags. The `itemLabel` attribute is what is displayed to the user, while the `itemValue` attribute is what is submitted to the server when the form is posted.

```
<h:selectManyCheckbox id="interests"
   value="#{customerBean.interests}" layout="lineDirection">
   <f:selectItem itemLabel="Java" itemValue="Java" />
   <f:selectItem itemLabel="Architecture" itemValue="Architecture" />
   <f:selectItem itemLabel="Web Design" itemValue="Web Design" />
   <f:selectItem itemLabel="GUI Development"
                 itemValue="GUI Development" />
   <f:selectItem itemLabel="Database" itemValue="Database" />
</h:selectManyCheckbox>
```

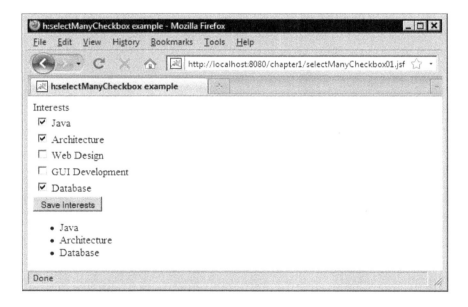

The same example can be rewritten to display the options horizontally instead of vertically by setting the `layout` attribute of the `<h:selectManyCheckox>` tag to `pageDirection` as follows:

```
<h:selectManyCheckbox id="interests"
   value="#{customerBean.interests}" layout="pageDirection">
   <f:selectItem itemLabel="Java" itemValue="Java" />
   <f:selectItem itemLabel="Architecture" itemValue="Architecture" />
   <f:selectItem itemLabel="Web Design" itemValue="Web Design" />
```

```
    <f:selectItem itemLabel="GUI Development"
                  itemValue="GUI Development" />
    <f:selectItem itemLabel="Database" itemValue="Database" />
</h:selectManyCheckbox>
```

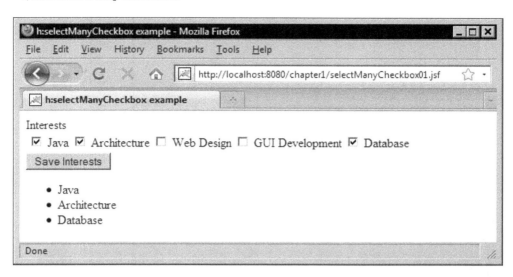

Rendering radio buttons

The following example for the `<h:selectOneRadio>` tag is interesting because it demonstrates a useful technique. The `<h:selectOneRadio>` tag renders a set of radio buttons in the view. These radio buttons represent mutually exclusive options within a set of predefined values. The Java `enum` type is a good choice for a data type here because it also represents a set of predefined values. JSF also includes a built-in converter class that specifically handles Java `enum` types. Therefore, we can define our `enum` as follows:

```
public enum SatisfactionLevel {
VERY_UNSATISFIED, SOMEWHAT_UNSATISFIED, NEUTRAL, SOMEWHAT_SATISFIED,
VERY_SATISFIED
}
```

Next, in our `Customer` class we define a new property of type `SatisfactionLevel`.

```
public class Customer implements Comparable<Customer>, Serializable {
   ...
   private SatisfactionLevel satisfactionLevel;
   ...
}
```

In our JSF page, we can now declare an `<h:selectOneRadio>` tag that is bound to this property. When the user submits the form, the selected value will be converted automatically to one of our enumerated values and stored in our model class.

```
<h:selectOneRadio id="survey"
  value="#{customerBean.customer.satisfactionLevel}"
  layout="pageDirection">
  <f:selectItem itemLabel="Very Unsatisfied"
    itemValue="VERY_UNSATISFIED" />
  <f:selectItem itemLabel="Somewhat Unsatisfied"
    itemValue="SOMEWHAT_UNSATISFIED" />
  <f:selectItem itemLabel="Neutral" itemValue="NEUTRAL" />
  <f:selectItem itemLabel="Somewhat Satisfied"
    itemValue="SOMEWHAT_SATISFIED" />
  <f:selectItem itemLabel="Very Satisfied"
    itemValue="VERY_SATISFIED" />
</h:selectOneRadio>
```

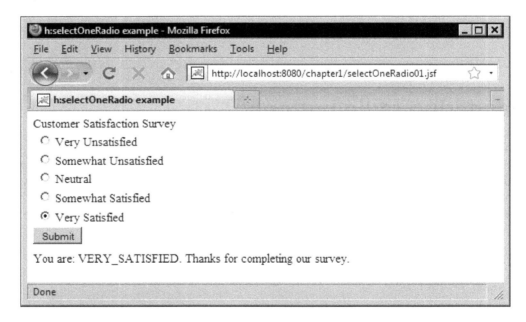

As we used a typesafe `enum` as our data type, only the values we defined in our Java code are acceptable. If we entered a new option value for the `<h:selectOneRadio>` tag, a conversion error would result when the form is submitted.

```
<h:selectOneRadio id="survey"
  value="#{customerBean.customer.satisfactionLevel}"
  layout="pageDirection">
```

```
    <f:selectItem itemLabel="Very Unsatisfied"
      itemValue="VERY_UNSATISFIED" />
    <f:selectItem itemLabel="Somewhat Unsatisfied"
      itemValue="SOMEWHAT_UNSATISFIED" />
    <f:selectItem itemLabel="Indifferent"
      itemValue="INDIFFERENT" />
    <f:selectItem itemLabel="Somewhat Satisfied"
      itemValue="SOMEWHAT_SATISFIED" />
    <f:selectItem itemLabel="Very Satisfied"
      itemValue="VERY_SATISFIED" />
</h:selectOneRadio>
```

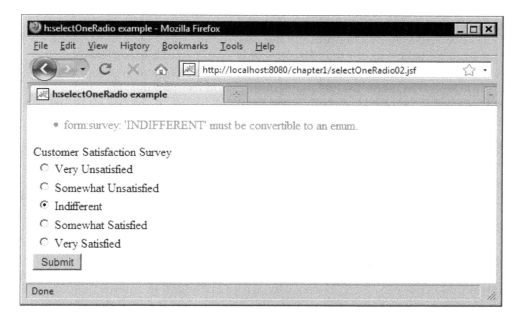

Selecting one or selecting many values

In addition to checkboxes and radio buttons, the HTML markup language includes another important selection control: the `<select>` element. The `<select>` element is useful because it can produce a number of different selection menus. Depending on the values of the `multiple` and `size` attributes, this element might display the following:

- A single selection menu with only one item visible
- A single selection menu with multiple items visible
- A multiple selection menu with only one item visible
- A multiple selection menu with many items visible

The menu items contained by the `<select>` element are specified by child `<option>` elements. The `<option>` element can have a selected state, and can declare a `label` and a `value`. The `label` attribute or the body of the `<option>` element is what is displayed to the user, while the `value` attribute is what is sent to the server during form submission. Multiple options can be grouped together using the `<optgroup>` element. The value of the `<optgroup>` element's `label` attribute is displayed as a header above the indented list of options. Grouping options together is an easy way to enhance the readability and usability of `<select>` elements in your forms.

JSF includes a number of components that represent the different states of the `<select>` element. The `<h:selectOneMenu>` tag renders the `HtmlSelectOneMenu` component as a single selection menu that displays only one item at a time. The `<h:selectManyMenu>` tag renders the `HtmlSelectManyMenu` component as a multiple selection menu that displays only one item at a time. The `<h:selectOneListbox>` tag renders the `HtmlSelectOneListbox` component as a single selection menu that displays multiple items at a time. The `<h:selectManyListbox>` tag renders the `HtmlSelectManyListbox` component as a multiple selection menu that displays multiple items at a time.

When would we use the `<h:selectOneMenu>` and `<h:selectManyMenu>` tags? The `<h:selectOneMenu>` tag is a good choice for a selection situation where the user may only choose one item from a long list of items, such as his or her country of origin. The `<h:selectManyMenu>` tag is intended for situations where it is preferable to display only one item at a time in the selection component, but where the user is allowed to make more than one selection.

Both of these menu components have an inherent size of one, meaning they will only display one item at a time. Unfortunately, the `<h:selectManyMenu>` tag produces a control that is not rendered consistently across browsers. In Internet Explorer, the component is rendered with a scrollbar allowing the user to scroll through the items in the list. In Firefox, however, the control is rendered without scrollbars, making it impossible for the user to make a selection. Therefore, it is not recommended to use the `<h:selectManyMenu>` tag at this time.

When should we use the `<h:selectOneListbox>` and `<h:selectManyListbox>` tags? If the user is only allowed to select one item and the list of options is greater than two but is still relatively short, then it may be preferable to use the `<h:selectOneListbox>` tag and to set the `size` attribute to the number of items in the list to ensure they will all be displayed without scrolling.

For example, if we were asking the user how they discovered our website, and the available options were "Television, Radio, Internet Search, Word of Mouth, Other", then displaying these options in a fully expanded single selection menu would actually increase the efficiency of our user interface by saving the user from having to click twice to make a selection (once to scroll, and once to select an option).

Choosing between the <h:selectOneListbox> and <h:selectManyListbox> tag is more straightforward than choosing between menu and list box components. It comes down to whether our application allows the user to select multiple options, or whether they must select only one option for a particular field. In the previous example, users may be allowed to select more than one source of information, in which case replacing the single selection component with its multiple selection variant is the obvious choice.

On the other hand, the decision to use the menu or list box selection components is a little more involved and ultimately depends on how well these components "fit" into our user interface as a whole. If there are several selection menus on the same screen, and all but one have long lists of items and are therefore rendered using the <h:selectOneMenu> tag, then it might look awkward to have a single <h:selectOneListbox> tag on the page. In this case, we may have to trade the user interface efficiency for consistency and use the <h:selectOneMenu> tag to render a component that makes our UI more aesthetically pleasing to user.

Rendering a list of countries

This example shows how to use the <h:selectOneMenu> tag to display a list of Country objects in the form. It obtains the country list from the backing bean and renders a blank item to prompt the user to make a selection. A custom converter is also registered on the HtmlSelectOneMenu component. The JSF framework calls our converter twice: once to convert each Country object to a string when the view is rendered, and once to convert the selected string back to a Country object when the form is submitted.

The following UML class diagram shows the design of our model classes:

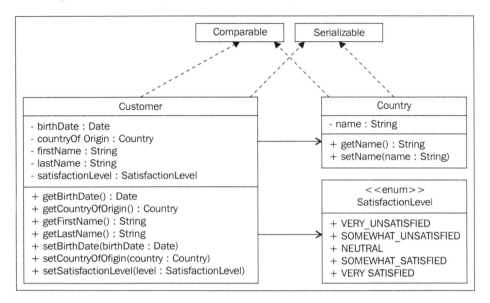

In this example, we rely on a custom JSF converter to convert Country objects to String objects and vice versa. In later chapters, we will see that many popular JSF component libraries include reusable converters that can eliminate the need for us to write our own. When the view is rendered, our Country objects are rendered as strings in an HTML <select> element.

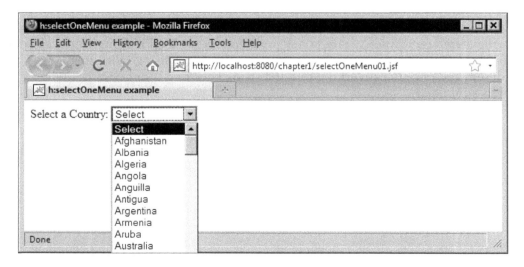

Rendering a single-select list of options

In this example, we use the `<h:selectOneListbox>` tag to render a single-selection list of items to the user.

```
<h:selectOneListbox id="option"
  value="#{customerBean.informationSource}">
  <f:selectItem itemLabel="Television" itemValue="Television" />
  <f:selectItem itemLabel="Radio" itemValue="Radio" />
  <f:selectItem itemLabel="Internet Search"
                itemValue="Internet Search" />
  <f:selectItem itemLabel="Word of Mouth" itemValue="Word of Mouth" />
  <f:selectItem itemLabel="Other" itemValue="Other" />
</h:selectOneListbox>
```

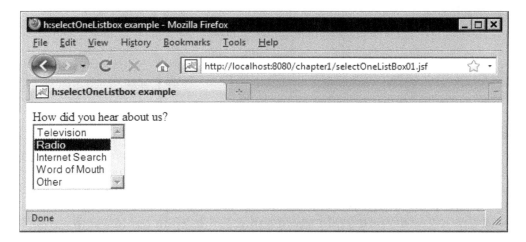

Rendering a multiple-select list of options

We can render the same set of options in a multiple selection mode using the `<h:selectManyListbox>` tag.

```
<h:selectManyListbox id="option"
  value="#{customerBean.informationSources}">
  <f:selectItem itemLabel="Television" itemValue="Television" />
  <f:selectItem itemLabel="Radio" itemValue="Radio" />
  <f:selectItem itemLabel="Internet Search"
                itemValue="Internet Search" />
```

```
    <f:selectItem itemLabel="Word of Mouth" itemValue="Word of Mouth" />
    <f:selectItem itemLabel="Other" itemValue="Other" />
</h:selectManyListbox>
```

Laying out components

The standard JSF HTML components that we have covered so far represent the basic building blocks of a JSF user interface. In GUI development terminology, the basic set of controls supported by HTML represents what can be described as base-level components, in the sense that buttons, checkboxes, and radio buttons cannot have other visible components nested inside them.

The organization of elements on the form is an essential step in the development of a JSF user interface. Determining the optimal arrangement, alignment, and distribution of user interface controls is an important decision-making process for UI designers that can have an impact on the usability of our application. Do we place labels to the left of controls or above them? Do we group components of the same type together on the screen, or do we group components together on the basis of their relationship to the data they are collecting?

One of the more powerful components in the JSF HTML component library is the `HtmlPanelGrid` component. This component is rendered by the `<h:panelGrid>` tag as an HTML `<table>` element. Java GUI programmers will recognize similarities between the `HtmlPanelGrid` component and the `GridLayout` layout manager class from the Java Swing/AWT toolkit. As the `<h:panelGrid>` tag renders an HTML table, let's start by taking a look at how to use a table-based approach to organize the components in our user interface.

The `<h:panelGrid>` tag has a `columns` attribute that specifies how many columns the component should render while it is laying out components on the screen. Understanding how to use this component is simple. Any child components that are nested within this component are arranged from left to right, then from top to bottom. The `HtmlPanelGrid` component iterates its children, rendering each one as a table cell. Once the desired number of columns is reached, the component begins a new table row and repeats the process until all child components have been rendered. The result is a grid of components rendered on the screen as an HTML layout table.

Let's consider an example that uses all the components we have seen so far, to demonstrate how to lay out components on the screen using the JSF `<h:panelGrid>` tag. Suppose we wanted to gather information from the user as part of a customer registration form. We need to collect the following information: the customer' s first and last names, date of birth, gender, phone number, e-mail address, country of origin, and relevant interests.

Rendering a complex layout table

In this example, we use the `<h:panelGrid>` tag to render a complex layout table that organizes other components into an attractive grid of controls on the screen.

```
<h:panelGrid columns="3">
  <h:outputLabel for="firstName" value="#{bundle.firstNameLabel}" />
  <h:inputText id="firstName" value="#{customerBean.customer.
    firstName}" required="true" />
  <h:message for="firstName" errorClass="error" showSummary="true"
          showDetail="false" />
  <h:outputLabel value="#{bundle.lastNameLabel}" for="lastName" />
  <h:inputText id="lastName" value="#{customerBean.customer.lastName}"
          required="true" />
  <h:message for="lastName" errorClass="error" showSummary="true"
          showDetail="false" />
  <h:outputLabel for="dateOfBirth"
              value="#{bundle.dateOfBirthLabel}" />
  <h:inputText id="dateOfBirth" value="#{customerBean.customer.
          birthDate}" required="true">
```

```
    <f:convertDateTime pattern="M/d/yyyy" />
    <f:validator validatorId="customDateValidator" />
</h:inputText>
<h:message for="dateOfBirth" errorClass="error"
           showSummary="true" showDetail="false" />
<h:outputLabel for="gender" value="#{bundle.genderLabel}" />
<h:selectOneRadio id="gender" value="#{customerBean.customer.male}"
                   required="true">
   <f:selectItem itemLabel="Male" itemValue="true" />
   <f:selectItem itemLabel="Female" itemValue="false" />
</h:selectOneRadio>
<h:message for="gender" errorClass="error" showSummary="true"
           showDetail="false" />
<h:outputLabel for="phoneNumber"
               value="#{bundle.phoneNumberLabel}" />
<h:inputText id="phoneNumber" value="#{customerBean.customer.
                                       phoneNumber}" />
<h:message for="phoneNumber" errorClass="error"
           showSummary="true" showDetail="false" />
<h:outputLabel for="emailAddress" value="#{bundle.
                                            emailAddressLabel}" />
<h:inputText id="emailAddress" value="#{customerBean.customer.
              emailAddress}" required="true" />
<h:message for="emailAddress" errorClass="error"
           showSummary="true" showDetail="false" />
<h:outputLabel value="#{bundle.countryLabel}" for="country"
               required="true" />
<h:selectOneMenu id="country" value="#{customerBean.customer.
                 countryOfOrigin}" required="true">
   <f:selectItem itemLabel="Select" itemValue="" />
   <f:selectItems value="#{customerBean.countrySelectItems}" />
     <f:converter converterId="countryConverter" />
</h:selectOneMenu>
<h:message for="country" errorClass="error" showSummary="true"
           showDetail="false" />
<h:outputLabel for="interests" value="#{bundle.interestsLabel}" />
<h:selectManyCheckbox id="interests" value="#{customerBean.
                      interests}" layout="pageDirection">
   <f:selectItem itemLabel="Java" itemValue="Java" />
   <f:selectItem itemLabel="Architecture" itemValue="Architecture" />
   <f:selectItem itemLabel="Web Design" itemValue="Web Design" />
   <f:selectItem itemLabel="GUI Development" itemValue="GUI
       Development" />
   <f:selectItem itemLabel="Database" itemValue="Database" />
</h:selectManyCheckbox>
```

```
<h:message for="interests" errorClass="error" showSummary="true"
          showDetail="false" />
</h:panelGrid>
```

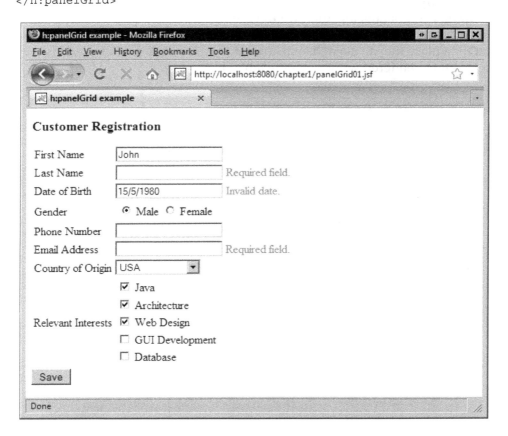

Sometimes, we may want to display more than one component in a particular table cell within the grid. For example, a common scenario is to render two or more buttons in a single column. We know the behavior of the HtmlPanelGrid component is to render each child component in a separate cell, so how do we render more than one component per column?

The standard JSF HTML component library includes the `HtmlPanelGroup` component for just this purpose. This component is rendered by the `<h:panelGroup>` tag and allows us to group two or more components together. By grouping components together, we can then treat them as a single component. Therefore, if we nest two `<h:commandButton>` tags within an `<h:panelGroup>` tag, we can then place the `<h:panelGroup>` inside the `<h:panelGrid>` tag and our two controls will be rendered within a single table cell.

Rendering a table column

This example shows how to use the `<h:panelGroup>` tag to group two buttons together in the same column in an `<h:panelGrid>` tag.

```
<h:panelGrid columns="3">
  <h:outputLabel for="firstName"
    value="#{bundle.firstNameLabel}" />
  <h:inputText id="firstName"
    value="#{customerBean.customer.firstName}"
    required="true" />
  <h:message for="firstName" errorClass="error"
    showSummary="true" showDetail="false" />
  <h:panelGroup>
    <h:commandButton value="Save"
      actionListener="#{customerBean.saveCustomer}"
      style="margin-right:5px" />
    <h:commandButton type="reset" value="Reset" />
  </h:panelGroup>
</h:panelGrid>
```

Displaying data

The JSF framework makes it easy to display tabular data to the user. The `HtmlDataTable` component abstracts many of the details involved in rendering a data set as HTML. For this reason, it is perhaps the most powerful standard JSF component.

As JSF is based on the Model-View-Controller pattern, it mandates a clear separation of concerns: the data structures and entities of our application are the "Models", the backing beans of our application are the "Controllers", and the UI components and JSF pages that constitute our presentation layer are the "Views".

The `HtmlDataTable` component is a good example of how JSF implements the MVC pattern. The `<h:dataTable>` tag renders this component as an HTML table and provides a nice adapter between the presentation and business tiers of our application. The JSF expression language in our JSF page is the glue that binds these two layers together.

The JSF `HtmlDataTable` component is a very basic data table component. We will see in later chapters a number of more specialized versions of this component included in third-party JSF component libraries that provide more full-featured data grid implementations, enabling advanced features such as column sorting, pagination, drag-and-drop, and more. For now, let's examine the basic functionality of the standard JSF HTML data table component.

Rendering an HTML table

The `<h:dataTable>` tag adopts a column-based approach to define the HTML table structure. This example shows how to render a list of customers as an HTML table using the `<h:dataTable>` tag.

```
<h:dataTable value="#{customerBean.customerList}"
  var="customer" rowClasses="row-even,row-odd"
  columnClasses="left-aligned,left-aligned,centered,
  left-aligned" border="2" cellpadding="5" cellspacing="2"
  rows="8">
  <h:column>
    <f:facet name="header">
      <h:outputText value="Full Name" />
    </f:facet>
    <h:outputText value="#{customer.fullName}" />
  </h:column>
  <h:column>
    <f:facet name="header">
      <h:outputText value="Birth Date" />
    </f:facet>
```

```
        <h:outputText value="#{customer.birthDate}">
          <f:convertDateTime type="date" dateStyle="medium" />
        </h:outputText>
      </h:column>
      <h:column>
        <f:facet name="header">
          <h:outputText value="Phone Number" />
        </f:facet>
        <h:outputText value="#{customer.phoneNumber}" />
      </h:column>
      <h:column>
        <f:facet name="header">
          <h:outputText value="Country of Origin" />
        </f:facet>
        <h:outputText value="#{customer.countryOfOrigin.name}" />
      </h:column>
    </h:dataTable>
```

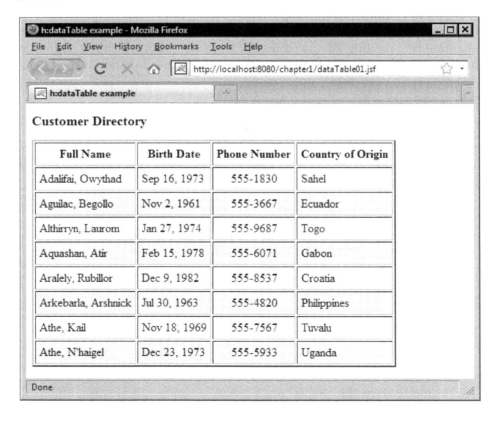

Summary

This chapter provided an introduction to the key concepts of the JavaServer Faces framework, and demonstrated how a number of common web development tasks can be implemented using JSF.

We introduced the Model-View-Controller (MVC) architecture that provides the conceptual framework of a JSF application. We also discussed the role of managed beans in JSF as event handlers that implement application logic and perform model updates in response to user gestures. We introduced the JSF Expression Language (EL) and JSF converters and validators.

Next, we looked at how to implement common web development tasks using JSF components. We examined a number of standard JSF components, and looked at several use cases such as gathering input from users using text fields and submitting HTML forms with buttons and links.

We also looked at how to display localized text and validation messages, and how to render field labels. We saw examples of how to make selections with menus, radio buttons, and checkboxes, and we discussed laying out components with panel grids. Finally, we studied an example of how to render tabular data using the JSF data table component.

Now that we have introduced JSF and covered standard JSF components, we can move on to more advanced topics such as Facelets and third-party JSF component libraries.

2
Facelets Components

In the previous chapter, we looked at how to use standard JavaServer Faces components to implement a number of common web development tasks, such as rendering forms containing simple UI components and accepting and validating input from users. We also discussed several features and extension points of the JSF framework, such as the managed beans facility and message bundle support.

Indeed, the JSF framework was designed with extensibility in mind, enabling both application and framework developers to leverage its infrastructure to build even more sophisticated technologies on top of an already excellent platform for web development. One of the most interesting extension points of the JSF framework is the **ViewHandler** mechanism.

In this chapter, we will discuss one of the most important technologies in the JSF ecosystem — the Facelets view definition framework. The Facelets framework includes a pluggable ViewHandler implementation that provides an alternative to **JavaServer Pages (JSP)**. Facelets also includes a number of useful JSF tags that can be used in place of the **JavaServer Pages Standard Tag Library (JSTL)**.

To gain a better appreciation for the role of Facelets in the JSF context, we will begin with a brief history of Java web development, paying attention to the similarities and differences between Facelets and JSP. We will also look at how to configure a JSF application to use Facelets.

The topics we will look at in this chapter include:

- Getting started with Facelets
- Rendering debug information
- Iterating data in a Facelets page
- Removing UI components and markup
- Including UI components and markup

- Passing parameters from one Facelet to another
- Rendering a UI composition
- Rendering a UI component
- Creating a Facelets UI composition template
- Decorating the user interface
- Rendering a UI fragment

A brief history of Java web development

Before we dive into the details of the Facelets framework, let's review a brief history of web development on the Java platform to understand how Facelets fits into this broader context.

Before Model-View-Controller (MVC) web frameworks and templating systems such as Struts, Tiles, Tapestry, JSF, and Facelets, building web applications on the Java platform involved writing Java Servlets and JavaServer Pages (JSPs).

JSP technology was introduced in 1999 as a competitor to Microsoft's Active Server Pages (ASP) and PHP. JSP made it easier for Java developers to separate programming logic from web page markup, and introduced the concept of custom tag libraries. Developers could now write custom tag classes that could encapsulate presentation logic, register them in a **Tag Library Descriptor** (TLD) file, and use them declaratively in a JSP page simply by adding an import directive at the top of the page.

The Struts framework was originally launched in 2000 and made extensive use of the Servlet API, JSP, and the JSP custom tag mechanism. Struts applied the MVC design pattern to the Servlet API, and introduced a class named the `ActionServlet` that acted as the **Front Controller** of the framework. The Struts `ActionServlet` handled all requests matching a particular URL pattern (usually *.do) by delegating request processing to a number of application-defined action classes implementing the Command pattern.

The Struts framework also introduced a number of custom tag libraries, which provided useful functionality that was common to web development. Some of these libraries included tags for working with JavaBeans, tags for working with HTML elements, and tags for implementing presentation logic such as data iteration and conditional rendering.

The popularity of the Struts framework in general and of the Struts custom tag libraries in particular suggested a widespread need in the Java developer community for tools to simplify the process of implementing Java web applications. This need was recognized by the Java Community Process, and in 2002 the JSP Standard Tag Library (JSTL) was released. It introduced standardized tag libraries for implementing conditional logic, data iteration, date/time and number formatting, internationalization, and more.

The JSTL also supported the **JSP Expression Language (JSP EL)**, a compact scripting language with a simple syntax that provided a less verbose and less error-prone alternative to JSP scriptlets for dynamic rendering.

Due to the similarities between the JSTL and the Struts custom tag libraries, the Struts documentation encouraged developers to adopt the JSTL over Struts tags, whenever there was redundancy between the two libraries.

The Struts framework also supported a templating system known as "Tiles". **Tiles** was an open source project that integrated into the Struts framework and had a plug-in to support the definition of user interface screens based on the Composite View design pattern.

The Composite View design pattern

Implementing web user interfaces often involves creating and reusing a number of repeating branding and navigational elements, such as organizational logos, headers, footers, and navigation menus. An effective strategy for managing these repeating elements is to use the Composite View design pattern. This pattern helps us to subdivide our user interface into smaller pieces, and to create new views by "compositing" these pieces back together in different ways.

As we will see, Facelets performs a role similar to Tiles in the JSF context, but includes many other features as well.

When JSF 1.0 was released in 2004, it introduced a number of enhancements over and above what the Struts framework was currently providing, such as automatic type conversion of strings to and from other Java data types, direct binding of user interface components to application domain models, and more. The Struts framework can be described as an action-based MVC framework due to its emphasis on action classes and the command pattern, while JSF can be described as an event-driven, component-based MVC framework due to its emphasis on UI components and the Observer pattern.

The Command pattern and the Observer pattern

Two popular software design patterns are the Command pattern and the Observer pattern. The **Command pattern** emphasizes the use of objects as executable actions. An object encapsulates a single action, typically by implementing a callback interface method such as execute(), and is invoked by a Controller object.

The **Observer pattern** is common in GUI programming and emphasizes events and event handlers. Another name for the Observer pattern is the Publisher/Subscriber model. A UI component such as a button or hyperlink publishes an event (such as a mouse click), and an event handler *observes* user interaction and processes the event.

The advantage of the Observer pattern is that a single object can manage state (the Model) more easily and can handle multiple events for a single user interface screen (the View). Also, a component can have multiple event handlers registered with it. The Observer pattern is also used in GUI toolkits such as Swing/AWT.

Like Struts, JSF is a highly extensible framework. JSF has a number of important extension points, such as managed beans, converters, validators, lifecycle phase listeners, UI components, render kits, and more. In JSF, even the view technology itself can be swapped out for an alternative ViewHandler implementation.

Comparing Facelets and JSP

Before we can appreciate the advantages that Facelets brings to a JSF application, let's consider the role of JSP as the presentation technology for JSF. By default, the JSF ViewHandler mechanism uses JSP. The ViewHandler is an infrastructural component of the JSF framework that performs an important role during the request processing lifecycle, specifically during the **Render Response** and **Restore View** phases. The ViewHandler is responsible for creating, restoring, and rendering the UI component tree for the current view.

JSP was originally designed to solve the problem of how to include dynamic content in a static HTML document. JSPs enable dynamic content to be inserted into an HTML document through the use of scriptlets, expressions, and JSP directives.

These are typically blocks of Java code interspersed with HTML markup. When the JSP page is requested by the browser, the Servlet/JSP container generates a Java servlet from the JSP source code, compiles it, and executes it to produce an HTML document that is sent to the browser for rendering. This is called the JSP translation process and depending on the speed of the computer, it can take approximately one or two seconds to complete. During JSF application development, we often make many changes to our JSF pages, resulting in frequent recompilation of our JSP pages, and this compile-time overhead can add up.

Facelets pages are simply XML documents (typically XHTML pages) that are never compiled to servlets. Instead, Facelets uses a fast SAX-based compilation process that constructs the UI component tree for our views, which is free from the JSP translation overhead.

Another issue with JSP as the view technology for JSF applications is the mismatch between the JSP compilation process and the UI component tree lifecycle. When a JSP containing JSF tags is rendered for the first time, the page is executed and the components are constructed and rendered at the same time. The problem is that some UI components, such as labels, depend on the presence of other UI components in the tree before they can properly render themselves. The result is that some UI components may render in a different order from the first JSP page request to the next.

Fortunately, Facelets was designed with the JSF UI component lifecycle in mind and, for many developers, it represents a much more intuitive view technology for JSF application development. All of the examples in this book are based on Facelets, so a proper introduction is in order. Let's take a look at how to configure a JSF application to use Facelets as the ViewHandler implementation.

Configuring a JSF application to use Facelets

Java web applications consist of compiled Java classes, XML configuration files, static resources, and other artifacts. To enable Facelets in our JSF application, we must configure our `web.xml` file with a few context parameters, which are used by the Facelets framework.

Mapping the FacesServlet

The `FacesServlet` is the front controller of the JSF application. Incoming requests are mapped to this servlet using different URI patterns. Although it is possible to map any arbitrary prefix and/or file extension to the `FacesServlet`, for simplicity, we have chosen to use the `.jsf` file extension for both the FacesServlet mapping pattern and for our Facelets XHTML documents.

Configuring web.xml

The following example demonstrates some of the context parameters that we set in `web.xml` to enable the Facelets ViewHandler. Notice that we set the `facelets.REFRESH_PERIOD` parameter to true to enable more verbose output during page development. This parameter should be set to false in a production environment.

We also set the `facelets.REFRESH_PERIOD` parameter to 1 second to ensure that Facelets detects and renders any changes that we make to our pages while the application is running. Whenever we make a change to a Facelets page, save it, copy it to our exploded web application deployment, and request it again in the browser; Facelets will compare the last modified date of the file with the date when the view was last compiled. If at least one second has elapsed, Facelets will recompile the view. Otherwise, it will render the previously compiled view.

The refresh behavior of the Facelets framework can be enabled in a development environment by setting the refresh period to 1 and disabled in a production environment by setting the refresh period to -1. As frequent changes to pages are not expected for a live application running on a production server, performance can be improved by disabling the refresh behavior using the -1 setting.

We also indicate that JSF should look for files with the `.jsf` extension when rendering our JSF pages. For simplicity, we chose to use the same file extension for the `FacesServlet` mapping pattern and the actual files that constitute our views, so all our JSF pages have the `.jsf` file extension.

The default behavior in Facelets is to exclude XML comments from the rendered response. This has some performance benefits, but can cause problems too. The `facelets.SKIP_COMMENTS` parameter when set to false indicates to Facelets that XML comments should be preserved from the rendered markup. One reason for preserving comments is to avoid breaking web pages that use legacy techniques such as wrapping JavaScript code with an HTML comment to hide it from older browsers. Another reason is simply to preserve HTML comments to improve the human readability of the rendered markup.

The following source code listing demonstrates how to configure Facelets in `web.xml` for a development environment. This configuration provides a simplified mapping relationship between JSF pages (`*.jsf`) and the `FacesServlet`, detailed error reporting and a refresh period that enables instant JSF view updates.

```xml
<context-param>
  <param-name>javax.faces.DEFAULT_SUFFIX</param-name>
  <param-value>.jsf</param-value>
</context-param>
<context-param>
  <param-name>javax.faces.STATE_SAVING_METHOD</param-name>
  <param-value>client</param-value>
</context-param>
<context-param>
  <param-name>facelets.DEVELOPMENT</param-name>
  <param-value>true</param-value>
</context-param>
<context-param>
  <param-name>facelets.REFRESH_PERIOD</param-name>
  <param-value>1</param-value>
</context-param>
<context-param>
  <param-name>facelets.SKIP_COMMENTS</param-name>
  <param-value>false</param-value>
</context-param>
<context-param>
  <param-name>facelets.VIEW_MAPPINGS</param-name>
  <param-value>*.jsf</param-value>
</context-param>
<servlet>
  <servlet-name>Faces Servlet</servlet-name>
  <servlet-class>javax.faces.webapp.FacesServlet</servlet-class>
  <load-on-startup>1</load-on-startup>
</servlet>
<servlet-mapping>
  <servlet-name>Faces Servlet</servlet-name>
  <url-pattern>/faces/*</url-pattern>
  <url-pattern>*.jsf</url-pattern>
</servlet-mapping>
```

Configuring faces-config.xml

The next step in configuring Facelets in our JSF application is to specify the Facelets ViewHandler in our `faces-config.xml` file. The following example demonstrates the XML required to enable Facelets in our JSF application:

```
<application>
      <message-bundle>messages</message-bundle>
      <view-handler>com.sun.facelets.FaceletViewHandler</view-handler>
      <locale-config>
          <default-locale>en</default-locale>
          <supported-locale>fr</supported-locale>
          <supported-locale>es</supported-locale>
      </locale-config>
</application>
```

Getting started with Facelets

One of the goals of the Facelets view definition framework is to simplify designing composite views in a JSF application. The Composite View design pattern is an approach to user interface development that encourages subdivision and reuse of view elements, such as headers, footers, navigation menus, and more. Let's examine how the Facelets framework supports this approach. Facelets includes a number of useful tags for assembling JSF views from smaller elements.

What is a Facelet?

We can think of a **Facelet** as a subset of a user interface comprised of zero or more UI components. In this chapter, we will begin by looking at some of the basic tags in the Facelets tag library and will progress towards a more complex composite view implementation based on advanced Facelets templating concepts.

Hello World Facelets

First, let's begin with a very simple example of a Facelets page to highlight some key similarities and differences between Facelets and JSP. The following Facelets example renders a simple welcome message:

```
<!DOCTYPE html PUBLIC "-//W3C//DTD XHTML 1.0 Transitional//EN"
"http://www.w3.org/TR/xhtml1/DTD/xhtml1-transitional.dtd">
<html xmlns="http://www.w3.org/1999/xhtml" xmlns:h="http://java.sun.
com/jsf/html">
<head>
```

```
<meta http-equiv="Content-Type" content="text/html; charset=utf-8" />
<title>Facelets Hello World Example</title>
</head>
<body>
<p>Hello, #{backingBean.username}!</p>
<p><h:outputText value="How are you today?" /></p>
</body>
</html>
```

There are a few details to note about this example. First, the document is a well-formed XHTML document and there are no scriptlets or JSP declarations on the page. Second, the root `<html>` tag imports the JSF HTML tag library by declaring an XML namespace with the prefix h and the URL `http://java.sun.com/jsf/html`. This is similar to importing a tag library in a JSP page using the `<%@ taglib %>` directive. Third, notice the absence of the `<f:view>` tag. This tag is not required in a Facelets page. Fourth, notice that Facelets supports inline JSF EL expressions. This enables page authors to render EL expressions mixed with plain HTML tags. Since JSP 2.0, inline EL expressions are also permitted in plain HTML and template text in JSP pages.

So, Facelets pages are very similar to JSP pages except:

- A Facelets page must be a well-formed XML document
- JSF tag libraries are imported using XML namespaces
- The `<f:view>` tag is not required
- No JSP expressions or directives are allowed
- Facelets pages are not compiled to generated servlets

Rendering debug information

It is often helpful to have diagnostic information about the pages in our web application for analyzing and resolving issues. Aside from the usual error reporting mechanism of our web container, the JSF framework lacks a reliable means of obtaining detailed and precise error information about the pages in our JSF application.

Fortunately, the Facelets framework provides comprehensive diagnostic information to simplify debugging our JSF pages. For example, Facelets can provide detailed information about invalid EL expressions in our views. First, we must set the `facelets.DEVELOPMENT` initialization parameter to true in `web.xml` to enable detailed error reporting.

The following Facelets page example contains an unbalanced EL expression. When the page is rendered, a Facelets error page will be displayed indicating the view ID, line, and column number on which an unbalanced EL expression was declared.

error01.jsf

```
<!DOCTYPE html PUBLIC "-//W3C//DTD XHTML 1.0 Transitional//EN"
"http://www.w3.org/TR/xhtml1/DTD/xhtml1-transitional.dtd">
<html xmlns="http://www.w3.org/1999/xhtml" xmlns:h="http://java.sun.
com/jsf/html" xmlns:ui="http://java.sun.com/jsf/facelets">
<head>
<meta http-equiv="Content-Type" content="text/html; charset=utf-8" />
<title>Facelets error page example</title>
</head>
<body>
<h:outputText value="There are #{customerBean.customerCount
customers." />
</body>
</html>
```

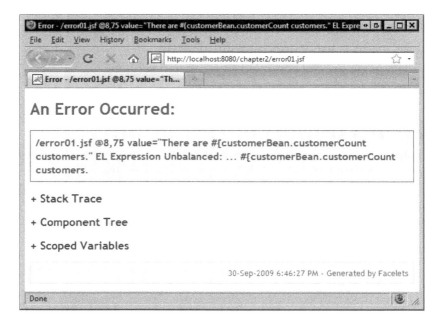

In addition to reporting errors about EL expressions, Facelets can also provide XML syntax checking information to help us ensure that our JSF markup is well formed. Unlike JSP, Facelets is based on pure XML, and therefore requires that all JSF pages (typically XHTML documents) are valid as per the XML specification. The following screenshot demonstrates Facelets' XML error reporting feature. In the next example, our EL expression is syntactically correct, but the `<h:outputText>` tag is missing an end tag.

error02.jsf

```
<!DOCTYPE html PUBLIC "-//W3C//DTD XHTML 1.0 Transitional//EN"
"http://www.w3.org/TR/xhtml1/DTD/xhtml1-transitional.dtd">
<html xmlns="http://www.w3.org/1999/xhtml"
      xmlns:h="http://java.sun.com/jsf/html"
      xmlns:ui="http://java.sun.com/jsf/facelets">
<head>
<meta http-equiv="Content-Type" content="text/html; charset=utf-8" />
<title>Facelets error page example</title>
</head>
<body>
<h:outputText value="There are #{customerBean.customerCount}
                                customers.">
</body>
</html>
```

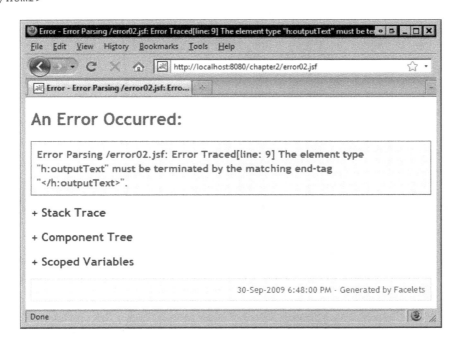

Facelets also includes a tag that can be used to render additional diagnostic information about our JSF pages even after we have corrected any invalid markup. The `<ui:debug>` tag has two important attributes. The `rendered` attribute supports conditional rendering of debug information. In the following example, we only enable this information if Facelets is running in development mode. This ensures that our application will not incur the overhead of generating debug information for each view while running in production mode.

The `hotkey` attribute is also an important attribute for this tag. It defines the key to use in combination with the control and shift keys to open a pop-up window that will display the diagnostic information. By default, it is the letter "D". The following example demonstrates how the Facelets debug page enables us to see the hierarchical structure of the UI component tree for our view. In this example, we include the Facelets debug component on our page and we press *Ctrl+Shift+D* to launch the debug window. Note that there are no errors on this page. The debug window is a useful tool for understanding the structure of the JSF UI component tree for the current view.

debug01.jsf

```
<!DOCTYPE html PUBLIC "-//W3C//DTD XHTML 1.0 Transitional//EN"
"http://www.w3.org/TR/xhtml1/DTD/xhtml1-transitional.dtd">
<html xmlns="http://www.w3.org/1999/xhtml" xmlns:h="http://java.sun.
com/jsf/html" xmlns:ui="http://java.sun.com/jsf/facelets">
<head>
<meta http-equiv="Content-Type" content="text/html; charset=utf-8" />
<title>ui:debug example</title>
</head>
<body>
<h:outputText value="There are #{customerBean.customerCount}
customers." />
<ui:debug hotkey="D"
          rendered="#{initParam['facelets.DEVELOPMENT']}" />
</body>
</html>
```

The following screenshot displays the result of pressing *Ctrl+Shift+D* to launch the Facelets debug window. Notice that a visualization of the UI component tree for the previous view is shown. For example, we can see the UIViewRoot component with a child HtmlOutputText component followed by the UIDebug component. We will use the Facelets debug window throughout this chapter to examine how Facelets tags can modify the UI component tree.

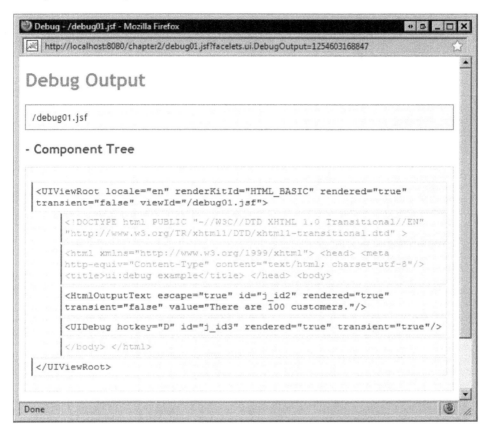

The Facelets debug page also displays any scoped variables such as request or session attributes that were used by the current view, as shown in the following screenshot. Notice the reference to the session-scoped `customerBean` object.

Iterating data in a Facelets page

The JSTL tag library includes a `<c:forEach>` tag that supports iterating dynamic data. While Facelets supports a subset of the JSTL, it provides the `<ui:repeat>` tag as an alternative to the JSTL `<c:forEach>` tag for data iteration. The following example demonstrates how to render an unordered list of customers using the Facelets `<ui:repeat>` tag and plain HTML tags:

repeat01.jsf

```
<!DOCTYPE html PUBLIC "-//W3C//DTD XHTML 1.0 Transitional//EN"
"http://www.w3.org/TR/xhtml1/DTD/xhtml1-transitional.dtd">
```

```
<html xmlns="http://www.w3.org/1999/xhtml"
      xmlns:h="http://java.sun.com/jsf/html"
      xmlns:ui="http://java.sun.com/jsf/facelets">
<head>
<meta http-equiv="Content-Type" content="text/html; charset=utf-8" />
<title>ui:repeat example</title>
</head>
<body>
<h:form>
    <ul>
        <ui:repeat value="#{customerBean.customerList}" var="customer">
            <li>#{customer.fullName}</li>
        </ui:repeat>
    </ul>
</h:form>
</body>
</html>
```

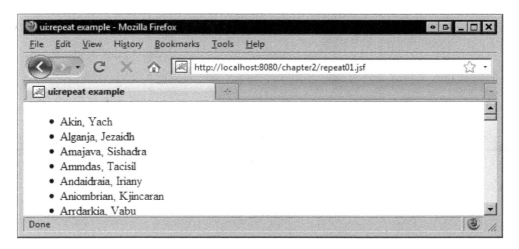

Removing UI components and markup

Sometimes, it is desirable to remove certain elements from a JSF page during development without necessarily deleting the markup. As developers we are accustomed to "commenting out" code, but standard JSF does not provide a simple way for us to remove markup without deleting it.

We can always set the `rendered` attribute to false for UI components, but what if the `rendered` attribute is already specified based on some EL expression? We can use HTML comments, but any EL expressions in those comments will still be evaluated, possibly resulting in runtime errors.

Facelets provides a simple solution to this problem: the <ui:remove> tag. Any markup wrapped by the <ui:remove> tag will literally be removed from the UI component tree at request time. The following example shows the difference between a button component that is not rendered, and a button component that is removed. In the first attempt, we set the button's rendered attribute to false.

remove01.jsf

```
<!DOCTYPE html PUBLIC "-//W3C//DTD XHTML 1.0 Transitional//EN"
"http://www.w3.org/TR/xhtml1/DTD/xhtml1-transitional.dtd">
<html xmlns="http://www.w3.org/1999/xhtml"
      xmlns:h="http://java.sun.com/jsf/html"
      xmlns:ui="http://java.sun.com/jsf/facelets">
<head>
<meta http-equiv="Content-Type" content="text/html; charset=utf-8" />
<title>ui:remove example</title>
</head>
<body>
<h:form>
    <h:outputText value="The button below is not rendered." />
    <h:commandButton rendered="false" />
    <ui:debug />
</h:form>
</body>
</html>
```

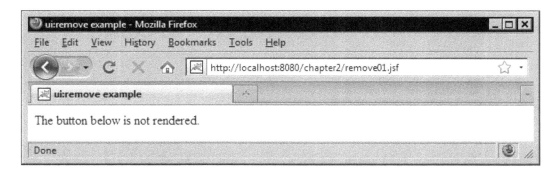

Notice that the button component is still included in the UI component tree even when it is not rendered.

In the second example, we surround the button component with the `<ui:remove>` tag. This is an effective way to remove UI components and markup from a JSF page.

remove02.jsf

```
<!DOCTYPE html PUBLIC "-//W3C//DTD XHTML 1.0 Transitional//EN"
"http://www.w3.org/TR/xhtml1/DTD/xhtml1-transitional.dtd">
<html xmlns="http://www.w3.org/1999/xhtml"
      xmlns:h="http://java.sun.com/jsf/html"
      xmlns:ui="http://java.sun.com/jsf/facelets">
<head>
<meta http-equiv="Content-Type" content="text/html; charset=utf-8" />
<title>ui:remove example</title>
</head>
<body>
<h:form>
```

```
      <h:outputText value="The button below is removed." />
      <ui:remove>
        <h:commandButton />
      </ui:remove>
      <ui:debug />
</h:form>
</body>
</html>
```

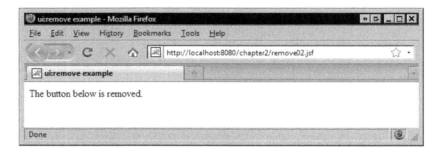

Notice that the button has now been removed from the UI component tree.

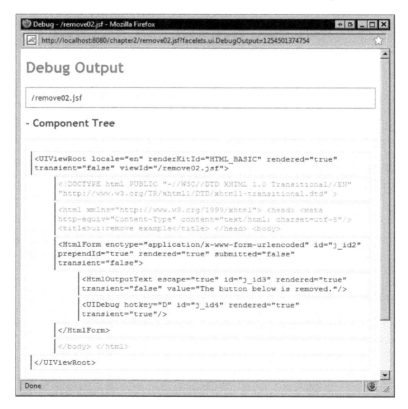

Including UI components and markup

One of the most common techniques for implementing the Composite View design pattern is the **Server Side Include (SSI)** technique. JSP supports the `<jsp:include>` server-side include element, and Facelets provides similar functionality through the `<ui:include>` tag. The tag's `src` attribute can be used to specify the path of a Facelets page to be included at request time. This technique enables us to externalize common view elements such as headers and footers as separate files and to reuse these by including them in other pages throughout our application.

Including a header and footer

The following example demonstrates how to create a simple composite view using the SSI approach. The header and footer files are included to create a complete view.

include01.jsf

```
<!DOCTYPE html PUBLIC "-//W3C//DTD XHTML 1.0 Transitional//EN"
"http://www.w3.org/TR/xhtml1/DTD/xhtml1-transitional.dtd">
<html xmlns="http://www.w3.org/1999/xhtml"
      xmlns:h="http://java.sun.com/jsf/html"
      xmlns:ui="http://java.sun.com/jsf/facelets">
<head>
<meta http-equiv="Content-Type" content="text/html; charset=utf-8" />
<title>ui:include example</title>
</head>
<body>
<h:form>
    <ui:include src="/WEB-INF/includes/header.jsf" />
    <div>This is the body</div>
    <ui:include src="/WEB-INF/includes/footer.jsf" />
</h:form>
</body>
</html>
```

Creating the header Facelet

Notice that the following header file is a complete XHTML document, so it can be edited using any XML editor. But as we are using the Facelets `<ui:composition>` tag, only the content inside this tag is included by the Facelets framework at request time; the content outside the `<ui:composition>` tag will be trimmed.

The use of the `<ui:composition>` tag makes it easier for us to edit complete XHTML documents in our favorite editor, while ensuring that Facelets uses only the content inside the composition to produce a valid composite view at runtime. If we did not wrap the header content shown in the following example with a `<ui:composition>` tag, the entire document would be included, resulting in invalid markup.

HTML editors such as Dreamweaver will ignore the `<ui:composition>` tag, enabling web designers to edit the header as if it was a complete document. When the `header.jsf` page is included by the `include01.jsf` page, only the desired content will be added to the document. We will discuss the `<ui:composition>` tag in more detail later on, in this chapter.

header.jsf

```
<!DOCTYPE html PUBLIC "-//W3C//DTD XHTML 1.0 Transitional//EN"
"http://www.w3.org/TR/xhtml1/DTD/xhtml1-transitional.dtd">
<html xmlns="http://www.w3.org/1999/xhtml"
      xmlns:ui="http://java.sun.com/jsf/facelets">
<head>
<meta http-equiv="Content-Type" content="text/html; charset=utf-8" />
<title>Untitled Document</title>
</head>
<body>
<ui:composition>
<h1>Header</h1>
<hr />
</ui:composition>
</body>
</html>
```

Creating the footer Facelet

The page footer can also be externalized as its own file and reused throughout the application.

footer.jsf

```
<!DOCTYPE html PUBLIC "-//W3C//DTD XHTML 1.0 Transitional//EN"
"http://www.w3.org/TR/xhtml1/DTD/xhtml1-transitional.dtd">
<html xmlns="http://www.w3.org/1999/xhtml"
      xmlns:ui="http://java.sun.com/jsf/facelets">
<head>
<meta http-equiv="Content-Type" content="text/html; charset=utf-8" />
<title>Untitled Document</title>
</head>
<body>
<ui:composition>
<hr />
<div>Footer</div>
</ui:composition>
</body>
</html>
```

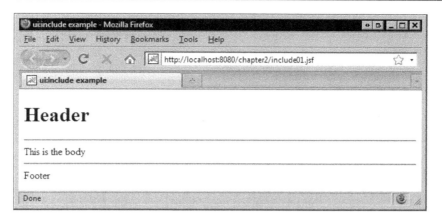

Passing parameters from one Facelet to another

Including static content declared in another document is fine for view elements such as headers and footers, but what if we wanted to pass an object from one Facelet to another? The `<ui:include>` tag is more than a simple SSI tag; it has enhanced functionality that makes it possible to pass arbitrary data from one page to another.

Facelets supports the ability to pass parameters from one Facelet to another by nesting the `<ui:param>` tag inside a `<ui:include>` tag. Using the `<ui:param>` tag's name and value attributes, we can define named content that can be referenced by the included Facelet.

The next example demonstrates how to pass parameters to an included Facelet by using the `<ui:param>` tag within a `<ui:include>` tag. In this case, we include a Facelet that renders a customer list twice, and we pass different parameters to each one. In the first case, we render a list of male customers, and in the second case we render a list of female customers.

This example demonstrates how we can create a Facelet that renders an unordered list of `Customer` objects using the `<ui:repeat>` tag. Instead of hardcoding the backing bean EL expression that obtains the list of customers in our `<ui:repeat>` tag's value attribute, we can introduce some indirection here by referencing a parameter named `customers` that will be defined by the including Facelet.

param01.jsf

```
<!DOCTYPE html PUBLIC "-//W3C//DTD XHTML 1.0 Transitional//EN"
"http://www.w3.org/TR/xhtml1/DTD/xhtml1-transitional.dtd">
<html xmlns="http://www.w3.org/1999/xhtml"
```

```
       xmlns:h="http://java.sun.com/jsf/html"
       xmlns:ui="http://java.sun.com/jsf/facelets">
<head>
<meta http-equiv="Content-Type" content="text/html; charset=utf-8" />
<title>ui:param example</title>
<link rel="stylesheet" type="text/css" href="css/style.css" />
</head>
<body>
<h:form>
   <h:panelGrid columns="2">
      <ui:include src="/WEB-INF/includes/customerList.jsf">
         <ui:param name="title" value="Male Customers" />
         <ui:param name="customers"
                   value="#{customerBean.maleCustomers}" />
      </ui:include>
      <ui:include src="/WEB-INF/includes/customerList.jsf">
         <ui:param name="title" value="Female Customers" />
         <ui:param name="customers"
                   value="#{customerBean.femaleCustomers}" />
      </ui:include>
   </h:panelGrid>
   <ui:debug rendered="true" />
</h:form>
</body>
</html>
```

The included customer list is defined in a separate Facelets document. Notice that the value expression for the `<ui:repeat>` is not bound to a backing bean directly, but indirectly using a parameter named `customers`.

By combining the Facelets `<ui:include>` tag with the `<ui:param>` tag, we can create dynamic, parameterized user interface elements that can be reused by other Facelets pages. The following example demonstrates how to create a reusable Facelet. Notice that the HTML `<h2>` element contains a parameter named `title` for the page header. Once again, we use the `<ui:composition>` tag to surround the content that we wish to be included. Any markup outside the `<ui:composition>` tag will be trimmed.

customerList.jsf

```
<!DOCTYPE html PUBLIC "-//W3C//DTD XHTML 1.0 Transitional//EN"
"http://www.w3.org/TR/xhtml1/DTD/xhtml1-transitional.dtd">
<html xmlns="http://www.w3.org/1999/xhtml"
      xmlns:ui="http://java.sun.com/jsf/facelets"
      xmlns:h="http://java.sun.com/jsf/html">
<head>
<meta http-equiv="Content-Type" content="text/html; charset=utf-8" />
<title>Untitled Document</title>
</head>
<body>
<ui:composition >
   <h2>#{title}</h2>
  <ul>
   <ui:repeat value="#{customers}" var="customer">
     <li>#{customer.fullName}</li>
   </ui:repeat>
   </ul>
</ui:composition>
</body>
</html>
```

Rendering a UI composition

In the previous example, we saw that content from one page could be included in another page by using a combination of the `<ui:include>` and `<ui:composition>` tags. Let's discuss the `<ui:composition>` tag in more detail.

When Facelets encounters a `<ui:composition>` tag, it includes the surrounded content and "trims" the content outside this tag. The surrounded content is included as is, and unlike the `<ui:component>` tag, is not wrapped in a UI component.

Including a UI composition

The following source code example demonstrates how to include a Facelets UI composition using the `<ui:include>` tag. When the markup in the file named composition.jsf is included, only the content inside the `<ui:composition>` tag is rendered.

```
<!DOCTYPE html PUBLIC "-//W3C//DTD XHTML 1.0 Transitional//EN"
"http://www.w3.org/TR/xhtml1/DTD/xhtml1-transitional.dtd">
<html xmlns="http://www.w3.org/1999/xhtml"
      xmlns:ui="http://java.sun.com/jsf/facelets">
<head>
<meta http-equiv="Content-Type" content="text/html; charset=utf-8" />
<title>ui:composition example</title>
</head>
<body>
<ui:include src="/WEB-INF/includes/composition.jsf" />
<ui:debug />
</body>
</html>
```

Declaring a UI composition

The Facelets UI composition from the previous example is declared here. Notice that the page is a complete XHTML document, so it can be edited by any XHTML editor, but as it is designed to be included by another page, the Facelets framework trims any content outside the `<ui:composition>` tag at runtime.

```
<!DOCTYPE html PUBLIC "-//W3C//DTD XHTML 1.0 Transitional//EN"
"http://www.w3.org/TR/xhtml1/DTD/xhtml1-transitional.dtd">
<html xmlns="http://www.w3.org/1999/xhtml"
      xmlns:f="http://java.sun.com/jsf/core"
      xmlns:h="http://java.sun.com/jsf/html"
      xmlns:ui="http://java.sun.com/jsf/facelets">
<head>
<meta http-equiv="Content-Type" content="text/html; charset=utf-8" />
<title>ui:composition example</title>
</head>
<body>
Text before will be removed.
<ui:composition>
   This text will NOT be rendered inside a UI component.
</ui:composition>
Text after will be removed.
</body>
</html>
```

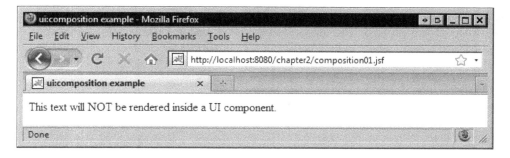

The output in the debug window shown in the next screenshot demonstrates that the included text within the `<ui:composition>` tag is inserted into the including Facelets page, but is not wrapped with a UI component.

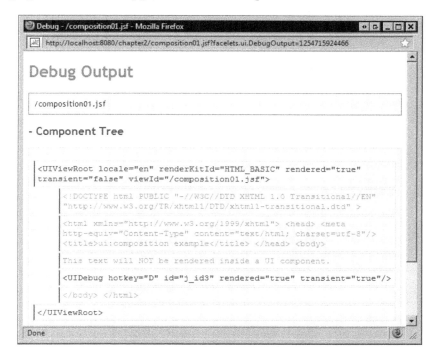

Rendering a UI component

Sometimes, it is desirable to include content from another view element as a single UI component. This enables us, for example, to use the `rendered` attribute on the included content to support conditionally rendered markup more easily, and is convenient for situations where a single component is expected (such as inside the `<h:panelGrid>` or `<f:facet>` tag).

The Facelets `<ui:component>` tag is similar to the `<ui:composition>` tag. In both cases, any content outside the tag is trimmed, but in the case of the `<ui:component>` tag, the content will be rendered within a UI component. Let's look at some examples of using the Facelets `<ui:component>` tag.

Including a UI component

The following example demonstrates that a Facelet containing a `<ui:component>` tag can be included just like a Facelet containing a `<ui:composition>` tag:

component01.jsf

```
<!DOCTYPE html PUBLIC "-//W3C//DTD XHTML 1.0 Transitional//EN"
"http://www.w3.org/TR/xhtml1/DTD/xhtml1-transitional.dtd">
<html xmlns="http://www.w3.org/1999/xhtml"
      xmlns:ui="http://java.sun.com/jsf/facelets">
<head>
<meta http-equiv="Content-Type" content="text/html; charset=utf-8" />
<title>ui:component example</title>
</head>
<body>
<ui:include src="/WEB-INF/includes/component.jsf" />
<ui:debug />
</body>
</html>
```

Declaring a UI component

The Facelet containing the `<ui:component>` tag is a complete XHTML document. It can be edited using any XHTML editor. The content outside the `<ui:component>` tag will be trimmed at runtime. The content inside the `<ui:component>` tag will be rendered inside a UIComponent instance.

component.jsf

```
<!DOCTYPE html PUBLIC "-//W3C//DTD XHTML 1.0 Transitional//EN"
"http://www.w3.org/TR/xhtml1/DTD/xhtml1-transitional.dtd">
<html xmlns="http://www.w3.org/1999/xhtml"
      xmlns:f="http://java.sun.com/jsf/core"
      xmlns:h="http://java.sun.com/jsf/html"
      xmlns:ui="http://java.sun.com/jsf/facelets">
<head>
<meta http-equiv="Content-Type" content="text/html; charset=utf-8" />
<title>ui:component example</title>
</head>
<body>
Text before will be removed.
<ui:component>
```

```
       This text will be rendered inside a UI component.
</ui:component>
Text after will be removed.
</body>
</html>
```

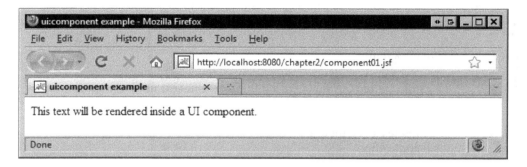

The next screenshot demonstrates that the content inside the `<ui:component>` tag is inserted into the including Facelets page within a UI component.

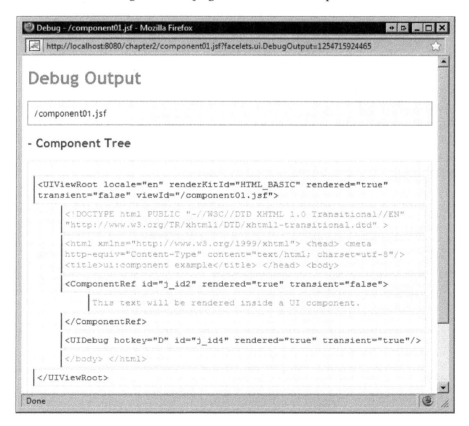

Creating a Facelets UI composition template

One of the more advanced features of the Facelets framework is the ability to define complex templates containing dynamic nested content.

What is a template?

The Merriam-Webster dictionary defines the word "template" as "a gauge, pattern, or mold (as a thin plate or board) used as a guide to the form of a piece being made" and as "something that establishes or serves as a pattern." In the context of user interface design for the Web, a template can be thought of as an abstraction of a set of pages in the web application.

A template does not define content, but rather it defines placeholders for content, and provides the layout, orientation, flow, structure, and logical organization of the elements on the page. We can also think of templates as documents with "blanks" that will be filled in with real data and user interface controls at request time. One of the benefits of *templating* is the separation of content from presentation, making the maintenance of the views in our web application much easier.

The `<ui:insert>` tag has a `name` attribute that is used to specify a dynamic content region that will be inserted by the template client. When Facelets renders a UI composition template, it attempts to substitute any `<ui:insert>` tags in the Facelets template document with corresponding `<ui:define>` tags from the Facelets template client document. Conceptually, the Facelets composition template transformation process can be visualized as follows:

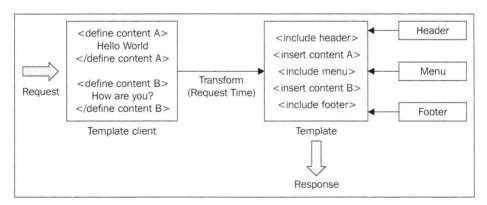

In this scenario, the browser requests a Facelets template client document in our JSF application. This document contains two `<ui:define>` tags that specify named content elements and references a Facelets template document using the `<ui:composition>` tag's `template` attribute. The Facelets template document contains two `<ui:insert>` tags that have the same names as the `<ui:define>` tags in the client document, and three `<ui:include>` tags for the header, footer, and navigation menu.

This is a good example of the excellent support that Facelets provides for the Composite View design pattern. Facelets transforms the template client document by merging any content it defines using `<ui:define>` tags with the content insertion points specified in the Facelets template document using the `<ui:insert>` tag. The result of merging the Facelets template client document with the Facelets template document is rendered in the browser as a composite view.

While this concept may seem a bit complicated at first, it is actually a powerful feature of the Facelets view definition framework that can greatly simplify user interface templating in a web application. In fact, the Facelets composition template document can itself be a template client by referencing another composition template. In this way, a complex hierarchy of templates can be used to construct a flexible, multi-layered presentation tier for a JSF application.

Without the Facelets templating system, we would have to copy and paste view elements such as headers, footers, and menus from one page to the next to achieve a consistent look and feel across our web application. Facelets templating enables us to define our look and feel in one document and to reuse it across multiple pages. Therefore, if we decide to change the look and feel, we only have to update one document and the change is immediately propagated to all the views of the JSF application.

Let's look at some examples of how to use the Facelets templating feature.

A simple Facelets template

The following is an example of a simple Facelets template. It simply renders a message within an HTML `<h2>` element. Facelets will replace the "unnamed" `<ui:insert>` tag (without the `name` attribute) in the template document with the content of the `<ui:composition>` tag from the template client document.

template01.jsf

```
<!DOCTYPE html PUBLIC "-//W3C//DTD XHTML 1.0 Transitional//EN"
"http://www.w3.org/TR/xhtml1/DTD/xhtml1-transitional.dtd">
<html xmlns="http://www.w3.org/1999/xhtml"
    xmlns:f="http://java.sun.com/jsf/core"
    xmlns:h="http://java.sun.com/jsf/html"
```

```
        xmlns:ui="http://java.sun.com/jsf/facelets">
<head>
<meta http-equiv="Content-Type" content="text/html; charset=utf-8" />
<title>Facelets template example</title>
<link rel="stylesheet" type="text/css" href="/css/style.css" />
</head>
<body>
<h2><ui:insert /></h2>
</body>
</html>
```

A simple Facelets template client

Let's look at a simple example of Facelets templating. The following page is a Facelets template client document. (Remember: you can identify a Facelets template client by looking for the existence of the `template` attribute on the `<ui:composition>` tag.) The `<ui:composition>` tag simply contains the text **Hello World**.

templateClient01.jsf

```
<!DOCTYPE html PUBLIC "-//W3C//DTD XHTML 1.0 Transitional//EN"
"http://www.w3.org/TR/xhtml1/DTD/xhtml1-transitional.dtd">
<html xmlns:h="http://java.sun.com/jsf/html"
      xmlns:ui="http://java.sun.com/jsf/facelets">
<head>
<meta http-equiv="Content-Type" content="text/html; charset=utf-8" />
<title>ui:composition example</title>
</head>
<body>
<ui:composition template="/WEB-INF/templates/template01.jsf">
   Hello World
</ui:composition>
<ui:debug />
</body>
</html>
```

The following screenshot displays the result of the Facelets UI composition template transformation when the browser requests `templateClient01.jsf`.

Another simple Facelets template client

The following Facelets template client example demonstrates how a template can be reused across multiple pages in the JSF application:

templateClient01a.jsf

```
<!DOCTYPE html PUBLIC "-//W3C//DTD XHTML 1.0 Transitional//EN"
"http://www.w3.org/TR/xhtml1/DTD/xhtml1-transitional.dtd">
<html xmlns:h="http://java.sun.com/jsf/html"
      xmlns:ui="http://java.sun.com/jsf/facelets">
<head>
<meta http-equiv="Content-Type" content="text/html; charset=utf-8" />
<title>ui:composition example</title>
</head>
<body>
<ui:composition template="/WEB-INF/templates/template01.jsf">
   How are you today?
</ui:composition>
<ui:debug />
</body>
</html>
```

The following screenshot displays the result of the Facelets UI composition template transformation when the browser requests `templateClient01a.jsf`:

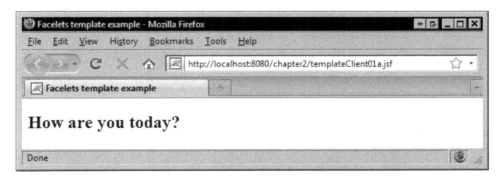

A more complex Facelets template

The Facelets template in the previous example is quite simple and does not demonstrate some of the more advanced capabilities of Facelets templating. In particular, the template in the previous example only has a single `<ui:insert>` tag, with no `name` attribute specified. The behavior of the unnamed `<ui:insert>` tag is to include any content in the referencing template client page.

In more complex templates, multiple `<ui:insert>` tags can be used to enable template client documents to define several custom content elements that will be inserted throughout the template. The following Facelets template document declares three named `<ui:insert>` elements. Notice carefully where these tags are located.

template02.jsf

```
<!DOCTYPE html PUBLIC "-//W3C//DTD XHTML 1.0 Transitional//EN"
"http://www.w3.org/TR/xhtml1/DTD/xhtml1-transitional.dtd">
<html xmlns="http://www.w3.org/1999/xhtml"
      xmlns:f="http://java.sun.com/jsf/core"
      xmlns:h="http://java.sun.com/jsf/html"
      xmlns:ui="http://java.sun.com/jsf/facelets">
<head>
<meta http-equiv="Content-Type" content="text/html; charset=utf-8" />
<title><ui:insert name="title" /></title>
<link rel="stylesheet" type="text/css" href="/css/style.css" />
</head>
<body>
<ui:include src="/WEB-INF/includes/header.jsf" />
<h2><ui:insert name="header" /></h2>
<ui:insert name="content" />
<ui:include src="/WEB-INF/includes/footer.jsf" />
</body>
</html>
```

In the following example, the template client document defines three content elements named `title`, `header`, and `content` using the `<ui:define>` tag. Their position in the client document is not important because the template document determines where this content will be positioned.

templateClient02.jsf

```
<!DOCTYPE html PUBLIC "-//W3C//DTD XHTML 1.0 Transitional//EN"
"http://www.w3.org/TR/xhtml1/DTD/xhtml1-transitional.dtd">
<html xmlns:h="http://java.sun.com/jsf/html"
      xmlns:ui="http://java.sun.com/jsf/facelets">
<head>
<meta http-equiv="Content-Type" content="text/html; charset=utf-8" />
<title>ui:composition example</title>
</head>
```

```
<body>
<ui:composition template="/WEB-INF/templates/template02.jsf">
   <ui:define name="title">Facelet template example</ui:define>
   <ui:define name="header">Hello World</ui:define>
  <ui:define name="content">Page content goes here.</ui:define>
</ui:composition>
<ui:debug />
</body>
</html>
```

The following screenshot displays the result of a more complex Facelets UI composition template transformation when the browser requests the page named `templateClient02.jsf`.

The next example demonstrates reusing a more advanced Facelets UI composition template. At this stage, we should have a good understanding of the basic concepts of Facelets templating and reuse.

templateClient02a.jsf

```
<!DOCTYPE html PUBLIC "-//W3C//DTD XHTML 1.0 Transitional//EN"
"http://www.w3.org/TR/xhtml1/DTD/xhtml1-transitional.dtd">
<html xmlns:h="http://java.sun.com/jsf/html"
      xmlns:ui="http://java.sun.com/jsf/facelets">
<head>
<meta http-equiv="Content-Type" content="text/html; charset=utf-8" />
<title>ui:composition example</title>
</head>
<body>
```

```
<ui:composition template="/WEB-INF/templates/template02.jsf">
   <ui:define name="title">Facelet template example</ui:define>
   <ui:define name="header">Thanks for visiting!</ui:define>
  <ui:define name="content">We hope you enjoyed our site.</ui:define>
</ui:composition>
<ui:debug />
</body>
</html>
```

The next screenshot displays the result of the Facelets UI composition transformation when the browser requests `templateClient02a.jsf`. We can follow this pattern to make a number of JSF pages reuse the template in this manner to achieve a consistent look and feel across our web application.

Decorating the user interface

The Facelets framework supports the definition of smaller, reusable view elements that can be combined at runtime using the Facelets UI tag library. Some of these tags, such as the `<ui:composition>` and `<ui:component>` tags, trim their surrounding content. This behavior is desirable when including content from one complete XHTML document within another complete XHTML document.

There are cases, however, when we do not want Facelets to trim the content outside the Facelets tag, such as when we are decorating content on one page with additional JSF or HTML markup defined in another page.

For example, suppose there is a section of content in our XHTML document that we want to wrap or "decorate" with an HTML `<div>` element defined in another Facelets page. In this scenario, we want all the content on the page to be displayed, and we are simply surrounding part of the content with additional markup defined in another Facelets template. Facelets provides the `<ui:decoration>` tag for this purpose.

Decorating content on a Facelets page

The following example demonstrates how to decorate content on a Facelets page with markup from another Facelets page using the `<ui:decoration>` tag. The `<ui:decoration>` tag has a `template` attribute and behaves like the `<ui:composition>` tag. Facelets templating typically uses the `<ui:composition>`. It references a Facelets template document that contains markup to be included in the current document. The main difference between the `<ui:composition>` tag and the `<ui:decoration>` tag is that Facelets trims the content outside the `<ui:composition>` tag but does not trim the content outside the `<ui:decoration>` tag.

```
<!DOCTYPE html PUBLIC "-//W3C//DTD XHTML 1.0 Transitional//EN"
"http://www.w3.org/TR/xhtml1/DTD/xhtml1-transitional.dtd">
<html xmlns="http://www.w3.org/1999/xhtml"
      xmlns:ui="http://java.sun.com/jsf/facelets">
<head>
<meta http-equiv="Content-Type" content="text/html; charset=utf-8" />
<title>ui:decorate example</title>
<link rel="stylesheet" type="text/css" href="css/style.css" />
</head>
<body>
  Text before will stay.
  <ui:decorate template="/WEB-INF/templates/box.jsf">
    <span class="header">Information Box</span>
    <p>This is the first line of information.</p>
    <p>This is the second line of information.</p>
    <p>This is the third line of information.</p>
  </ui:decorate>
  Text after will stay.
  <ui:debug />
</body>
</html>
```

Creating a Facelets decoration

Let's examine the Facelets decoration template referenced by the previous example. The following source code demonstrates how to create a Facelets template to provide the decoration that will surround the content on another page.

As we are using a `<ui:composition>` tag, only the content inside this tag will be used. In this example, we declare an HTML `<div>` element with the "box" CSS style class that contains a single Facelets `<ui:insert>` tag. When Facelets renders the above Facelets page, it encounters the `<ui:decorate>` tag that references the `box.jsf` page. The `<ui:decorate>` tag will be merged together with the associated decoration template and then rendered in the view. In this scenario, Facelets will insert the child content of the `<ui:decorate>` tag into the Facelets decoration template where the `<ui:insert>` tag is declared.

```
<!DOCTYPE html PUBLIC "-//W3C//DTD XHTML 1.0 Transitional//EN"
"http://www.w3.org/TR/xhtml1/DTD/xhtml1-transitional.dtd">
<html xmlns="http://www.w3.org/1999/xhtml"
      xmlns:ui="http://java.sun.com/jsf/facelets"
      xmlns:f="http://java.sun.com/jsf/core"
      xmlns:h="http://java.sun.com/jsf/html"
      xmlns:c="http://java.sun.com/jstl/core">
<head>
<meta http-equiv="Content-Type" content="text/html; charset=utf-8" />
<title>Box</title>
</head>
<body>
<ui:composition>
   <div class="box">
      <ui:insert />
   </div>
</ui:composition>
</body>
</html>
```

The result is that our content is surrounded or "decorated" by the `<div>` element. Any text before or after the `<ui:decoration>` is still rendered on the page, as shown in the next screenshot:

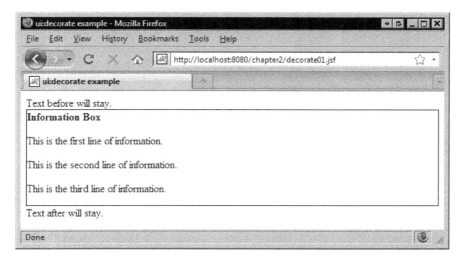

The included decoration is rendered as is, and is not nested inside a UI component as demonstrated in the following Facelets debug page:

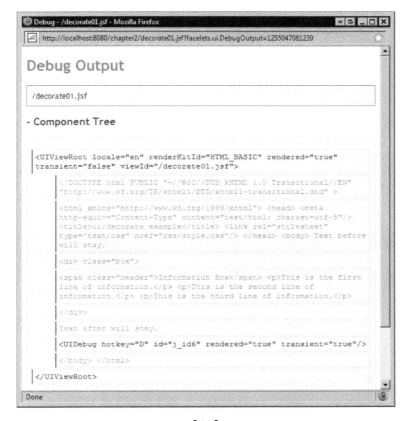

Rendering a UI fragment

Like the `<ui:decorate>` tag, the `<ui:fragment>` tag is also a non-trimming tag. Facelets preserves the markup outside this tag.

One difference between the `<ui:decoration>` and the `<ui:fragment>` tags, however, is that Facelets includes the content of the `<ui:fragment>` tag inside a UI component. In this way, the `<ui:fragment>` and the `<ui:component>` tag have similar behavior.

Another difference between the `<ui:decorate>` and the `<ui:fragment>` tags is that the `<ui:fragment>` tag does not support the `template` attribute, but instead has a `binding` attribute that gives us the ability to bind the tag to a UI component in our backing bean.

```
<!DOCTYPE html PUBLIC "-//W3C//DTD XHTML 1.0 Transitional//EN"
"http://www.w3.org/TR/xhtml1/DTD/xhtml1-transitional.dtd">
<html xmlns="http://www.w3.org/1999/xhtml"
      xmlns:h="http://java.sun.com/jsf/html"
      xmlns:ui="http://java.sun.com/jsf/facelets">
<head>
<meta http-equiv="Content-Type" content="text/html; charset=utf-8" />
<title>ui:fragment example</title>
</head>
<body>
<h:form>
  Text before will be rendered.
  <ui:fragment>
  <p>A fragment adds a component to the view but does not trim any
      content.</p>
  </ui:fragment>
  Text after will be rendered.
   <ui:debug />
</h:form>
</body>
</html>
```

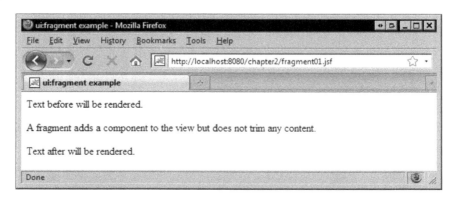

The non-trimming and UI component-based behavior of the `<ui:fragment>` tag is demonstrated in the Facelets debug page shown in the next screenshot.

As Facelets renders the content of the `<ui:fragment>` tag within a UI component, we can use this tag whenever we want to group multiple components (and markup) together as a single UI component, such as within the `<h:panelGrid>` and `<f:facet>` tags.

An advanced Facelets composition template

The following example demonstrates an advanced Facelets composition template and uses the majority of Facelets tags in a single composite view. In this example, the template client document specifies a number of named content elements using the <ui:define> tag and reuses multiple UI elements.

The <ui:define> tag named title specifies the document title. The links element uses a <ui:include> tag to include the navigation menu that will be inserted into the links section of the template. The header element simply defines the page header. The content element defines the paragraph text to be rendered by the template. Finally, the data element defines the data to be displayed by re-using the external links.jsf template that renders a parameterized list of customers.

```
<!DOCTYPE html PUBLIC "-//W3C//DTD XHTML 1.0 Transitional//EN"
"http://www.w3.org/TR/xhtml1/DTD/xhtml1-transitional.dtd">
<html xmlns="http://www.w3.org/1999/xhtml"
     xmlns:f="http://java.sun.com/jsf/core"
     xmlns:h="http://java.sun.com/jsf/html"
     xmlns:ui="http://java.sun.com/jsf/facelets">
<head>
<meta http-equiv="Content-Type" content="text/html; charset=utf-8" />
<title>Facelets template example</title>
</head>
<body>
<ui:composition template="/WEB-INF/templates/template03.jsf">
   <ui:define name="title">Facelets template example</ui:define>
   <ui:define name="links">
      <ui:include src="/WEB-INF/includes/links.jsf" />
   </ui:define>
    <ui:define name="header">Customer Listing</ui:define>
   <ui:define name="content">
    <p>Our company has #{customerBean.customerCount} customers.</p>
     <p>They have been separated into two lists shown below.</p>
   </ui:define>
   <ui:define name="data">
     <h:panelGrid columns="2">
     <ui:fragment>
        <ui:include src="/WEB-INF/includes/customerList.jsf">
          <ui:param name="title" value="Male Customers" />
          <ui:param name="customers" value="#{customerBean.
                                            maleCustomers}" />
        </ui:include>
     </ui:fragment>
     <ui:fragment>
        <ui:include src="/WEB-INF/includes/customerList.jsf">
```

```
                <ui:param name="title" value="Female Customers" />
                <ui:param name="customers" value="#{customerBean.
                                              femaleCustomers}" />
            </ui:include>
        </ui:fragment>
      </h:panelGrid>
      </ui:define>
    </ui:composition>
    </body>
    </html>
```

The corresponding Facelets UI composition template for this example uses the <ui:include> tag to render a header defined in an external Facelets page. The main content of the page is rendered using the <h:panelGrid> tag to render a single-column layout table. (CSS-based layouts are generally preferred to table-based layouts; this example is for demonstration only.)

The first row of the panel grid renders the links element by using the <ui:insert> tag named links. Notice that the content is wrapped in a <ui:fragment> tag to ensure that any included content is wrapped with a single UI component so the content is rendered in a single column within the panel grid component.

The second row of the panel grid renders a title inside the HTML <h2> element. The third row of the panel grid renders a box decoration around the named data element provided by the template client. The page footer is rendered using a <ui:include> tag.

Finally, we declare the <ui:debug> tag and set the rendered attribute to true based on the value of the facelets.DEVELOPMENT initialization parameter. This way, debugging support can be enabled conditionally whenever Facelets error handling is turned on during the development cycle.

```
<!DOCTYPE html PUBLIC "-//W3C//DTD XHTML 1.0 Transitional//EN"
"http://www.w3.org/TR/xhtml1/DTD/xhtml1-transitional.dtd">
<html xmlns="http://www.w3.org/1999/xhtml"
      xmlns:f="http://java.sun.com/jsf/core"
      xmlns:h="http://java.sun.com/jsf/html"
      xmlns:ui="http://java.sun.com/jsf/facelets">
<head>
<meta http-equiv="Content-Type" content="text/html; charset=utf-8" />
<title><ui:insert name="title" /></title>
<link rel="stylesheet" type="text/css" href="/chapter2/css/style.css"
/>
</head>
<body>
<ui:include src="/WEB-INF/includes/header.jsf" />
<h:panelGrid width="100%">
  <ui:fragment>
      <ui:insert name="links" />
```

```
    </ui:fragment>
    <ui:fragment>
     <h2><ui:insert name="header" /></h2>
     <ui:insert name="content" />
    </ui:fragment>
    <ui:fragment>
      <ui:decorate template="/WEB-INF/templates/box.jsf">
        <ui:insert name="data" />
      </ui:decorate>
    </ui:fragment>
  </h:panelGrid>
  <ui:include src="/WEB-INF/includes/footer.jsf" />
  <ui:debug hotkey="D" rendered="#{initParam['facelets.DEVELOPMENT']}"
  />
  </body>
  </html>
```

The result of the Facelets UI composition transformation is a complex composite view arrangement containing multiple reusable UI elements, such as headers, footers, navigation menus, and box decorations.

Summary

In this chapter, we explored how the Facelets view definition framework can be used to enhance presentation tier development in a JSF application.

We looked at a brief history of web development on the Java platform and compared Facelets with JSP technology to understand the advantages that Facelets offers to the JSF developer.

Facelets provides a fresh and compelling alternative to JSP as the view technology for JSF. Designed specifically to support the UI component tree lifecycle, Facelets is a highly optimized technology that greatly simplifies user interface development with the JSF framework.

Facelets pages are different from JSP pages because they are not compiled to generate servlets and they do not contain JSP expressions and directives. JSF tag libraries can be included in Facelets pages by using XML namespaces. Faceletsand JSP (since JSP 2.0) both support inline JSF EL expressions.

Our discussion included tips on how to configure a JSF application to use Facelets by specifying initialization parameters in `web.xml` and by configuring JSF to use the Facelets ViewHandler implementation in `faces-config.xml`. We can enable the Facelets refresh behavior during development, and disable it in production for best performance.

We studied examples of how to perform common tasks with the Facelets framework, such as enabling detailed error reporting with line number and attribute information, examining the UI component tree at runtime, iterating data in a Facelets page, including components and markup, removing components and markup, and decorating content in a Facelets page. We also looked at how to render advanced UI composition templates using the Facelets framework. Facelets templates can be reused by multiple client documents, simplifying the task of implementing a consistent look and feel across all the pages in our JSF application.

Based on the Composite View design pattern, Facelets is a sophisticated framework that makes it easy to create reusable user interface elements for a JSF application. Facelets supports a declarative approach to component-based development. As Facelets is supported by all major JSF component libraries, we will use it extensively throughout this book.

3
Apache MyFaces Tomahawk Components

In the previous chapter, we learned how to use the Facelets view definition framework as a templating system for JSF. In this chapter, we will look at how to implement a number of typical web application development scenarios using the Tomahawk JSF component library.

What is a component library? The JSF framework is highly extensible, and this is especially true for UI components. JSF includes a flexible class hierarchy that developers can extend to create their own custom components. The Tomahawk component library is an excellent example of the extensibility of JSF as a UI component framework.

The Tomahawk library contains more than 75 custom JSF components. We will look at a subset of these components to highlight some of the strengths of this library and how it can be used to implement common web development use cases, such as:

- Validating user input
- Accepting time information from the user
- Working with files
- Using tree components
- Creating navigation menus
- Securing our user interfaces
- Displaying tabular data

Validating user input

In Chapter 1, we saw how to use some of the converters and validators included in the JSF framework, and we saw how to create our own custom converters and validators.

In one example, we looked at a customer registration form that required the user to enter their name, contact information, date of birth, country of origin, and relevant interests. We registered our custom date validator on the date of birth field to ensure that the date entered by the user was correctly formatted and represented a legitimate birth date.

What we didn't do, however, was validate the phone number and e-mail address entered by the user. Let's look at this example again to see how we can validate these form fields using the Tomahawk validation tags.

The Tomahawk component library includes several validation tags based on the **Jakarta Commons Validator** utility class library for Java. Tomahawk includes built-in validator tags, such as `<t:validateCreditCard>` for verifying credit card numbers, `<t:validateEmail>` for validating e-mail addresses, and `<t:validateRegExpr>` for validating arbitrary regular expression patterns.

Tomahawk also includes the `<t:validateEqual>` tag for comparing one field with another field within the same form in our user interface. This can be useful for situations where we need to validate the same user input twice, such as when accepting a password or an e-mail address from the user.

Validating e-mail addresses

The example from the previous chapter could be improved by using the Tomahawk e-mail validator tag to ensure that the user's e-mail address is well formed. In the next code, we will render a form to accept an e-mail address from the user and validate it. If the e-mail address is correct, we will accept it, else we will display a customized error message. Note that a localized error message could be retrieved from a message bundle using an EL expression instead of hardcoding it in the `message` attribute.

```
<h:form>
  <h:panelGrid columns="1">
    <h:panelGroup>
      <h:outputLabel for="emailAddress"
        value="#{bundle.emailAddressLabel}" />
      <h:inputText id="emailAddress"
        value="#{customerBean.customer.emailAddress}"
        required="true">
```

```
    <t:validateEmail message="The email address you have
        entered is not valid." />
    </h:inputText>
    <h:commandButton value="Submit" />
  </h:panelGroup>
  <h:message for="emailAddress" errorClass="error"
    showSummary="false" showDetail="true" />
  </h:panelGrid>
</h:form>
```

The next screenshot shows our customized error message that will be displayed if the user enters an invalid e-mail address:

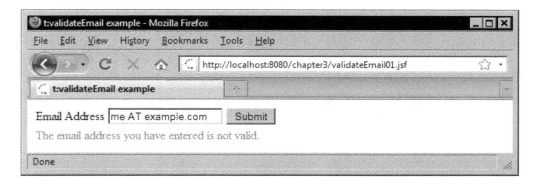

Validating a phone number with a regular expression pattern

Similarly, we can make our customer information more robust by using the Tomahawk regular expression validator tag to verify the customer's phone number. In this example, we provide a regular expression pattern that expects three digits followed by a space or a dash, followed by three digits, followed by a space or a dash, followed by four digits.

Also note that we have replaced the standard JSF `HtmlInputText` component with the Tomahawk `HtmlInputTextHelp` component because this component allows us to display help text to the user. This text is defined by the `helpText` attribute of the `<t:inputTextHelp>` tag and will be displayed initially in the text field when the form is rendered in the browser. Once the text field gains focus, the help text will disappear.

```
<h:form>
  <h:panelGrid columns="1">
    <h:panelGroup>
      <h:outputLabel for="phoneNumber"
```

```
                value="#{bundle.phoneNumberLabel}" />
            <t:inputTextHelp id="phoneNumber"
                value="#{customerBean.customer.phoneNumber}"
                helpText="XXX-XXX-XXXX">
                <t:validateRegExpr
                    message="#{bundle.invalidPhoneNumber}"
                    pattern="\d{3}[\-\s]\d{3}[\-\s]\d{4}" />
            </t:inputTextHelp>
            <h:commandButton value="Submit" />
        </h:panelGroup>
        <h:message for="phoneNumber" errorClass="error"
            showSummary="false" showDetail="true" />
    </h:panelGrid>
</h:form>
```

In the following screenshot, we can see the result of this source code. A text field is rendered in the browser with an input mask representing a correct phone number. Once the text field gains focus, the input mask disappears.

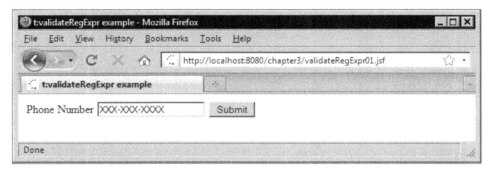

If the user enters an invalid phone number, the Tomahawk regular expression validation fails and the validation message we specified is displayed in the view.

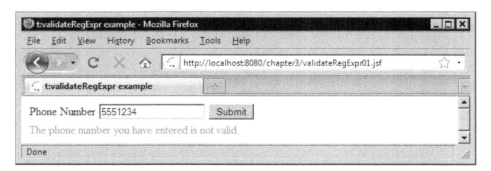

Validating that two fields have an equal value

It is a good practice to validate certain types of information twice, such as passwords and e-mail addresses, to ensure that the value entered by the user is what the user intended. Conveniently, Tomahawk includes a validator for just this purpose. In this example, we improve the customer information form (from Chapter 1) by adding a second field for capturing the user's e-mail address. We use the Tomahawk `<t:validateEqual>` tag to ensure that the two e-mail addresses entered by the user are equal.

```
<h:form>
  <h:panelGrid columns="1">
    <h:panelGroup>
      <h:outputLabel for="emailAddress"
        value="#{bundle.emailAddressLabel}" />
      <h:inputText id="emailAddress"
        value="#{customerBean.customer.emailAddress}"
        required="true">
        <t:validateEmail message="The email address you have
          entered is not valid." />
      </h:inputText>
    </h:panelGroup>
    <h:panelGroup>
      <h:outputLabel for="emailAddressConfirm"
        value="#{bundle.emailAddressConfirmLabel}" />
      <h:inputText id="emailAddressConfirm"
        required="true">
        <t:validateEqual for="emailAddress" message="The email
          addresses you have entered do not match." />
      </h:inputText>
    </h:panelGroup>
    <h:commandButton value="Submit" />
    <h:message for="emailAddress" errorClass="error"
      showSummary="false" showDetail="true" />
    <h:message for="emailAddressConfirm" errorClass="error"
      showSummary="false" showDetail="true" />
  </h:panelGrid>
</h:form>
```

As with the previous example, if the user inputs incorrect information (in this case, an incorrect e-mail address in the confirmation field), the Tomahawk regular expression validator will fail and the custom validation message we defined for this component is displayed in the view.

Managing date and time selection

The `<h:inputText>` tag in the standard JSF HTML tag library, when used with a nested `<f:convertDateTime>` tag, can be used to accept arbitrarily formatted date and time information from the user. Many desktop applications, however, offer users a richer set of controls for entering date and time information. If we want to make our web applications more like desktop software, enhancing date/time selection is a good place to start.

The Tomahawk component library includes several powerful components that support date and time selection. The `HtmlInputDate` component offers a convenient set of text fields that are mapped to the different components in a date, such as the day, the month, the year, and the time.

The `HtmlInputCalendar` component can render an attractive pop-up calendar that users can interact with to select a date or time in our user interface. Finally, the Tomahawk `HtmlSchedule` component offers a full-featured scheduling control similar to popular calendaring applications for the desktop such as Microsoft Outlook and Mozilla Sunbird.

Selecting a date

In this example, we use the Tomahawk `HtmlInputDate` component to render a date input field in our form. This enables the user to use a more intuitive type of control for entering date/time information. Notice that we reuse our existing custom date validator to ensure that the user enters a valid birth date.

```
<h:form>
  <h:panelGrid columns="1">
    <h:panelGroup>
      <h:outputLabel for="dateOfBirth"
        value="#{bundle.dateOfBirthLabel}" />
      <t:inputDate id="dateOfBirth"
        value="#{customerBean.customer.birthDate}" type="date"
        required="true">
        <f:validator validatorId="customDateValidator" />
      </t:inputDate>
      <h:commandButton value="Submit" />
    </h:panelGroup>
    <h:message for="dateOfBirth" errorClass="error"
      showSummary="false" showDetail="true" />
    <h:panelGroup rendered="#{customerBean.customer.birthDate
      ne null}">
      <h:outputText value="Your birth date is " />
      <h:outputText
        value="#{customerBean.customer.birthDate}">
        <f:convertDateTime dateStyle="full" type="date" />
      </h:outputText>
    </h:panelGroup>
  </h:panelGrid>
</h:form>
```

As shown in the following screenshot, the Tomahawk `HtmlInputDate` component renders input date fields for the day, month, and year, with restricted possible values. The date format used (for example, mm/dd/yyyy) is also customizable.

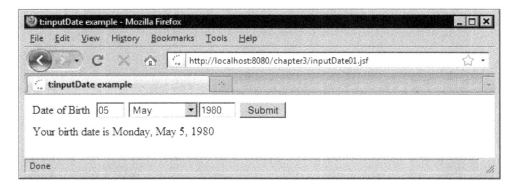

The Tomahawk `HtmlInputDate` component is quite flexible. We can also use it to render an attractive pop-up calendar to improve the interactivity of our JSF page by setting the `popupCalendar` attribute to true.

```
<h:form>
  <h:panelGrid columns="1">
    <h:panelGroup>
      <h:outputLabel for="dateOfBirth"
        value="#{bundle.dateOfBirthLabel}" />
      <t:inputDate id="dateOfBirth"
        value="#{customerBean.customer.birthDate}"
        type="date" required="true"
        popupCalendar="true">
        <f:validator validatorId="customDateValidator" />
      </t:inputDate>
      <h:commandButton value="Submit" />
    </h:panelGroup>
    <h:message for="dateOfBirth" errorClass="error"
      showSummary="false" showDetail="true" />
    <h:panelGroup rendered="#{customerBean.customer.birthDate
      ne null}">
      <h:outputText value="Your birth date is " />
      <h:outputText
        value="#{customerBean.customer.birthDate}">
        <f:convertDateTime dateStyle="full" type="date" />
      </h:outputText>
    </h:panelGroup>
  </h:panelGrid>
</h:form>
```

The following screenshot shows the pop-up calendar rendered in the view. The Tomahawk calendar component provides an interactive user interface for selecting a date.

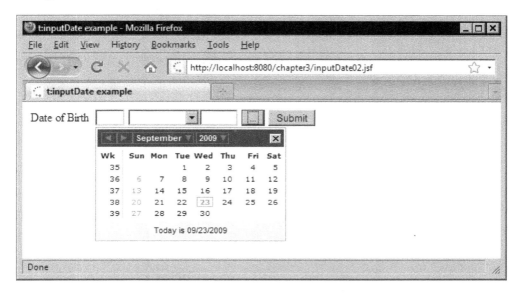

Rendering a simple calendar

The `HtmlInputCalendar` component, rendered by the `<t:inputCalendar>` tag, is another useful date/time component in the Tomahawk library. It can render a date selection control in one of two ways. When the `renderAsPopup` attribute is set to true, a text field is rendered with a button that displays a JavaScript calendar for date selection. When the `renderAsPopup` attribute is set to false (the default), a calendar is rendered as an element on the page. This component also supports a number of CSS properties to enable customization of the appearance of the calendar.

```
<h:form>
  <h:panelGrid columns="1">
    <h:panelGroup>
      <h:outputLabel for="date" value="Select a Date" />
      <t:inputCalendar id="date" type="date"
        required="true" styleClass="calendar" />
      <h:commandButton value="Submit" />
    </h:panelGroup>
    <h:message for="date" errorClass="error"
      showSummary="false" showDetail="true" />
  </h:panelGrid>
</h:form>
```

The `<t:inputCalendar>` tag renders a calendar component in one of two ways. It can render a static calendar on the JSF page, or it can render a pop-up calendar identical to the one produced by the `<t:inputDate>` tag. The following screenshot demonstrates rendering a static calendar on the page by omitting the `renderAsPopup` attribute or by setting it to false.

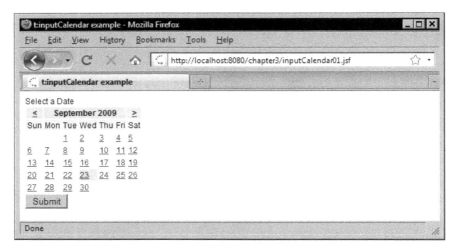

Rendering an appointment schedule

The Tomahawk `HtmlSchedule` component is a powerful and feature-rich date/time control. In the first example, we use the `<t:schedule>` tag to render a monthly appointment calendar using the default theme with tooltips.

```
<h:form>
  <t:schedule
    value="#{customerBean.monthlyAppointmentsScheduleModel}"
    tooltip="true" />
</h:form>
```

The value expression for this tag returns a Tomahawk `ScheduleModel` object from our backing bean that contains the appointment data to be displayed on the schedule. This model object is also configured to display the appointments and the monthly schedule view. The following code example demonstrates how to construct a monthly schedule model object using the Tomahawk API (see the sample Eclipse project for this chapter for the complete source code):

```
ScheduleModel model = new SimpleScheduleModel();
model.setMode(ScheduleModel.MONTH);
```

To populate the schedule model with appointments, we can use the Tomahawk `DefaultScheduleEntry` class. In the next example, we create a `DefaultScheduleEntry` object, set the appointment information such as start time and end time, and add it to the schedule model.

```
DefaultScheduleEntry entry = new DefaultScheduleEntry();
entry.setId(UUID.randomUUID().toString());
entry.setStartTime(start);
entry.setEndTime(end);
entry.setTitle("Meeting with " + customer.getFirstName() + " "
    + customer.getLastName());
entry.setSubtitle("Follow-up appointment");
entry.setDescription("Meeting to discuss project
                    opportunity.");
model.addEntry(entry);
```

The result is a fully populated monthly appointment schedule that displays a tooltip when the mouse cursor is hovered over a particular appointment. Here we use the default theme for the schedule.

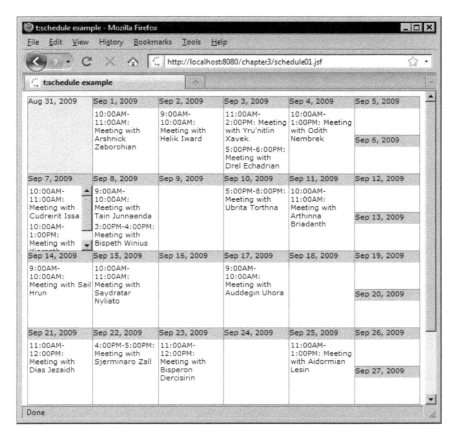

In the next example, we use the `<t:schedule>` tag to render a daily schedule of appointments using the `outlookxp` theme with tooltips. We can also control the start and end time for the workday.

```
<h:form>
  <t:schedule
    value="#{customerBean.dailyAppointmentsScheduleModel}"
    tooltip="true" workingStartHour="8" workingEndHour="17"
    theme="outlookxp" />
</h:form>
```

This time when we construct the schedule model, we set the mode to the `ScheduleModel.DAY` constant.

```
ScheduleModel model = new SimpleScheduleModel();
model.setMode(ScheduleModel.DAY);
```

This component generates a full-featured day planner with clickable, user-defined events that can span multiple hours and provide rollover tooltip information, as shown in the following screenshot:

Next, we use the `<t:schedule>` tag to render a weekly schedule of appointments using the default theme with tooltips.

```
<h:form>
  <t:schedule
    value="#{customerBean.weeklyAppointmentsScheduleModel}"
    tooltip="true" />
</h:form>
```

The schedule model is set to the `ScheduleModel.WEEK` mode.

```
ScheduleModel model = new SimpleScheduleModel();
model.setMode(ScheduleModel.WEEK);
```

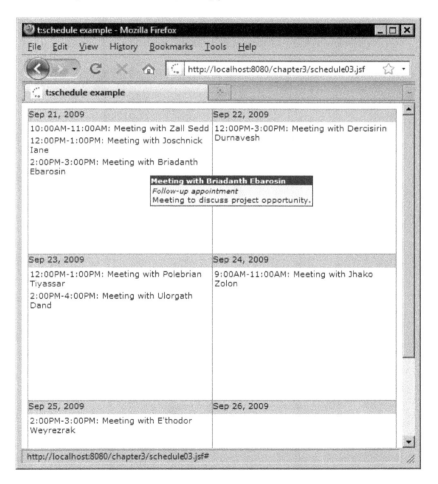

Finally, we use the `<t:schedule>` tag to render a schedule of appointments for the workweek using the `outlookxp` theme with tooltips.

```
<h:form>
  <t:schedule
    value="#{customerBean.workweekAppointmentsScheduleModel}"
    tooltip="true" theme="outlookxp" />
</h:form>
```

The schedule model is set to the `ScheduleModel.WORKWEEK` mode.

```
ScheduleModel model = new SimpleScheduleModel();
model.setMode(ScheduleModel.WORKWEEK);
```

The following screenshot shows the Tomahawk schedule component in a workweek mode using the `evolution` theme:

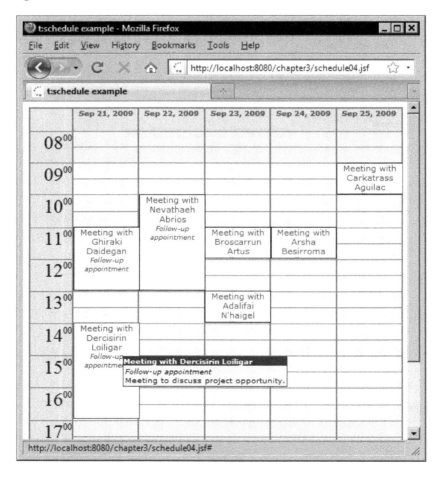

File management

Working with files is another common scenario for web developers. Many web applications and content management systems enable users to upload files from their desktop to a remote server. HTML includes support for file transfer through the use of a form tag with an `enctype` attribute set to `multipart/form-data`. By properly setting the encoding of our HTML forms, this enables the browser to send file data to a web server. The JSF `HtmlForm` component also supports this behavior, and when combined with the Tomahawk `HtmlInputFileUpload` component, we can add file management capabilities to our web application fairly easily.

To enable file upload with the Tomahawk library, we need to declare the **MyFaces Extension Filter** in our web application's configuration file (`web.xml`). The Extension Filter is an important web-tier component of the Tomahawk library, and is responsible for inserting the resources needed for rendering Tomahawk UI components (such as JavaScript files and Cascading Style Sheets) into the HTML document before it is sent to the browser. We must add the following filter to our `web.xml` file:

```xml
<filter>
  <filter-name>MyFacesExtensionsFilter</filter-name>
  <filter-class>org.apache.myfaces.webapp.filter.ExtensionsFilter
   </filter-class>
  <init-param>
    <param-name>maxFileSize</param-name>
    <param-value>20m</param-value>
  </init-param>
</filter>
<filter-mapping>
  <filter-name>MyFacesExtensionsFilter</filter-name>
  <servlet-name>Faces Servlet</servlet-name>
</filter-mapping>
<filter-mapping>
  <filter-name>MyFacesExtensionsFilter</filter-name>
  <url-pattern>/faces/myFacesExtensionResource/*</url-pattern>
</filter-mapping>
<filter-mapping>
  <filter-name>MyFacesExtensionsFilter</filter-name>
  <url-pattern>*.jsf</url-pattern>
</filter-mapping>
<filter-mapping>
  <filter-name>MyFacesExtensionsFilter</filter-name>
  <url-pattern>/faces/*</url-pattern>
</filter-mapping>
```

Notice that we can limit the uploaded file size by setting the `maxFileSize` initialization parameter. In this case, we set the maximum size to `20` megabytes.

Uploading a file

In this example, we use the `<t:inputFileUpload>` tag to render the file upload component on our JSF page. The value expression for this tag is bound to a property in our backing bean of type `UploadedFile`. When the user clicks on the submit button labeled **Upload**, the browser sends the file data to our web application and the JSF framework invokes our `uploadFile` backing bean method.

The following markup demonstrates how to use the `<t:inputFileUpload>` tag in our JSF page:

```
<h:form enctype="multipart/form-data">
  <h:panelGrid columns="1">
    <h:panelGroup>
      <t:inputFileUpload value="#{backingBean.uploadedFile}" />
      <h:commandButton value="Upload"
        actionListener="#{backingBean.uploadFile}" />
    </h:panelGroup>
    <h:panelGroup>
      <h:outputText value="Directory listing for:
        #{backingBean.uploadDirectory.name}" />
      <t:dataList value="#{backingBean.uploadedFiles}"
        var="file" layout="unorderedList">
        <h:outputLink value="file:///#{file.path}">
          <h:outputText value="#{file.name}" />
        </h:outputLink>
      </t:dataList>
    </h:panelGroup>
  </h:panelGrid>
</h:form>
```

The following Java source code demonstrates how to handle the file upload event in our backing bean:

```
public void uploadFile(ActionEvent event) {
    InputStream in = null;
    OutputStream out = null;
    try {
        if (uploadedFile != null) {
          in = uploadedFile.getInputStream();
          File dir = getUploadDirectory();
          if (!dir.exists()) {
            if (!dir.mkdir()) {
              throw new IOException("Unable to make directory: " +
                                    dir);
            }
          }
```

```
            File file = new File(dir, uploadedFile.getName());
            out = new FileOutputStream(file);
            byte[] buffer = new byte[1024];
            while (in.read(buffer) != -1) {
              out.write(buffer);
            }
            out.flush();
            out.close();
            in.close();
        }
    } catch (Exception e) {
       e.printStackTrace();
    } finally {
        try {
            if (out != null) {
                out.flush();
                out.close();
            }
            if (in != null) {
                in.close();
            }
        } catch (Exception e) {
        }
    }
}
```

When the page is rendered again, we iterate all the files contained in the upload directory as an unordered list as seen in the following screenshot:

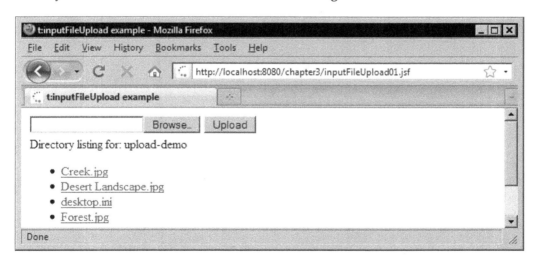

Working with trees

In desktop software applications, trees represent a convenient and intuitive type of control that users can interact with to perform a variety of tasks, such as navigating a file system, managing operating system users and groups, browsing threaded messages on an Internet newsgroup, exploring an XML document, and working with other types of hierarchically structured data.

The Tomahawk component library includes a number of components that can be used to implement tree controls for our JSF applications. Let's look at some examples of how we can integrate a tree component with our file management example to enable users to browse the files that they've uploaded to our web application.

Creating a tree

In this example, the `<t:tree>` tag is used to render a tree component on our JSF page. This time, instead of rendering the uploaded files as an ordered list, we render them as a dynamic tree.

```
<h:form enctype="multipart/form-data">
  <h:panelGrid columns="1">
    <h:panelGroup>
      <t:inputFileUpload value="#{backingBean.uploadedFile}" />
      <h:commandButton value="Upload"
        actionListener="#{backingBean.uploadFile}" />
    </h:panelGroup>
    <h:panelGroup>
      <h:outputText value="Directory listing for:
        #{backingBean.uploadDirectory.name}" />
      <t:tree value="#{backingBean.uploadedFilesTreeModel}"
        expandRoot="true" />
    </h:panelGroup>
  </h:panelGrid>
</h:form>
```

The Java code required to provide the model data for the tree component is as follows. In this case, we get a reference to a `java.io.File` object representing the file upload directory. Next, we construct a Tomahawk `DefaultMutableTreeNode` object and pass the directory name to the constructor. This constructor argument provides the string to be rendered as the tree node's label. Next, we set the `userObject` property of the tree node, passing in our `FileAdapter` object wrapped around the `File` object. Then, we call the recursive `buildTreeModel()` method to perform the tree initialization based on the files contained in the upload directory.

```
public org.apache.myfaces.custom.tree.model.TreeModel
```

```
getUploadedFilesTreeModel() {
File dir = getUploadDirectory();
DefaultMutableTreeNode root = new
  DefaultMutableTreeNode(dir.getName());
root.setUserObject(new FileAdapter(dir));
buildTreeModel(dir, root);
org.apache.myfaces.custom.tree.model.TreeModel model = new
  DefaultTreeModel(root);
return model;
}
```

The `buildTreeModel()` method iterates the files in a directory, and creates a `DefaultMutableTreeNode` for each file. If a file is a directory, we call the method recursively to add that directory's files to the current tree node. The result is a Tomahawk tree model object that represents the uploaded files on the file system.

```
private void buildTreeModel(File dir, DefaultMutableTreeNode root) {
  File[] files = dir.listFiles();
  if (files != null) {
    for (File file : files) {
      DefaultMutableTreeNode node = new
        DefaultMutableTreeNode(file.getName());
      node.setUserObject(new FileAdapter(file));
      root.insert(node);
      if (file.isDirectory()) {
        buildTreeModel(file, node);
      }
    }
  }
}
```

 Adapter design pattern: There are many software design patterns that can be used effectively to implement JSF applications. Sometimes, it is necessary to adapt a class for use in another context that it was not originally written for. This is similar to the way we can purchase a power adapter for an electric shaver or hairdryer when we travel overseas.

Here, we use the adapter design pattern to wrap the `java.io.File` class with another class that exposes JavaBeans-style properties to our JSF page.

```
package chapter2.model;
import java.net.URLConnection;
import java.util.Date;
/**
 * This class is a model adapter for the java.io.File class.
 * It makes it easier to render the file's information in the
```

```
 *   view.
 *
 * @author Ian
 *
 */
public class FileAdapter {
    private java.io.File file;
    public FileAdapter(java.io.File file) {
        this.file = file;
    }
    public Date getLastModified() {
        return new Date(file.lastModified());
    }
    public String getName() {
        return file.getName();
    }
    public long getSize() {
        return file.length();
    }
    public String getUrl() {
        String url = null;
        try {
            url = file.toURL().toExternalForm();
        } catch (Exception e) {
            e.printStackTrace();
        }
        return url;
    }
    public String getType() {
        String type = "file";
        if (file.isDirectory()) {
            type = "directory";
        }
        return type;
    }
    public String getContentType() {
        String contentType = null;
        try {
            URLConnection connection =
                file.toURL().openConnection();
            contentType = connection.getContentType();
        } catch (Exception e) {
            e.printStackTrace();
        }
        return contentType;
    }
    public String toString() {
        return file.getName();
```

```
    };
  }
```

The following is an example of a file system folder hierarchy rendered by the Tomahawk tree component:

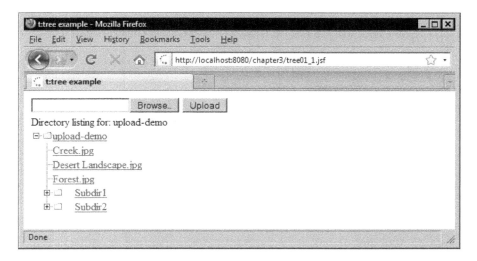

Creating a tree column

The `<t:tree>` tag also accepts nested `<t:treeColumn>` and `<h:column>` tags. This combination of tags can be used effectively to create a tree table component, where some of the data is rendered as a dynamic tree and some of it is rendered as table columns. This is similar to the way file browser windows behave on desktop operating systems. By using this technique, we can make our JSF application behave more like a desktop application.

The `<t:tree>` tag has a `value` attribute that expects a value expression of type `TreeModel` and a `var` attribute that defines the name of the variable used to iterate the nodes of the tree model. Inside the tag, we can reference the user object property of the current tree node by using this variable. In our example, the `node` variable will have a reference to a `FileAdapter` object at request time. We can use this variable to display specific information about each file, such as the file type, the file size, and the last modified date.

```
<h:form enctype="multipart/form-data">
  <h:panelGrid columns="1">
    <h:panelGroup>
      <t:inputFileUpload value="#{backingBean.uploadedFile}" />
```

```
        <h:commandButton value="Upload"
          actionListener="#{backingBean.uploadFile}" />
      </h:panelGroup>
      <h:panelGroup>
        <h:outputText value="Directory listing for:
          #{backingBean.uploadDirectory.name}" />
        <t:tree
          value="#{backingBean.uploadedFilesTreeModel}"
          var="node" expandRoot="true"
          columnClasses="right-aligned,centered"
          styleClass="treeTable">
          <t:treeColumn>
            <f:facet name="header">
              <h:outputText value="File Name" />
            </f:facet>
            <h:outputText value="#{node.name}" />
          </t:treeColumn>
          <h:column>
            <f:facet name="header">
              <h:outputText value="Size (KB)" />
            </f:facet>
            <h:outputText value="#{node.size}">
              <f:convertNumber type="number"
                maxFractionDigits="2" groupingUsed="true" />
            </h:outputText>
          </h:column>
          <h:column>
            <f:facet name="header">
              <h:outputText value="Last Modified" />
            </f:facet>
            <h:outputText value="#{node.lastModified}">
              <f:convertDateTime dateStyle="full"
                type="both" />
            </h:outputText>
          </h:column>
        </t:tree>
      </h:panelGroup>
    </h:panelGrid>
</h:form>
```

The following screenshot shows the rendered Tomahawk `<t:tree>` tag combined with `<t:treeColumn>` tags to produce a dynamic tree table:

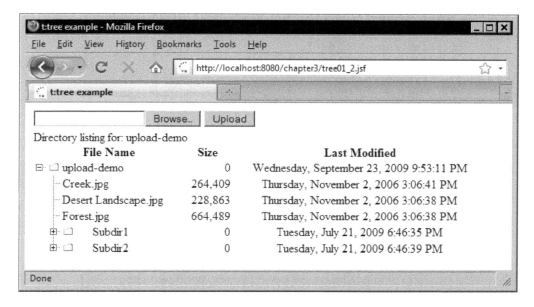

Customizing the tree component

The `<t:tree2>` tag in the Tomahawk component library also renders a tree component and is more customizable than the `<t:tree>` tag. It is important to note that the two tree components in the Tomahawk library have similar but also different behavior. In this example, we use the `<t:tree2>` tag to render a tree component with custom icons for files and folders.

Custom tree node icons can be defined by declaring a named facet for each node type that we are displaying in the tree. When the component is rendered, the graphic image in each facet will be rendered for the corresponding tree node. In our backing bean, we have to construct the tree model in a different way, as shown in the following markup:

```
<h:form enctype="multipart/form-data">
  <h:panelGrid columns="1">
    <h:panelGroup>
      <t:inputFileUpload value="#{backingBean.uploadedFile}" />
      <h:commandButton value="Upload"
        actionListener="#{backingBean.uploadFile}" />
    </h:panelGroup>
```

```
<h:panelGroup>
<h:outputText value="Directory listing for:
  #{backingBean.uploadDirectory.name}" />
<t:tree2 value="#{backingBean.uploadedFilesTree2Model}"
  var="node">
  <f:facet name="folder">
    <h:panelGroup>
      <f:facet name="expand">
        <h:graphicImage value="images/yellow-folder-
          open.png" />
      </f:facet>
      <f:facet name="collapse">
        <h:graphicImage value="images/yellow-folder-
          closed.png" />
      </f:facet>
      <h:outputText value="#{node.description}" />
    </h:panelGroup>
  </f:facet>
  <f:facet name="file">
    <h:panelGroup>
      <h:graphicImage value="images/document.png" />
      <h:outputText value="#{node.description}" />
    </h:panelGroup>
  </f:facet>
</t:tree2>
  </h:panelGroup>
 </h:panelGrid>
</h:form>
```

The Java code required to produce a tree model for this component is as
follows. Notice that we use recursion to build the tree model for both the tree
component examples.

```
public TreeNode getUploadedFilesTree2Model() {
  File dir = getUploadDirectory();
  TreeNode root = new TreeNodeBase("folder", dir.getName(),
    false);
  buildTree2Model(dir, root);
  return root;
}

@SuppressWarnings("unchecked")
private void buildTree2Model(File dir, TreeNode root) {
  File[] files = dir.listFiles();
  if (files != null) {
    for (File file : files) {
```

```
        boolean leaf = false;
        String name = file.getName();
        String type = null;
        if (file.isDirectory()) {
          type = "folder";
        } else {
          type = "file";
          leaf = true;
        }
        TreeNode node = new TreeNodeBase(type, name, leaf);
        root.getChildren().add(node);
        if (file.isDirectory()) {
          buildTree2Model(file, node);
        }
      }
    }
  }
```

The <t:tree2> tag is similar to the <t:tree> tag, but it is easier to customize the node icons with this tag.

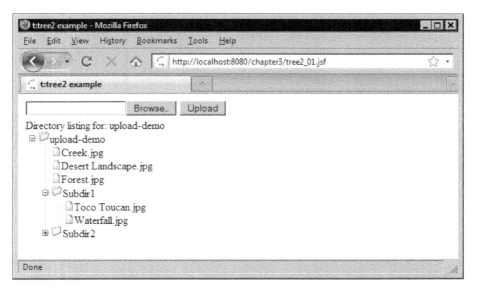

Navigation menus

The Tomahawk component library includes a number of useful components for creating navigation menus for our JSF applications. Depending on the information architecture of the website, and the number of static and dynamic views within the application, a navigation menu may be simple or complex. It may have a small set of top-level menu items, or it may have a large number of submenus and submenu items.

The navigation components in the Tomahawk component library integrate with the declarative navigation and page flow support provided by the JSF framework. A typical JSF application will have navigation rules declared in `faces-config.xml` that specify the page flow for the use cases supported by the application.

```
<navigation-rule>
  <display-name>*</display-name>
  <from-view-id>*</from-view-id>
  <navigation-case>
    <from-outcome>products</from-outcome>
    <to-view-id>/products.jsf</to-view-id>
    <redirect />
  </navigation-case>
</navigation-rule>
<navigation-rule>
  <display-name>products.jsf</display-name>
  <from-view-id>/products.jsf</from-view-id>
  <navigation-case>
    <from-outcome>outofstock</from-outcome>
    <to-view-id>/outofstock.jsf</to-view-id>
    <redirect />
  </navigation-case>
</navigation-rule>
<navigation-rule>
  <display-name>products.jsf</display-name>
  <from-view-id>/products.jsf</from-view-id>
  <navigation-case>
    <from-outcome>order</from-outcome>
    <to-view-id>/orderform.jsf</to-view-id>
    <redirect />
  </navigation-case>
</navigation-rule>
```

The navigation rules declared in `faces-config.xml` can be visualized using a graphical page flow tool such as the Eclipse **Web Tools Platform** (**WTP**) with JSF support. In this example, we define a global navigation rule and two navigation rules to handle two different outcomes related to placing an order for a particular product from the products page.

In the first case, we redirect to the product page from any other page in the site when the outcome of an action is "products". In the second and third cases, if the user has selected a product and that product is out of stock, we redirect the browser to a page that displays an appropriate message to the user. If the inventory level for the selected product is greater than zero, then we redirect the browser to an order form page.

The following screenshot shows how to design a JSF page flow visually using the WTP JSF tooling:

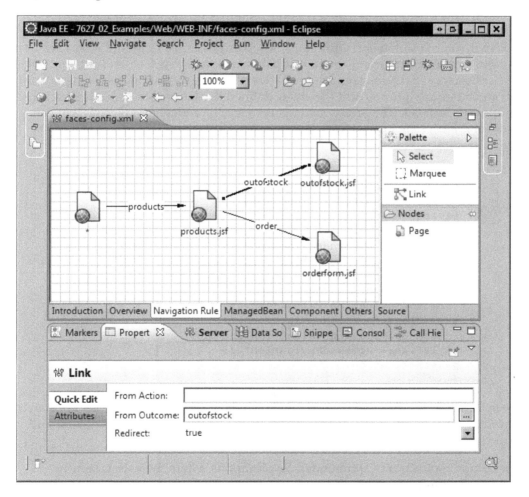

The previous screenshot demonstrates the Eclipse IDE's visualization of a few simple navigation rules for our application. These include a global navigation rule from any page (indicated by the asterisk symbol) to the "products" page, and two specific outcomes from the products page: one for an "out-of-stock" page and one for an "order" page. Now that we have some navigation rules declared, we can discuss how to use the various navigation components within the Tomahawk component library.

Creating a navigation menu

The HtmlPanelNavigation component is rendered by the <t:panelNavigation> tag as a vertical navigation menu. This component renders its children as rows in an HTML <table> element. Optionally, a separator can be rendered after each item by defining the style or styleClass attributes of the <t:panelNavigation> tag. If <t:commandNavigation> tags are used to render the navigation items, the separator CSS attributes are ignored and the styles defined by the <t:commandNavigation> tag are used instead. The HtmlCommandNavigation renders a hyperlink that can invoke a JSF backing bean action method. The return value of the action method determines the next view to be displayed in the browser.

```
<h:form>
  <t:panelNavigation>
    <t:commandNavigation value="Home"
      styleClass="commandNavigation" />
    <t:commandNavigation value="About"
      styleClass="commandNavigation" />
    <t:commandNavigation value="Products"
      action="#{productBean.findAllProducts}"
      styleClass="commandNavigation" />
    <t:commandNavigation value="Services"
      styleClass="commandNavigation" />
    <t:commandNavigation value="Contact Us"
      styleClass="commandNavigation" />
  </t:panelNavigation>
</h:form>
```

The HtmlPanelNavigation is ideal for cases where the push-style MVC approach is needed, such as when a list of products must be retrieved from a database and processed in memory before being displayed in the view.

This component is not recommended for situations where the user is simply navigating from one view to the next, and where no data processing is required in between requests. For simple navigation scenarios, the HtmlPanelNavigationMenu component offers several advantages over the HtmlPanelNavigation component.

Push-style versus pull-style MVC pattern

The push-style MVC approach is limited because (a) it requires a form POST submission that cannot be bookmarked easily by users or indexed by search engines, (b) it requires additional effort to implement the Post-Redirect-Get pattern to solve the double submit problem, and (c) it requires that any data prepared by the backing bean is stored in session scope so that it can survive two HTTP requests, increasing memory usage on the application server.

In general, the pull-style MVC approach is superior because (a) it defers data access to the rendering phase of the JSF request processing lifecycle, (b) it supports RESTful, bookmarkable, and search engine friendly URLs, (c) it only requires a GET request and so does not suffer from the double submit problem, and (d) it does not require session scope as data can be retrieved conveniently in a single HTTP request.

The following screenshot shows the navigation menu produced by the `<t:panelNavigation>` tag:

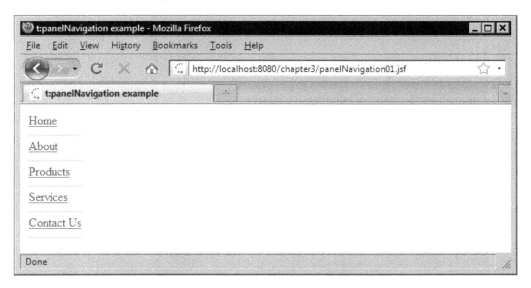

Creating bookmarkable navigation menus

The `HtmlPanelNavigationMenu` component, rendered by the `<t:panelNavigation2>` tag, is a powerful navigation control in the Tomahawk component library. It is compatible with the `HtmlCommandNavigationItem` component, an enhanced version of the `HtmlCommandNavigation` component that supports menu item activation states, submenus, horizontal and vertical layouts, dynamically generated menu items, bookmarkable URLs, and more.

For simple navigation links, we can use the `externalLink` attribute of the `<t:commandNavigation2>` tag to render hyperlinks in the navigation menu. These links will produce GET requests so they can be bookmarked more easily by users. Additionally, we can use the `activeOnViewIds` attribute of this tag to indicate which views in our application should cause the menu items to appear activated.

In this example, we also use the `<t:navigationMenuItems>` tag to render a dynamically generated navigation menu from a list of products. This component can be used to implement both push-style and pull-style MVC patterns. Using a push-style MVC approach, we would invoke an action method in our backing bean to select a product before redirecting the user to another view.

```
<h:form>
  <t:panelNavigation2 layout="list" itemClass="mypage"
    activeItemClass="selected" openItemClass="selected"
    renderAll="true">
    <t:commandNavigation2 externalLink="index.jsf"
      activeOnViewIds="/index.jsf">
      <h:outputText value="Home" />
    </t:commandNavigation2>
    <t:commandNavigation2 externalLink="about.jsf"
      activeOnViewIds="/about.jsf">
      <h:outputText value="About" />
    </t:commandNavigation2>
    <t:navigationMenuItems
      value="#{productBean.productsNavigationMenuItemPull}" />
    <t:commandNavigation2 externalLink="services.jsf"
      activeOnViewIds="/services.jsf">
      <h:outputText value="Services" />
      <t:commandNavigation2 externalLink="integration.jsf"
        activeOnViewIds="/integration.jsf">
        <h:outputText value="Integration" />
      </t:commandNavigation2>
      <t:commandNavigation2 externalLink="training.jsf"
        activeOnViewIds="/training.jsf">
        <h:outputText value="Training" />
      </t:commandNavigation2>
      <t:commandNavigation2 externalLink="support.jsf"
        activeOnViewIds="/support.jsf">
```

```
        <h:outputText value="Support" />
      </t:commandNavigation2>
    </t:commandNavigation2>
    <t:commandNavigation2 externalLink="contact.jsf"
      activeOnViewIds="/contact.jsf">
        <h:outputText value="Contact Us" />
    </t:commandNavigation2>
  </t:panelNavigation2>
</h:form>
```

The Java code required to render a dynamic navigation menu that supports product selection is as follows:

```
public NavigationMenuItem getProductsNavigationMenuItemPush()
{
String context =
  FacesContext.getCurrentInstance().getExternalContext().
  getRequestContextPath();
String view = context + "/products.jsf";
NavigationMenuItem menu = new NavigationMenuItem();
menu.setLabel("Products");
menu.setActiveOnViewIds("/products.jsf");
menu.setExternalLink(view);
List<Product> products = getProducts();
for (Product product : products) {
  NavigationMenuItem item = new NavigationMenuItem();
  item.setAction("products");
  item.setLabel(product.getName());
  item.setActionListener("#{productBean.selectProduct}");
  item.setValue(product);
  menu.add(item);
}
return menu;
}
```

When the user clicks on a product in our navigation menu, the selectProduct method in our backing bean is invoked. We obtain the value from the component and assign it to our selectedProduct property before redirecting the user to the view indicated by the "products" action outcome.

```
public void selectProduct(ActionEvent event) {
  UIComponent comp = event.getComponent();
  if (comp instanceof UICommand) {
    UICommand command = (UICommand) comp;
    Object value = command.getValue();
    if (value instanceof Product) {
      setSelectedProduct((Product) value);
    }
  }
}
```

Using a pull-style MVC approach, each product hyperlink will be rendered as a submenu item in the **Products** navigation menu and will pass a unique identifier for each product as a form parameter on the query string. This example demonstrates how to use pull-style MVC to implement a more RESTful approach to web development.

```
<t:navigationMenuItems
    value="#{productBean.productsNavigationMenuItemPull}" />
```

The Java code required to render bookmarkable product URLs in our navigation menu is as follows:

```
public NavigationMenuItem getProductsNavigationMenuItemPull()
  {
    String context =
      FacesContext.getCurrentInstance().getExternalContext().
      getRequestContextPath();
    String view = context + "/products.jsf";
    NavigationMenuItem menu = new NavigationMenuItem();
    menu.setLabel("Products");
    menu.setActiveOnViewIds("/products.jsf");
    menu.setExternalLink(view);
    List<Product> products = getProducts();
    for (Product product : products) {
      NavigationMenuItem item = new NavigationMenuItem();
      item.setAction("products");
      item.setLabel(product.getName());
      item.setExternalLink(view + "?product=" +
        product.getId());
      item.setValue(product);
      menu.add(item);
    }
    return menu;
  }
```

When the user clicks on a hyperlink, the browser sends a GET request to our web application that includes a "product" request parameter, that is, the product ID. The Java code required to look up the product by ID is as follows. In this example, we simply look up the product by ID in a hash map, but in a real application we could also perform a database query to retrieve the data.

```
public Product getSelectedProduct() {
  FacesContext context = FacesContext.getCurrentInstance();
  ExternalContext external = context.getExternalContext();
  String param =
    external.getRequestParameterMap().get("product");
  if (param != null && !param.equals("")) {
    selectedProduct = productsById.get(param);
  }
  return selectedProduct;
}
```

After clicking on **Products**, the user is redirected to the **Products** page where more information about the selected product is displayed, as seen in the next screenshot:

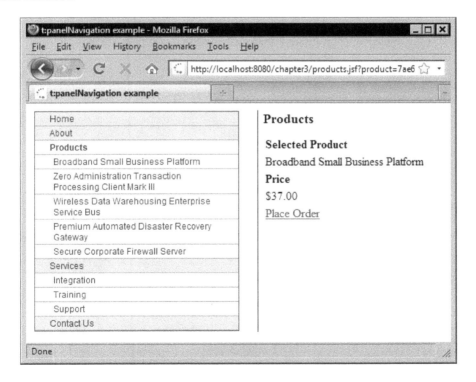

Notice the **Place Order** link on the **Products** page. This is a standard
`<h:commandLink>` tag rendering an `HtmlCommandLink` component that invokes a
JSF action method in our backing bean. Depending on the outcome of the method,
the user may be redirected to one of two pages. If the inventory level for the selected
product is greater than zero, the user will be redirected to an order form page, if the
inventory level is zero, then he/she will be redirected to an "out-of-stock" page.

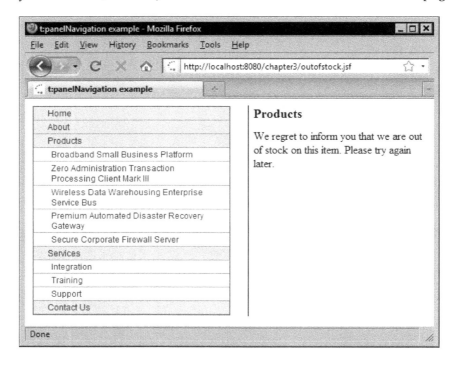

The `HtmlPanelNavigationMenu` component rendered by the `<t:panelNavigation2>`
tag can also display a horizontal menu with the creative use of CSS styling, as shown
in the next screenshot:

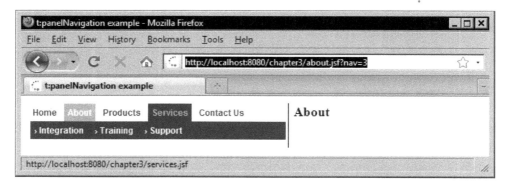

Populating a navigation menu

The `<t:navigationMenuItem>` tag adds a `NavigationMenuItem` object to its parent component. A `NavigationMenuItem` is a subclass of the standard JSF `SelectItem` class that is used to represent a menu item in a navigation menu tree. This tag can be used to render a single menu item. For dynamic navigation menus, we can use the `<t:navigationMenuItems>` tag and bind it to a property in our backing bean.

Generating dynamic navigation menus

The `<t:navigationMenuItems>` tag can be used to generate dynamic navigation menus. The `value` attribute of this tag accepts a value expression that evaluates to an `HtmlNavigationMenuItem` or a collection of `HtmlNavigationMenuItem` objects.

Using the JSCookMenu component

The `JSCookMenu` is a popular, open source JavaScript menu system that can be used to render simple or complex navigation menus for a web application using different layouts. The Tomahawk component library supports this menu through the `<t:jscookMenu>` tag.

In the following example, we render a horizontal navigation menu that includes a combination of `<t:navigationMenuItem>` and `<t:navigationMenuItems>` tags to produce a navigation menu that has both static and dynamic elements.

 For this component to function properly, all navigation menu items must have corresponding navigation rules in `faces-config.xml`.

```
<h:form>
  <t:jscookMenu theme="ThemeOffice" layout="hbr">
    <t:navigationMenuItem itemLabel="Home" action="home" />
    <t:navigationMenuItem itemLabel="About" action="about" />
    <t:navigationMenuItems
      value="#{productBean.productsJsCookMenuItem}" />
    <t:navigationMenuItem itemLabel="Services"
      action="services" />
    <t:navigationMenuItem itemLabel="Contact Us"
      action="contact" />
  </t:jscookMenu>
  <input type="hidden" name="jscook_action" />
</h:form>
```

Additionally, the code required to produce a dynamic navigation menu is slightly different for this example. As the `NavigationMenuItem` object's value is encoded as a string in the HTML response sent to the browser, we must provide the appropriate string representation of our product object using the product's `id` property.

```
public NavigationMenuItem getProductsJsCookMenuItem() {
  String context =
    FacesContext.getCurrentInstance().getExternalContext().
    getRequestContextPath();
  String view = context + "/products.jsf";
  NavigationMenuItem menu = new NavigationMenuItem();
  menu.setLabel("Products");
  menu.setActiveOnViewIds("/products.jsf");
  menu.setExternalLink(view);
  List<Product> products = getProducts();
  for (Product product : products) {
    NavigationMenuItem item = new NavigationMenuItem();
    item.setAction("products");
    item.setLabel(product.getName());
    item.setActionListener("#{productBean.selectProduct}");
    item.setValue(product.getId());
    menu.add(item);
  }
  return menu;
}
```

When the user clicks on the **Products** link in the navigation menu, our backing bean method is invoked and the selected product is stored for rendering in the view.

```
public void selectProduct(ActionEvent event) {
  UIComponent comp = event.getComponent();
  if (comp instanceof UICommand) {
    UICommand command = (UICommand) comp;
    Object value = command.getValue();
    if (value instanceof Product) {
      setSelectedProduct((Product) value);
    } else if (value instanceof String) {
      String id = (String) value;
      Product product = productsById.get(id);
      setSelectedProduct(product);
    }
  }
}
```

The `<t:jsCookMenu>` tag renders an interactive JavaScript menu system based on the `JSCookMenu` library as shown in the following screenshot:

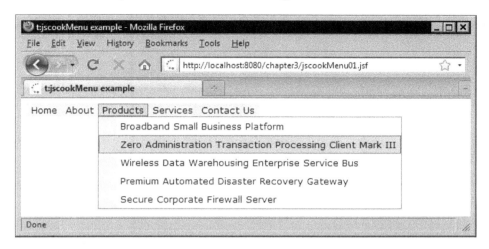

In the next example, we modify the `JSCookMenu` component to use a different theme and a vertical orientation by changing the `layout` attribute from "hbr" (horizontally, bottom-right) to "vbr" (vertically, bottom-right).

```
<h:form>
  <t:jscookMenu theme="ThemeOffice" layout="vbr">
    <t:navigationMenuItem itemLabel="Home" action="home" />
    <t:navigationMenuItem itemLabel="About" action="about" />
    <t:navigationMenuItems
      value="#{productBean.productsJsCookMenuItem}" />
    <t:navigationMenuItem itemLabel="Services"
      action="services" />
    <t:navigationMenuItem itemLabel="Contact Us"
      action="contact" />
  </t:jscookMenu>
  <input type="hidden" name="jscook_action" />
</h:form>
```

The following screenshot shows the JSCookMenu rendered in a vertical orientation with the "ThemeOffice" look and feel:

User interface security

Security is an important consideration that should be at the forefront of our minds when we design our user interfaces. Fortunately, many components in the Tomahawk component library have built-in security features that help to integrate our user interfaces with the Java security architecture.

For example, we may want to display certain controls on our screen only for certain users when they login to our application. An administrative user may be able to modify other users' accounts while a normal user cannot. How do we ensure that the UI components associated with higher privileged users and use cases are not exposed to users with insufficient privileges?

Before we discuss how to implement user interface security using Tomahawk components, let's examine the underlying security mechanisms of the Java EE runtime environment.

JSF applications run inside what is known as a web container. A **web container** is a standardized Java EE runtime environment for web applications that is capable of processing HTTP requests from a web browser, invoking Java Servlets and JSP pages, and serving a response, typically an HTML document, back to the browser.

One of the most popular open source web containers for Java is the Apache Tomcat Servlet/JSP engine. We will be using Apache Tomcat to run the examples for several chapters in this book. In later chapters, we will use the JBoss application server to demonstrate how to integrate a JSF application with EJB 3 components to access a relational database.

A Java web container can use a number of mechanisms to implement web application security. We will look at how to use the **Java Authentication and Authorization Service (JAAS)** in an Apache Tomcat environment to implement **role-based access control (RBAC)** using Tomahawk components. The first step is to configure our web application's deployment descriptor, the web.xml file, in our WEB-INF folder, to define the roles and security constraints required by our application.

Configuring web.xml

The first step in securing our user interface is to declare some roles and security constraints in our web application deployment descriptor. On its own, Java EE declarative security only allows us to implement role-based access control at the page or resource level of our web application. What if we want a more fine-grained role-based access control at the UI component level? Tomahawk components allow us to implement Java EE declarative security at the user interface component level.

To demonstrate, the roles declared in our web.xml file will be enforced at the page level of our application by applying Java security constraints to resource collections. At the same time, we will enforce these same role-based permissions at the level of user interface controls in some of our views using the Tomahawk HtmlCommandButton and HtmlCommandLink components.

In the following example from our web.xml file, we declare a user role and an administrator role and we indicate that HTTP basic authentication is required when the user accesses the /user/* and /admin/* resource collections within the web application.

```
<login-config>
  <auth-method>BASIC</auth-method>
  <realm-name>Authentication Required</realm-name>
</login-config>
<security-role>
  <description>The User role.</description>
  <role-name>User</role-name>
</security-role>
<security-role>
  <description>The Administrator role.</description>
    <role-name>Administrator</role-name>
```

```
    </security-role>

    <security-constraint>
      <display-name>Administrator access only</display-name>
      <web-resource-collection>
        <web-resource-name>The Admin area</web-resource-name>
        <url-pattern>/admin/*</url-pattern>
      </web-resource-collection>
      <auth-constraint>
        <description>Required roles for the Admin
          area.</description>
        <role-name>Administrator</role-name>
      </auth-constraint>
    </security-constraint>

    <security-constraint>
      <display-name>Authenticated users only</display-name>
      <web-resource-collection>
      <web-resource-name>The User area</web-resource-name>
        <url-pattern>/users/*</url-pattern>
      </web-resource-collection>
      <auth-constraint>
        <description>Required roles for the Admin
          area.</description>
        <role-name>User</role-name>
      </auth-constraint>
    </security-constraint>
```

Next, we enable Tomcat's built-in user database JAAS login module to handle our authentication attempts. This is achieved by replacing the tomcat-users.xml file with the following XML:

```
    <tomcat-users>
      <role rolename="User"/>
      <role rolename="Administrator"/>
      <user username="user" password="user" roles="User"/>
      <user username="admin" password="admin"
        roles="User,Administrator"/>
    </tomcat-users>
```

When we attempt to access the admin area of the website we get the following authentication dialog in the browser:

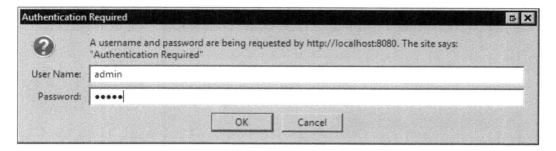

Security-enabled components

To demonstrate how the Tomahawk component library extends the concept of container-managed security to the user interface level, let's look at a simple example of how to render components conditionally based on the user's authenticated roles.

Once we have been authenticated as an administrator by Tomcat, our browser session will be associated with a JAAS subject with two security principles—one representing our "Administrator" role and the other representing our "User" role.

On the administrator page, we render a form with four controls on it. The first row in the panel grid contains two buttons, one that is enabled for users with the "Administrator" role, and one that is enabled for users with the "User" role. The second row in the grid contains two links, one that is visible for users with the "Administrator" role, and one that is visible for users with the "User" role. As our administrator account has both roles, all the controls are enabled and visible on the screen.

```
<h:form>
  <h:panelGrid columns="2">
    <t:commandButton enabledOnUserRole="Administrator"
      value="Administrator Button" />
    <t:commandButton enabledOnUserRole="User" value="User
      Button" />
    <t:commandLink value="Administrator Link"
      visibleOnUserRole="Administrator" />
    <t:commandLink value="User Link" visibleOnUserRole="User" />
  </h:panelGrid>
</h:form>
```

The following screenshot shows the administrator screen. Note that all the controls are visible.

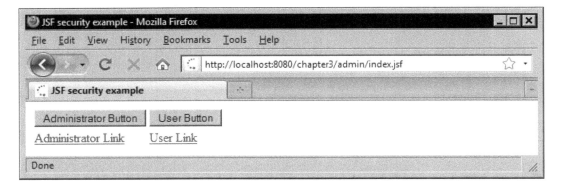

Suppose we close and reopen our browser, and then attempt login once again to the admin area of the application. This time, let's enter the "user" account credentials, as shown in this screenshot:

The standard web container security mechanism prevents us from accessing the admin area due to insufficient privileges associated with our account, and we get an **HTTP status 403** error page instead as shown in the next screenshot:

Let's navigate to the user's area of the application. The following screenshot displays the user page. This page contains an exact duplicate of the admin area page. Now we can see only three controls on the screen: the administrator button is disabled and the administrator link is no longer visible.

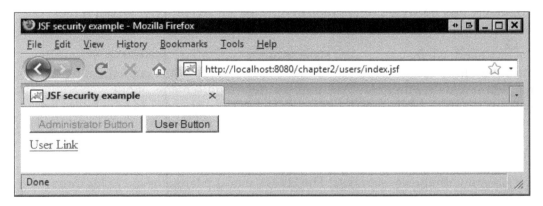

Tomahawk SecurityContext EL extension

The Tomahawk library includes an extension to the JSF Expression Language that introduces the #{securityContext} object, which provides access to container-managed security context information. Unlike the Tomahawk visibleOnUserRole and enabledOnUserRole attributes, this information is available to any JSF UI component. For more information, please see the MyFaces website (http://wiki.apache.org/myfaces/SecurityContext).

Displaying data

There are many ways to display data to the user with HTML. For example, we can use an inline series of text values, an unordered list, an ordered list, a definition list, or a table to present the same information. In the previous chapter, we looked at an example that used an HTML <table> element rendered by the <h:dataTable> tag. In this chapter, we will look at several Tomahawk components that support iterating Java data structures and rendering data to the user in interesting ways.

Let's begin by studying the HTML tags available for presenting lists and collections of information before we look at the Tomahawk components that utilize these particular tags during the rendering phase of the JSF request processing lifecycle.

When implementing a web page that displays data to the user, how do we know which are the right HTML elements to use? The answer to this question depends on a number of factors, such as the volume and type of information being presented, and how the presentation of information fits into the overall context of our application.

On one hand, we may have very clear requirements from our users as to how the information should be displayed; in which case our job is just implementing what they want. On the other hand, the user interface requirements of our web application may not specify exactly how information should be displayed, in which case we must use our judgment to choose the correct set of HTML elements for a particular screen. In either case, it helps us to understand the different HTML tags available and when they should be used.

Let's begin with the list elements. The HTML markup language includes three list elements:

- <ul> represents an unordered list
- <ol> represents an ordered list
- <dl> represents a definition list

As the name suggests, an unordered list contains a series of items in no particular order, such as a shopping list. Browsers typically render this element as a bulleted list, and support customization of the bullet icons through cascading style sheets. An ordered list contains a series of items arranged in a particular order, such as a set of instructions for completing a task. A definition list represents a series of terms with corresponding definitions, such as a technical glossary.

Rendering an unordered list

The `HtmlDataList` component is ideally suited for rendering different types of dynamic lists of information. Let's look at three examples of how to use this tag to render HTML list elements. In the first example, we render a list of files as an unordered list.

```
<t:dataList value="#{backingBean.uploadedFiles}" var="file"
  layout="unorderedList">
  <h:outputLink value="file:///#{file.path}">
    <h:outputText value="#{file.name}" />
  </h:outputLink>
</t:dataList>
```

The `<t:dataList>` tag is rendered in the browser as an unordered list backed by our managed bean. We render a hyperlink control for each file in the list that navigates to the file on the local file system.

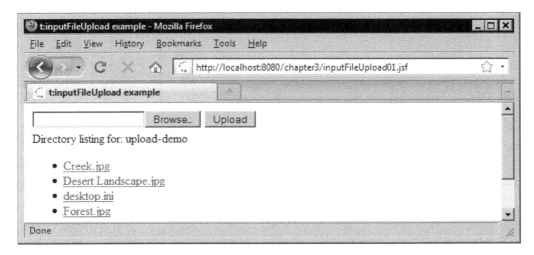

In the second example, we render the same collection of files as an ordered list.

```
<t:dataList value="#{backingBean.uploadedFiles}" var="file"
  layout="orderedList">
  <h:outputLink value="file:///#{file.path}">
    <h:outputText value="#{file.name}" />
  </h:outputLink>
</t:dataList>
```

The following screenshot shows that by setting the `layout` attribute to `orderedList`, the behavior of the tag can be changed to render an HTML ordered list for the same backing bean data.

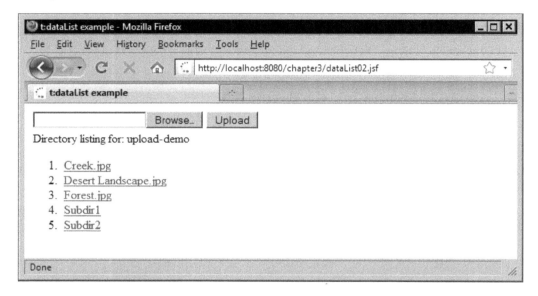

Rendering a definition list

The Tomahawk `<t:dataList>` tag does not support rendering definition lists out of the box, so we will have to use another Tomahawk tag to achieve this result. The `HtmlTag` component rendered by the `<t:htmlTag>` tag is a very flexible and useful component in the Tomahawk tag library.

It can be used to render any arbitrary HTML tag conditionally, giving us greater control over HTML rendering than is typically available when using plain HTML. In this example, we use the `HtmlTag` component together with the `HtmlDataList` component to render a definition list dynamically.

```
<t:htmlTag value="dl" rendered="#{not empty
  backingBean.adaptedUploadedFiles}">
  <t:dataList value="#{backingBean.adaptedUploadedFiles}"
    var="file" layout="simple">
  <dt>#{file.name}</dt>
  <dd>
    This #{file.type} has a content type of
    #{file.contentType}. It was last modified on
    #{file.lastModified} and contains #{file.size} bytes
    of data.
  </dd>
  </t:dataList>
</t:htmlTag>
```

The following screenshot shows a definition list rendered by combining
the `<t:dataList>` and the `<t:htmlTag>` Tomahawk tags:

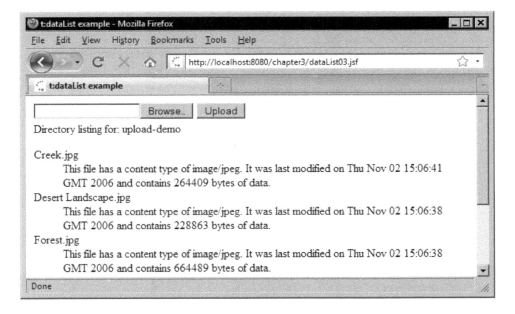

Rendering a data table

Sometimes, the data we are trying to display on a web page is too complex to
display as a list. In HTML, tables are better than lists for rendering certain types of
information. The Tomahawk component library includes several table components
that can be used to render tabular data. Let's begin by looking at the extended data
table.

The `<t:dataTable>` tag renders the Tomahawk `HtmlDataTable` component as an HTML table that introduces a number of performance and functionality improvements to the standard JSF HTML data table component.

The Tomahawk `HtmlDataTable` component includes a more sophisticated state preservation feature that enables the component to maintain its model state between HTTP requests. Additionally, this component supports column sort ordering—and conditional rendering based on user roles.

The following JSF markup demonstrates how to construct an HTML data table using the Tomahawk `<t:dataTable>` tag. The approach is similar to the standard JSF HTML data table component. The `<h:column>` tag is used to define each column, the `<t:dataTable>` tag's `value` attribute is bound to a backing bean `List` or `DataModel` property, and the `var` attribute specifies the variable name to use while rendering the rows. Notice that we have set the `sortable` attribute to true to enable column sorting.

```
<t:dataTable value="#{customerBean.customerList}"
  var="customer" rowClasses="row-even,row-odd"
  columnClasses="left-aligned,left-aligned,centered,left-
  aligned" border="2" cellpadding="5" cellspacing="2" rows="8"
  sortable="true">
  <h:column>
    <f:facet name="header">
      <h:outputText value="Full Name" />
    </f:facet>
    <h:outputText value="#{customer.fullName}" />
  </h:column>
  <h:column>
    <f:facet name="header">
      <h:outputText value="Birth Date" />
    </f:facet>
    <h:outputText value="#{customer.birthDate}">
      <f:convertDateTime type="date" dateStyle="medium" />
    </h:outputText>
  </h:column>
  <h:column>
    <f:facet name="header">
      <h:outputText value="Phone Number" />
    </f:facet>
    <h:outputText value="#{customer.phoneNumber}" />
  </h:column>
  <h:column>
    <f:facet name="header">
      <h:outputText value="Country of Origin" />
```

```
    </f:facet>
    <h:outputText value="#{customer.countryOfOrigin.name}" />
  </h:column>
</t:dataTable>
```

This screenshot displays a dynamic data table displaying customer information. The Tomahawk data table component has built-in support for column sorting. The headers are clickable links that sort the data in the table by that column.

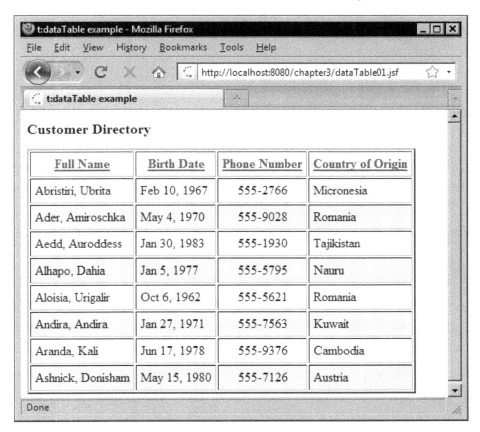

Paginating a data table

There are also situations where we have more data than we can render at once in our view. Instead of trying to display hundreds of rows in a data table, a common approach is to implement a "paging" system that allows users to navigate through a data set, one screen at a time. Conveniently, data-oriented Tomahawk components can support paging and data set navigation using the HtmlDataScroller component.

Notice in the next example that we actually use two `HtmlDataScroller` components, one to render pagination numbers, and one to render the current page and page index information.

```
<h:panelGrid columns="2" styleClass="dataTable"
  columnClasses="left-aligned,right-aligned">
  <t:dataScroller for="dataTable" paginator="true"
    paginatorMaxPages="10" paginatorActiveColumnStyle="font-
    weight:bold;" immediate="true" />
  <t:dataScroller for="dataTable" paginator="false"
    pageCountVar="pageCount" pageIndexVar="pageIndex">
    <h:outputFormat value="Page {0} of {1}">
      <f:param value="#{pageIndex}" />
      <f:param value="#{pageCount}" />
    </h:outputFormat>
  </t:dataScroller>
</h:panelGrid>
```

The next screenshot shows the Tomahawk data table component rendered with two paginator controls—one in the bottom-left corner displaying paging controls, and one in the bottom-right corner displaying the current page and total page count. This example also demonstrates the customizability of the `<t:dataScroller>` tag.

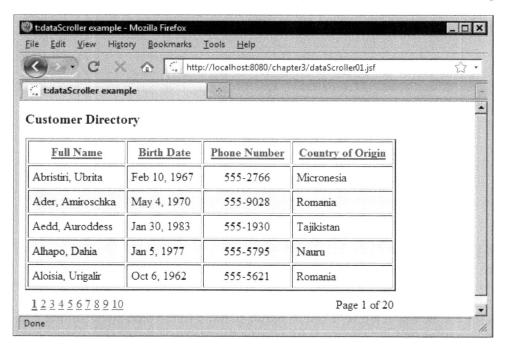

Rendering a multi-column data table with a newspaper layout

Another interesting table component within the Tomahawk component library is the `HtmlNewspaperTable` component rendered by the `<t:newspaperTable>` tag. This component is ideal for situations where we need to render dynamic data across several columns, similar to the way a newspaper displays the text for a particular story using several columns of text across the page.

```
<t:newspaperTable id="dataTable"
  value="#{customerBean.customerList}" newspaperColumns="3"
  var="customer" border="2"
  columnClasses="column-odd,column-even" cellpadding="5"
cellspacing="2"
  rows="9" sortable="true">
  <h:column>
    <h:outputLink value="##{customer.fullName}">
      <h:outputText value="#{customer.fullName}" />
    </h:outputLink>
    <h:outputText value=" was born on " />
    <h:outputText value="#{customer.birthDate}">
      <f:convertDateTime type="date" dateStyle="short" />
    </h:outputText>
    <h:outputText value=" in #{customer.countryOfOrigin}. " />
    <h:outputText value="To reach him, call
      #{customer.phoneNumber}." rendered="#{customer.male}" />
    <h:outputText value="To reach her, call
      #{customer.phoneNumber}." rendered="#{!customer.male}"
      />
  </h:column>
</t:newspaperTable>
```

The following screenshot demonstrates the Tomahawk `HtmlNewspaperTable` component. The data is rendered column by column, from top to bottom and then from left to right. Like the previous example, this table is paginated using the Tomahawk `HtmlDataScroller` component.

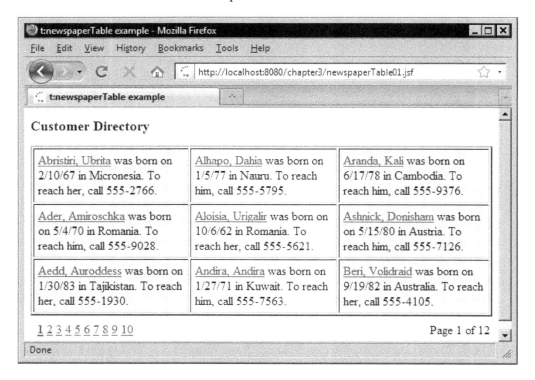

Summary

In this chapter, we examined the Tomahawk JSF component library. We looked at a number of interesting components in this library and learned how to implement common web development use cases, such as validating user input, accepting time information from the user, working with files, using tree components, creating navigation menus, securing our user interfaces, and displaying tabular data.

4
Apache MyFaces Trinidad Components

The Trinidad component library is an exciting set of over 100 rich user interface controls, including color choosers, calendars, trees, data tables, shuttle components, navigation menus, panels, and more. Trinidad also includes a number of powerful converters and validators, a templating framework, a dialog system, and is compatible with both Facelets and JSP.

In this chapter, we will look at how to build user interfaces for a JSF application using the Trinidad component library. Some of the web development tasks we will cover include:

- Receiving input from the user
- Performing client-side conversion and validation
- Enabling Ajax functionality
- Laying out components on the screen
- Shuttling selections between lists
- Working with hierarchical data using tree and tree table components
- Creating navigation menus
- Skinning and theme selection
- Implementing dialog windows for our application

As Trinidad is the first JSF component library introduced in this book that uses the popular Ajax approach for implementing a Rich Internet Application (RIA), a short introduction to Ajax is in order.

Installation and Configuration

The first step to getting started with the Apache MyFaces Trinidad framework is to download and install the necessary JAR files. These files can be obtained from the Apache website (`http://myfaces.apache.org/trinidad/index.html`). The example application for this chapter included with this book contains a fully functional Java web application with the necessary JAR files and configuration changes in `web.xml` for reference purposes. To highlight the key steps needed to use Trinidad, the following steps are needed:

1. Copy the Trinidad JAR files to the `WEB-INF/lib` directory.

2. Add the following to `web.xml`. Notice that we are specifying that we are using Facelets by setting the `org.apache.myfaces.trinidad.ALTERNATE_VIEW_HANDLER` parameter. We are also disabling view caching and enabling file modification checking for development purposes. We also specify the HTTP session for change persistence and we disable content compression to simplify debugging the Trinidad framework's JavaScript files (for example with a utility such as Firebug for the Mozilla FireFox web browser). Subsequently we register the TrinidadFilter and ResourceServlet.

```
<context-param>
  <param-name>org.apache.myfaces.trinidad.ALTERNATE_VIEW_HANDLER
  </param-name>
  <param-value>com.sun.facelets.FaceletViewHandler</param-value>
</context-param>
<context-param>
  <param-name>
    org.apache.myfaces.trinidad.USE_APPLICATION_VIEW_CACHE
  </param-name>
  <param-value>false</param-value>
</context-param>
<context-param>
  <param-name>
    org.apache.myfaces.trinidad.CHECK_FILE_MODIFICATION
  </param-name>
  <param-value>true</param-value>
</context-param>
<context-param>
  <param-name>org.apache.myfaces.trinidad.CHANGE_PERSISTENCE
  </param-name>
  <param-value>session</param-value>
</context-param>
<context-param>
  <param-name>
    org.apache.myfaces.trinidad.DISABLE_CONTENT_COMPRESSION
  </param-name>
  <param-value>true</param-value>
```

```
    </context-param>
  ...
  <filter>
    <filter-name>trinidad</filter-name>
    <filter-class>
        org.apache.myfaces.trinidad.webapp.TrinidadFilter
    </filter-class>
  </filter>
    <filter-mapping>
      <filter-name>trinidad</filter-name>
      <servlet-name>Faces Servlet</servlet-name>
    </filter-mapping>
  ...
  </filter>
  <servlet>
    <servlet-name>resources</servlet-name>
    <servlet-class>
        org.apache.myfaces.trinidad.webapp.ResourceServlet
    </servlet-class>
  </servlet>
    <servlet-mapping>
      <servlet-name>resources</servlet-name>
      <url-pattern>/adf/*</url-pattern>
    </servlet-mapping>
  ...
  </servlet>
```

What is Ajax?

Ajax is an acronym for **Asynchronous JavaScript and XML** that describes a web development technique for enhancing user interactivity and client/server communication in a web application. The term Ajax was first coined in 2005 and since then it has become one of the dominant approaches today for building **Rich Internet Applications (RIAs)**. What Ajax does is allow us to create pages that can update themselves in response to a wide variety of user interactions, creating a more responsive user interface and richer web experience for our users.

Ajax involves JavaScript code that sends asynchronous HTTP requests to the server using the XMLHttpRequest object API supported by modern browsers, then it waits a response from the server, and then it performs changes to the HTML Document Object Model (DOM) to update the web page in the browser (an approach also known as Dynamic HTML or DHTML). When the user clicks on a button, for example, the button invokes a JavaScript function that sends an HTTP request directly to the server and waits for a response. The response from the server may include XML, or it may be a plain text response in the **JavaScript Object Notation (JSON)** format.

When the JavaScript function that initiated the request receives a response, it can then update the HTML document however it chooses. For example, it may re-render an element such as a <div> tag, change some text on the page, or modify CSS attributes to create interesting visual effects. To the user, this appears almost magical. The browser has suddenly updated itself in visually appealing ways without the user having to click on the refresh button.

One of the key value propositions of JSF components is their ability to encapsulate rich behavior such as Ajax capabilities without requiring the developer to learn an Ajax API or even write a single line of JavaScript. All this good stuff is provided "right out of the box". As Ajax is supported by many JSF component libraries, such as Trinidad, ICEfaces, JBoss RichFaces/Ajax4jsf, and JSF 2.0, we will be discussing Ajax concepts throughout this book.

Receiving input from the user

The Trinidad framework introduces a rich, innovative, and intuitive set of UI components for receiving input from users. Trinidad provides components for receiving color information, date/time values, numeric input, and text from users. These components can be used to enhance the usability and appeal of an existing JSF application.

Rendering a color picker

Handling color selection can be a challenging task for web applications. The CoreInputColor component simplifies color selection in our user interface by providing an intuitive control for specifying color information.

The Trinidad framework provides the <tr:inputColor> tag to handle color selection in a JSF application. The <tr:inputColor> tag can be used in several ways. We will look at two examples of how to use this tag: one that involves a pop-up color chooser dialog, and one that renders a color selection palette on the same page.

In the first example, we use the <tr:inputColor> tag to render the CoreInputColor component as a color selection field in our form. It displays a text field with a color selection button beside it that launches a color selection window. The field is bound to a property in our backing bean of type java.awt.Color. The Trinidad framework handles the conversion of this data type for us automatically.

```
<tr:form>
    <tr:outputFormatted styleUsage="instruction" value="inputColor" />
    <tr:inputColor id="sic3" label="Enter or select color"
        value="#{customerBean.customer.favoriteColor}">
        <f:facet name="help">
```

```
                <tr:outputText value="Use format (#RRGGBB) or (r,g,b)" />
            </f:facet>
        </tr:inputColor>
            <tr:commandButton text="Submit" />
        </tr:form>
    <tr:form>
```

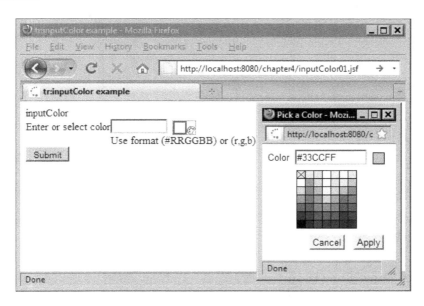

When the `<tr:inputColor>` tag is combined with the `<tr:chooseColor>` tag, Trinidad renders the color selection palette on the same page as the text field, and so does not require the use of an external window for color selection in this case. Combining these tags can be useful in situations where we want to limit the use of external windows in our user interface. The next example demonstrates this technique. Notice that we associate the `<tr:inputColor>` tag with the `<tr:colorChooser>` tag by specifying its ID in the `chooseId` attribute. We also set the `compact` and `simple` attributes to true to minimize the appearance of this control on the screen.

```
<tr:form>
    <h:panelGrid>
        <tr:outputFormatted styleUsage="instruction" value="Select a
            Color" />
        <tr:inputColor id="inputColor" compact="true" simple="true"
            value="#{customerBean.customer.favoriteColor}"
            chooseId="chooseColor" />
        <tr:colorChooser> id="chooseColor" />
```

```
            <tr:commandButton text="Submit" />
     </h:panelGrid>
  </tr:form>
```

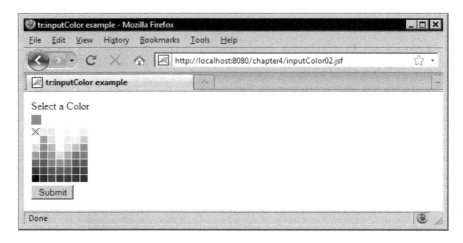

Rendering a calendar

Date and time entry is a very common task for web applications. Like the Tomahawk component library, Trinidad includes a date/time control that facilitates selecting a valid date by presenting an interactive calendar to the user.

There are several differences between the date/time components in the Apache MyFaces Tomahawk component library and those provided by the Trinidad framework. For instance, Trinidad includes only one date/time component—the `CoreInputDate` component rendered by the `<tr:inputDate>` tag—while Tomahawk includes several date/time components provided by tags such as `<t:inputDate>`, `<t:inputCalendar>`, and `<t:schedule>`.

By itself, Trinidad's `<tr:inputDate>` tag renders a text field with a button beside it that pops up a calendar window for the user to interact with. When this tag is combined with the `<tr:chooseDate>` tag, the calendar can be rendered on the same page as the text field without requiring a pop-up window. This is similar to the way the `<tr:inputColor>` tag behaves when it is combined with the `<tr:chooseColor>` tag.

The following example demonstrates how to render a Trinidad calendar inline on our JSF page.

```
     <h:panelGrid columns="1">
          <tr:outputFormatted styleUsage="instruction"
             value="Please enter your birthdate." />
```

```
        <h:panelGroup>
          <tr:chooseDate id="chooseDate"
             minValue="#{backingBean.minimumDate}" />
          <tr:inputDate chooseId="chooseDate"
             value="#{customerBean.customer.birthDate}"
             required="#{true}"
             label="#{bundle.dateOfBirthLabel}">
             <tr:validateDateTimeRange
                minimum="#{backingBean.minimumDate}" />
          </tr:inputDate>
        </h:panelGroup>
        <h:commandButton value="Submit" />
        <h:panelGroup rendered="#{customerBean.customer.birthDate ne
                                  null}">
          <h:outputText value="Your birth date is " />
          <h:outputText value="#{customerBean.customer.birthDate}">
             <f:convertDateTime dateStyle="full" type="date" />
          </h:outputText>
        </h:panelGroup>
      </h:panelGrid>
```

Another distinguishing feature of the Trinidad `<tr:inputDate>` tag is its inherent ability to use Ajax to communicate between the browser and the server more transparently and less disruptively. This behavior is evident when we attempt to change years or months in the calendar control.

What is actually happening is that the JavaScript rendered by the component is initiating an asynchronous HTTP request and processing the result without requiring a full-page refresh as is normally the case in browser/server communication. In Trinidad terminology, this behavior is also known as **Partial Page Rendering** (PPR). We will be covering this topic in more detail later on in this chapter.

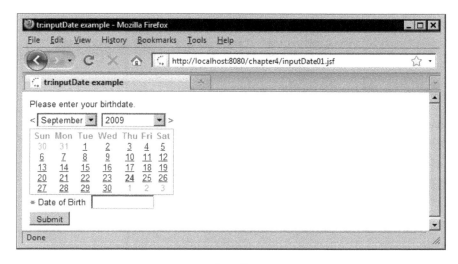

Rendering a number spinbox

Accepting numeric input from users is a very common task that can be implemented using standard JSF HTML components. There are, however, several limitations to using a text field for numeric data entry. First, it is difficult to restrict the range of values entered by the user without submitting a request to the server for form validation or implementing custom JavaScript to check the value. (Trinidad supports client-side converters and validators. We will cover these later in the chapter.)

Secondly, typing in a number into a text field is not always the most intuitive way to enter this type of information. Desktop application users have access to a wider range of numeric UI components such as sliders and spinboxes.

Fortunately, the Trinidad `CoreInputNumberSpinbox` component solves these problems gracefully and provides a way for users to enter numeric data within a specific range. The input can be validated on the client side using an intuitive control that mimics desktop application component behavior.

As shown in the following example, the `<tr:inputNumberSpinbox>` tag renders a numeric UI component that restricts data entry to a particular range on the client side and provides an interesting UI component for our JSF applications that extend beyond the limited set of HTML components supported by the browser.

```
<tr:form>
    <tr:inputNumberSpinbox label="Enter Number between 1976 and
        2010 " value="2000" minimum="1976" maximum="2010" stepSize="1"
        shortDesc="enter # between 1976 and 2010">
        <f:validateLongRange minimum="1976" maximum="2010" />
    </tr:inputNumberSpinbox>
    <tr:commandButton text="Submit" />
</tr:form>
```

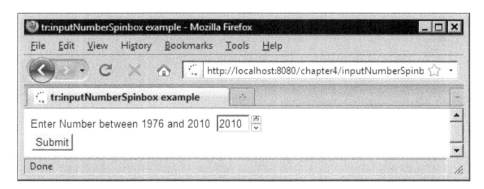

Rendering a text field

The Trinidad `<tr:inputText>` tag renders the `CoreInputText` component as an HTML `<input>` element or `<textarea>` element, depending on the number of rows specified in the `rows` attribute. In fact, this component can also be used to render a password field by setting the `secret` attribute to true. Therefore, any textual input required by a JSF application can be implemented using this component.

Additionally, this component can render its own label and message, further simplifying the task of writing JSF markup to render a properly formatted text component that displays a validation message. By default, this component will render its own label and message, but these features can be disabled by setting the `simple` attribute to true. The additional functionality of the Trinidad `CoreInputText` component far extends beyond the basic capabilities of the standard JSF input text component.

```
<tr:form>
    <tr:inputText value="#{backingBean.name}" label="Enter Name: " />
    <tr:commandButton text="Submit" />
    <tr:outputText styleClass="AFInstructionText"
                   value="The submitted value was: " />
    <tr:outputText styleClass="AFInstructionText"
                   value="#{backingBean.name}" />
</tr:form>
```

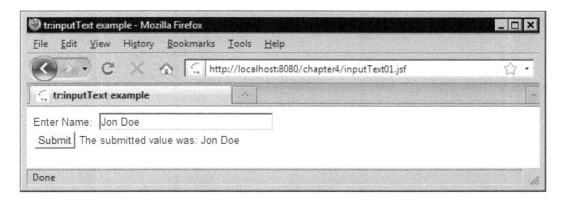

Rendering a selectable list of values

The Trinidad framework also provides innovative components for rendering selection lists to the user. The `<tr:inputListOfValues>` tag renders the `CoreInputListOfValues` component as an HTML table with radio buttons that can be displayed in a dialog window to assist in the selection of an item from a list of a predetermined values.

In this example, we use the `<tr:inputListOfValues>` tag to render a text field with a button beside it that launches a new browser window to render a list of predefined values to the user. This also demonstrates the Trinidad dialog framework that leverages the JSF navigation rules defined in `faces-config.xml`. We will cover this concept in more detail further on in this chapter, so for now let's concentrate on the list of values rendered in the window rather than how the dialog window was opened in the first place and how the selected value is passed back to the original page.

```
<tr:form partialTriggers="inputListOfValues">
    <tr:inputListOfValues label="Select Product:"
        id="inputListOfValues"
        value="(Empty)" searchDesc="Pick an element" columns="50"
        action="dialog:showProductSelectionDialog" />
    <tr:panelGroupLayout
        rendered="#{productBean.selectedProduct nenull}"
        inlineStyle="display:block">
        <tr:outputText value="You Selected: " />
        <tr:outputText value="#{productBean.selectedProduct.name}" />
    </tr:panelGroupLayout>
</tr:form>
```

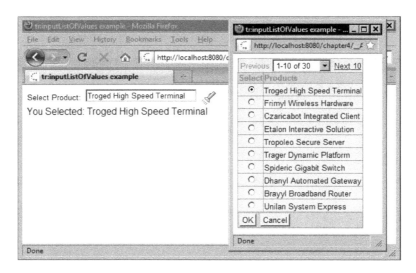

Client-side conversion and validation

There are a number of ways by which the Trinidad framework can enhance the interactivity and improve the performance of a JSF web application. One of those ways is through the use of client-side form validation. This concept is not new, and there are many JavaScript examples on the Internet that demonstrate how to convert and validate form fields in the browser before the form data is submitted to the server.

What is interesting is how easy it is to enable client-side form conversion and validation for built-in components using the Trinidad framework. Trinidad also allows us to create our own custom client-side converters and validators through a set of Java and JavaScript interfaces. Let's look at how to enable client-side conversion and validation for built-in Trinidad components.

Enabling client-side validation in trinidad-config.xml

To demonstrate, all we have to do is add a single XML element to our `trinidad-config.xml` file. This file is where a number of Trinidad-specific configuration settings are defined. It should be located in the `WEB-INF` directory, in the same location as the `faces-config.xml` file. By setting the "client-validation" element value to "ALERT", we turn on JavaScript alert box client-side form validation for all Trinidad components. Trinidad's default client-validation mode is "INLINE" and this supports a more streamlined style of rendering error messages on the page. We will see how to use the INLINE client-side form validation mode later in this chapter. We can disable client-side validation by setting this value to `DISABLED`. The default value is `INLINE` and causes server-side validation messages to appear inline within the JSF page.

```
<trinidad-config xmlns="http://myfaces.apache.org/trinidad/config">
  . . .
  <client-validation>ALERT</client-validation>
  . . .
</trinidad-config>
```

As shown in the following screenshot, this change results in a JavaScript alert box being presented to the user when form validation fails. This saves us a trip to the server when we are validating our form and can improve both the interactivity and the performance of our application.

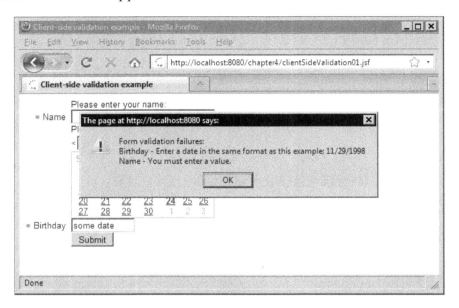

Validating one field at a time

Trinidad also supports event-based client-side validation. For example, sometimes it is nice to display validation messages to the user immediately after they have tabbed over or entered a value into a field. For text fields, we can use the `onblur` JavaScript event to fire the validation. For menus and other selection components, we can use the `onchange` event to fire the validation. Trinidad provides a JavaScript function named `_validateInput(event)` that invokes validation for the current field. To enable partial form validation, we should set the `<client-validation>` element to `INLINE` (the default value). Then, we can markup our Trinidad page as follows:

```
<tr:form>
    <tr:panelFormLayout>
        <tr:outputLabel for="name" value="Please enter your name: " />
        <tr:inputText id="name" required="#{true}" label="Name"
            onblur="_validateInput(event);" />
        <tr:outputLabel for="birthdate" value="Please enter your
                                                birthday: " />
```

```
        <tr:chooseDate id="chooseDate"
            minValue="#{backingBean.minimumDate}" />
        <tr:inputDate chooseId="chooseDate"
            value="#{customerBean.customer.birthDate}"
            required="#{true}" label="Birthday"
            onblur="_validateInput(event);">
          <tr:validateDateTimeRange
            minimum="#{backingBean.minimumDate}" />
        </tr:inputDate>
        <tr:commandButton text="Submit" />
      </tr:panelFormLayout>
  </tr:form>
```

The next screenshot demonstrates the result of calling the `_validateInput()` JavaScript function after the first name text field loses focus. When the `onblur` event is raised, the Trinidad framework validates the field and renders the inline validation message. Validating one field at a time is not compatible with the ALERT client-side validation mode.

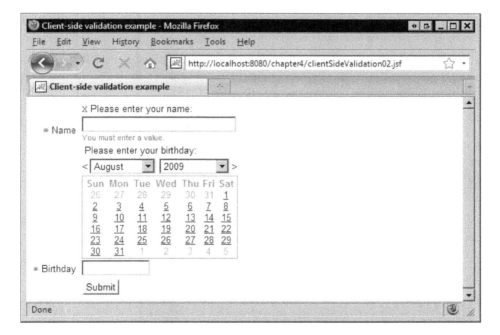

Enabling Ajax functionality

One of the most enticing features of the Trinidad component library is its support for Ajax. Many Trinidad components support Ajax functionality out of the box, and do not require any JavaScript coding or knowledge of Ajax techniques on the part of developers. In Trinidad terminology, the Ajax behavior of these components is known as Partial Page Rendering, or PPR for short.

Implementing Ajax-enabled JSF pages with Trinidad components is a two-step process. The first step is identifying which components should fire events asynchronously. The second part of the process is identifying which components should be updated in response to the events that fired asynchronously.

In some cases, the Ajax behavior of Trinidad components is built-in and is automatically enabled, requiring no additional effort from the developer. Some of these components include table and tree table components, the date chooser component, the poll component, and the Trinidad dialog framework. Additionally, all input components support an `autoSubmit` attribute that, when set to true, results in Ajax request that automatically updates a backing bean while the user is interacting with the view.

In other cases, we must decide which components should fire asynchronously and which components should be updated asynchronously. Let's look at a simple example.

Partial submit and partial triggers

Trinidad components that support partial page rendering have either the `partialSubmit` or `partialTriggers` tag attributes, or both. These attributes establish a "publisher/subscriber" relationship between one or more components. (A component can publish and subscribe to its own Ajax events.)

When a component that has the `partialSubmit` tag attribute set to true is invoked, any components that have a `partialTriggers` attribute containing the identifier of the component will be "refreshed" when the Ajax response is received by the browser. To see this in action, let's examine the following example.

We have a simple Trinidad command button with the `partialSubmit` attribute set to true inside a form that has the button component's identifier listed in its `partialTriggers` attribute. (A PPR-enabled component can subscribe to multiple Ajax event publishers by including their identifiers in a space separated list in the `partialTriggers` attribute.)

In our example, we establish a relationship between the button component and the form component. The button component is now the publisher of an asynchronous event, and the form is a subscriber to this event.

```
<tr:form partialTriggers="button">
    <tr:commandButton text="Refresh Date" id="button"
        partialSubmit="#{true}" />
    <tr:outputText value="#{backingBean.today}">
        <tr:convertDateTime type="both" timeStyle="full" />
    </tr:outputText>
</tr:form>
```

After the button is pressed, the form element's partial page rendering is triggered by the Ajax response and any components contained by the form will also be refreshed. This includes the output text component beside the button that is rendering the current date and time returned from the backing bean. When the user clicks the button, the text displaying the date is instantly updated with the current date and time.

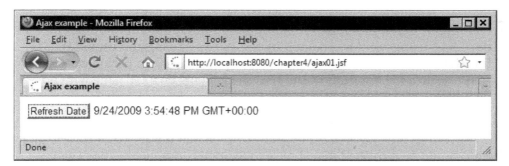

Polling the server

The Trinidad framework also includes sophisticated components that can fire Ajax events without user interaction. For example, sometimes we want the page to be refreshed on a regular basis while we wait for a long-running background activity to be completed on the server side, or for some other server-side state change to occur.

Ajax Polling versus Comet-Style Ajax Push

While polling is a nice Ajax feature to add to a web application, it can generate a lot of unnecessary traffic on the web server. Therefore, contemporary Ajax development today typically favors the "Comet" style, also known as "Reverse Ajax", for updating a page without user interaction in response to some server-side event. The Comet approach is so named because it refers to a competing household cleaning product that is similar to Ajax, but is somewhat different in its implementation.

Comet-style Ajax push involves an Ajax-enabled web page sending an asynchronous HTTP request to the web server, typically to a special servlet that handles the request, blocks indefinitely on its request handling thread, waits for a server-side event to occur (for example, a state change in the database), and then sends back data to the client when it is available. When the initial Ajax request finally returns, the client renders the result in the usual Ajax manner and then immediately sends another Ajax request to the blocking servlet. The result is that the web page can update itself more efficiently when a long running process is actually completed or when data becomes available.

The `CorePoll` component is rendered by the `<tr:poll>` tag and provides this functionality out of the box. With this component, we can periodically send Ajax requests to a JSF application and refresh elements on a JSF page with no user involvement.

In this example, we set the polling interval to one second (`1000` ms), and we indicate in the `<tr:form>` tag's `partialTriggers` attribute that the HTML form and all its children should be refreshed in response to the poll component's Ajax event.

```
<tr:form partialTriggers="poll">
    <tr:poll interval="1000"
        pollListener="#{backingBean.pollListener}" id="poll" />
    <tr:outputText value="#{backingBean.message}"
        inlineStyle="display:block" />
    <tr:outputText value="Count: #{backingBean.number}" />
</tr:form>
```

We also register a Trinidad poll event listener with the component to handle the periodic polling requests in our backing bean. The `<tr:poll>` tag has a `pollListener` attribute that expects a method expression bound to a JSF backing bean method with the appropriate signature (see the following). In this example, we simply increment an integer variable until the value reaches five and then we start the count all over again from one.

```
public void pollListener(PollEvent event) {
    System.out.println("Event received: " + event);
    number++;
```

```
    if (number < 5) {
      message = "Processing...";
    } else if (number == 5) {
      message = "Processing complete.";
    } else {
      message = "Processing...";
      number = 1;
    }
  }
```

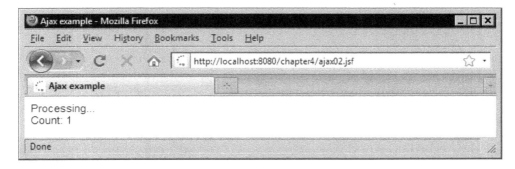

The effect of this example is that a text message on the page will be changed every five requests. This is to simulate a long-running process on the server side, where our managed bean could be processing data in the background, listening on a JMS message destination, querying a database, observing the file system for changes, or calling an external web service.

In other words, we can use the Trinidad poll component to periodically update our user interface without user intervention, making our JSF application capable of responding to outside events in a way that exceeds the limitations of conventional web applications.

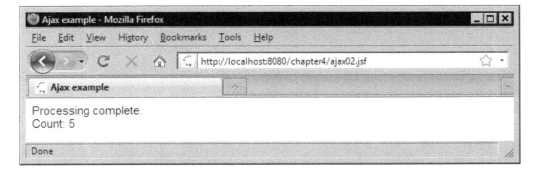

Rendering a status indicator

Polling the server periodically using Ajax is great, but what happens if our backing bean method does not return right away? Let's suppose we perform an intensive computation when we receive the polling event. What will happen to our user interface while the bean is working?

On the client side, the JavaScript rendered by the poll component will wait for the Trinidad request queue to return to a ready state before sending the next Ajax request. On the server side, the backing bean will continue processing data until it is finished, at which point the method returns, and HTTP response is sent back to the browser.

To avoid the appearance of an unresponsive user interface during asynchronous request processing, Trinidad includes several components that can be used to provide immediate feedback to users. One of these components is the CoreStatusIndicator. This component is rendered by the <tr:statusIndicator> tag as an icon or a text message on the page.

Let's look at how to use the <tr:statusIndicator> tag to provide visual feedback to users while a long-running Ajax request is being processed. In this example, we use the <tr:poll> tag to send an Ajax request to the server every second. This time, we invoke a poll listener method that has been intentionally designed to pause for three seconds before incrementing the integer variable.

```
<tr:form partialTriggers="poll">
    <tr:poll interval="1000"
        pollListener="#{backingBean.slowPollListener}"
        id="poll" />
    <tr:outputText value="#{backingBean.name}"
        inlineStyle="display:block" />
    <tr:outputText value="Count: #{backingBean.number}"
        inlineStyle="display:block" />
    <tr:statusIndicator>
        <f:facet message="busy">
            <tr:outputText value="Loading, please wait..." />
        </f:facet>
        <f:facet message="ready">
            <tr:outputText value="Ready." />
        </f:facet>
    </tr:statusIndicator>
</tr:form>
```

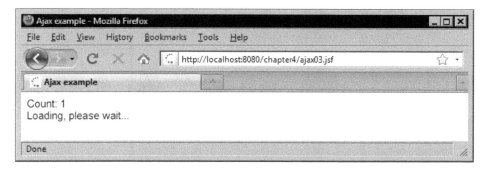

We use the `<tr:statusIndicator>` tag to display a "busy" message while the request is being handled, and a "ready" message when the response is received. Custom messages can be defined using the `busy` and `ready` facets.

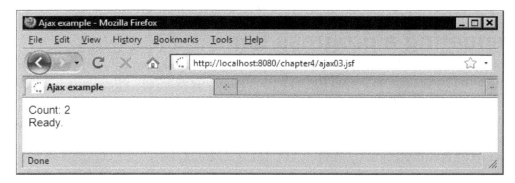

We can also use the default Trinidad status icon to render the busy and ready states of the page by omitting the facets of `<tr:statusIndicator>` tag. We could also provide our own busy and ready state icons by rendering an image in the `busy` and `ready` facets. Another option is to combine the default status icon with custom text messages by using two `<tr:statusIndicator>` tags, as shown in the next example:

```
<tr:form partialTriggers="poll">
    <tr:poll interval="1000"
        pollListener="#{backingBean.pollListener}"
        id="poll" />
    <tr:statusIndicator inlineStyle="padding-right:5px;" />
    <tr:statusIndicator>
        <f:facet name="busy">
            <tr:outputText value="Processing..." />
        </f:facet>
        <f:facet name="ready">
            <tr:outputText value="Processing complete." />
        </f:facet>
```

```
        </tr:statusIndicator>
        <tr:outputText value="Count: #{backingBean.slowNumber}"
            inlineStyle="display:block" />
</tr:form>
```

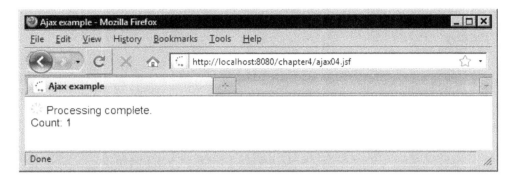

Rendering a progress bar

Trinidad also includes a progress indicator component that can be used to render an incremental progress bar on the screen. This component can optionally invoke an action or an action method once the progress reaches 100%.

For this component to work properly, we need to define a bounded range model that represents a finite amount of work and the current status of the work's completion. This can be accomplished by binding the CoreProgressIndicator component to a BoundedRangeModel object using the <tr:progressIndicator> tag's value attribute.

```
<tr:form partialTriggers="poll">
        <tr:poll interval="1000"
            pollListener="#{backingBean.pollListener}"
            id="poll" />
        <tr:progressIndicator inlineStyle="font-weight:bold"
            value="#{backingBean.progressModel}" />
</tr:form>
```

In this example, we construct a DefaultBoundedRangeModel instance in our backing bean and set the maximum value to 10.

```
public DefaultBoundedRangeModel getProgressModel() {
        if (progressModel == null) {
            progressModel = new DefaultBoundedRangeModel();
            progressModel.setMaximum(10);
        }
        return progressModel;
    }
```

Next, we write a poll event listener method that increments the model's value by one each time it is called. This enables us to increment the progress to indicate the completion of work.

```
public void progressListener(PollEvent event) {
    DefaultBoundedRangeModel model = getProgressModel();
    long value = model.getValue();
    value++;
    model.setValue(value);
}
```

The result is an Ajax-enabled progress bar that updates itself on the screen asynchronously whenever the Trinidad poll component in the same form fires a periodic Ajax request.

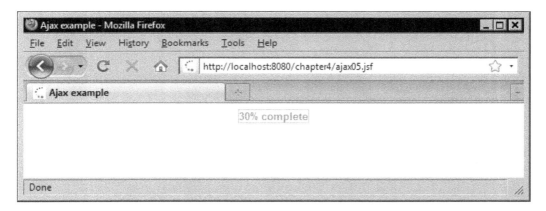

Laying out components on the screen

The Trinidad framework includes a number of useful tags for laying out components on the screen. Some of these tags handle more specific tasks such as laying out a set of controls horizontally, vertically, or in some other arrangement, while other tags handle more general tasks such as abstracting the "page" concept and breaking it up into smaller, more manageable sections.

Let's look at how to use Trinidad components to handle some of the more specific layout situations we may encounter in our web development activities.

Rendering a row layout

The HtmlRowLayout component is rendered as a sequence of HTML <tr> and <td> elements using the <trh:rowLayout> tag. This tag's layout logic is to render each of its child tags as a single HTML table cell within a single HTML table row.

```
<trh:rowLayout styleClass="row-layout">
        <tr:outputText value="Hello" />
        <tr:outputText value="World" />
        <tr:outputText value="How" />
        <tr:outputText value="Are" />
        <tr:outputText value="You?" />
</trh:rowLayout>
```

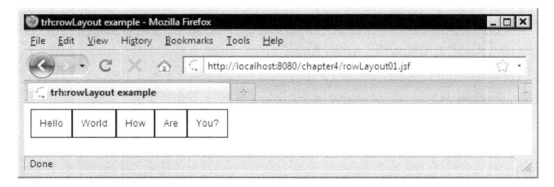

Rendering a complex table layout

If multiple rows are desired, several <trh:rowLayout> tags can be nested inside a <trh:tableLayout> tag. The HtmlTableLayout component also supports complex layout table arrangements with column span definitions when combined with the HtmlCellFormat component. The <trh:tableLayout> tag is more powerful for table-based layouts than the standard JSF <h:panelGrid> tag, as it enables column and row spans to be defined. The HtmlCellFormat component is rendered by the <trh:cellFormat> tag and can be nested inside a <trh:rowLayout> tag to specify table cell attributes. In the following example, we specify a layout using three rows where the first two rows have two columns each, and the third row has one column with a column span of two.

```
<trh:tableLayout>
      <trh:rowLayout styleClass="row-layout">
          <tr:outputText value="Hello" />
          <tr:outputText value="World" />
      </trh:rowLayout>
```

```
        <trh:rowLayout styleClass="row-layout">
            <tr:outputText value="How" />
            <tr:outputText value="Are" />
        </trh:rowLayout>
        <trh:rowLayout styleClass="row-layout">
            <trh:cellFormat columnSpan="2" halign="center">
                <tr:outputText value="You?" />
            </trh:cellFormat>
        </trh:rowLayout>
    </trh:tableLayout>
```

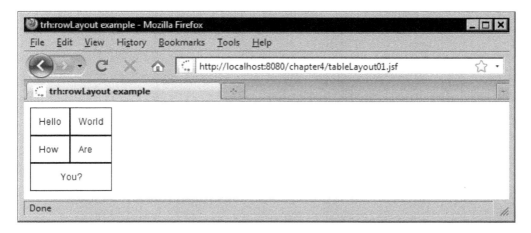

Rendering a form layout

The `CorePanelFormLayout` component is one of the most interesting layout components in the Trinidad component library. This component is rendered by the `<tr:panelFormLayout>` tag as an HTML table with an arbitrary number of rows and columns.

The purpose of this component is to simplify the task of laying out form fields, labels, and validation messages neatly and in an ordered way so that all the elements on the screen have a consistent alignment and arrangement. The `<tr:panelFormLayout>` component is ideally suited for laying out other Trinidad input components in a form, as it takes advantage of the built-in label and validation message features rendered by these components. It can, however, be used to render non-Trinidad input components as well.

In this example, we render a customer information form using Trinidad input component tags, such as `<tr:inputText>` and `<tr:selectOneChoice>`, with one exception that all the fields are required. This is reflected by the required icon rendered in these fields. In one case, we use a `help` facet to display a hint below the phone number field to suggest the correct input format to the user.

```
<tr:form id="orderForm">
    <tr:panelFormLayout>
        <tr:inputText id="firstName" label="First Name"
            value="#{productBean.order.customer.firstName}"
            required="#{true}" />
        <tr:inputText id="lastName" label="Last Name"
            value="#{productBean.order.customer.lastName}"
            required="#{true}" />
        <tr:inputText id="phoneNumber" label="Phone Number "
            value="#{productBean.order.customer.phoneNumber}">
            <f:facet name="help">
                <h:outputText value="XXX-XXX-XXXX" />
            </f:facet>
            <tr:validateRegExp pattern="\d{3}[\-\s]\d{3}[\-\s]\d{4}"
                messageDetailNoMatch="The phone number must be 10
                                      digits long (e.g. 123-555-1234)." />
        </tr:inputText>
        <tr:inputText id="emailAddress" label="Email Address "
            value="#{productBean.order.customer.emailAddress}"
            required="#{true}">
            <t:validateEmail message="The email address you have
                                      entered is not valid." />
        </tr:inputText>
        <tr:inputText id="emailAddressConfirm"
            label="Confirm Email "
            required="#{true}">
            <t:validateEqual for="emailAddress"
                message="The email addresses you have entered do not
                         match." />
        </tr:inputText>
        <tr:selectOneChoice label="Country" id="country"
            value="#{productBean.order.customer.countryOfOrigin}"
            required="#{true}">
            <f:selectItem itemLabel="Select" itemValue="" />
            <f:selectItems value="#{customerBean.countrySelectItems}" />
            <f:converter converterId="countryConverter" />
        </tr:selectOneChoice>
```

```
    <tr:commandButton text="Submit Order"
        action="#{productBean.submitOrder}" />
    </tr:panelFormLayout>
</tr:form>
```

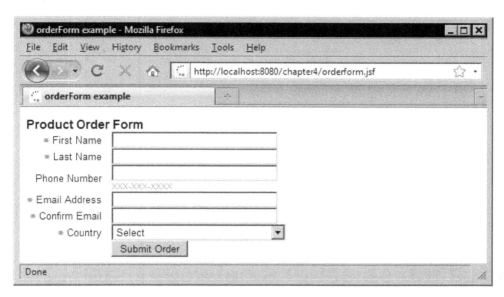

Rendering a panel group layout

Another powerful layout component in the Trinidad component library is
the CorePanelGroupLayout component. This component is rendered by the
<tr:panelGroupLayout> tag and employs some straightforward logic when laying
out components.

A single <div> tag is rendered containing each child component rendered
sequentially with a separator <div> after each child (except the last one). The
separator can be customized using the separator facet of this tag. In the following
example, we use the <tr:spacer> tag to render a transparent image with a height of
1 and a width of 150 inside each separator <div> element.

```
<tr:panelGroupLayout layout="vertical"
    styleClass="panel-group-layout">
        <f:facet name="separator">
          <tr:spacer height="1" width="150" />
        </f:facet>
          <tr:outputText value="Hello" />
          <tr:outputText value="World" />
          <tr:outputText value="How" />
```

```
        <tr:outputText value="Are" />
        <tr:outputText value="You?" />
    </tr:panelGroupLayout>
```

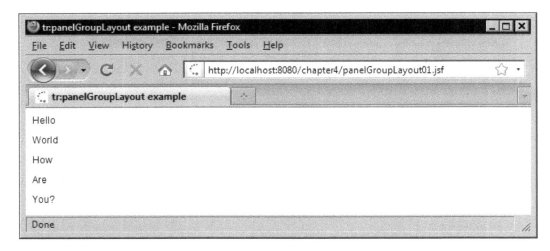

Shuttling selections between lists

There are situations where users need to sort and manage items between two separate lists. For example, an e-commerce application for a computer hardware vendor might offer customers the ability to customize a system by selecting one or more components from a list of available hardware upgrades. The Trinidad framework includes two components that can be used to "shuttle" list items between two selection list boxes.

Rendering a multiple selection shuttle

The CoreSelectManyShuttle component is rendered by the <tr:selectManyShuttle> tag and allows users to move items back and forth between two lists, one item at a time or multiple items at a time.

```
<tr:form>
    <tr:selectManyShuttle id="shuttle" label="Selected Values"
        leadingHeader="Available values:"
        trailingHeader="Selected values:"
        value="#{productBean.selectedProducts}">
        <f:selectItems value="#{productBean.productSelectItems}" />
    </tr:selectManyShuttle>
```

```
    <tr:commandButton text="Submit"
        actionListener="#{productBean.saveSortedProducts}" />
    <tr:message for="shuttle" />
</tr:form>
```

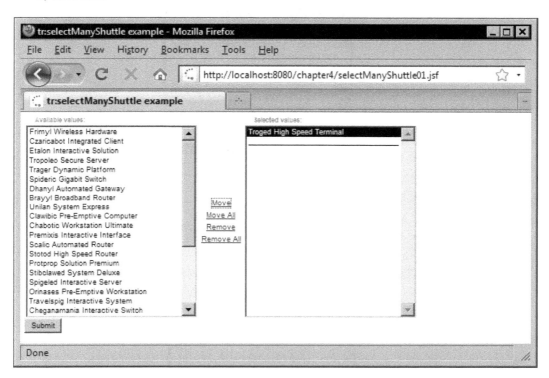

Rendering an ordered shuttle

The `CoreSelectOrderShuttle` component, rendered by the
`<tr:selectOrderShuttle>` tag, is similar to the `CoreSelectManyShuttle`
component except that it also allows the user to reorder the items in the list.

```
    <tr:form>
        <tr:selectOrderShuttle id="shuttle" label="Selected Values"
            leadingHeader="Available values:"
            trailingHeader="Selected values:"
            value="#{productBean.sortedProducts}">
            <f:selectItems value="#{productBean.productSelectItems}" />
        </tr:selectOrderShuttle>
        <tr:commandButton text="Submit"
```

```
        actionListener="#{productBean.saveSortedProducts}" />
    <tr:message for="shuttle" />
</tr:form>
```

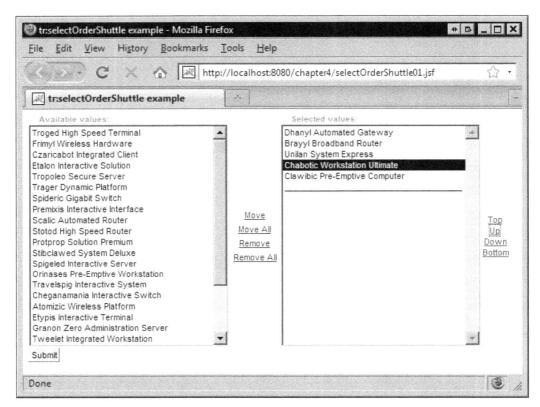

Working with tree and tree table components

A next generation web application component library would not be complete without at least one tree component, and the Trinidad framework is no exception in this case. Trinidad includes a powerful tree component that can be used to model hierarchical data such as a file system or a navigation menu. It also includes a tree table component that can be used to render detailed information about the elements in the tree.

Rendering a tree

The `CoreTree` component is a truly powerful JSF UI component that renders a rich, customizable tree element on the screen. This component includes built-in Ajax support that enables the tree to communicate with the server asynchronously when the user opens and closes tree nodes without any additional configuration. This component is rendered using the `<tr:tree>` tag and has a `value` attribute that expects a `TreeModel` object. In this example, we bind the tree component to a `ChildPropertyTreeModel` object, a specialized implementation of the `TreeModel` interface that uses reflection to define a graph of objects. Note that more examples of how to use the `ChildPropertyTreeModel` class are available in the Trinidad Javadoc documentation.

```
<tr:tree var="node"
    value="#{backingBean.uploadedFilesTrinidadTreeModel}">
        <f:facet name="nodeStamp">
            <tr:outputText value="#{node.name}" />
        </f:facet>
</tr:tree>
```

This example demonstrates the power of the Trinidad tree component. With only a few lines of code, we can construct a model object that Trinidad can render as a complex tree component.

```
public org.apache.myfaces.trinidad.model.TreeModel
getUploadedFilesTrinidadTreeModel() {
    org.apache.myfaces.trinidad.model.TreeModel model = null;
    File dir = getUploadDirectory();
    FileAdapter adapter = new FileAdapter(dir);
    model = new ChildPropertyTreeModel(adapter, "files");
    return model;
}
```

Our custom `FileAdapter` class plays an important role in this example. It provides a JavaBeans API compatible wrapper for the `java.io.File` class and it also provides the hierarchical object model needed by the tree component. The first argument to the `ChildPropertyTreeModel` constructor is a reference to a `FileAdapter` object that essentially wraps the root file upload directory. The second argument is a string representing the name of the property that provides child objects to be iterated when rendering the tree.

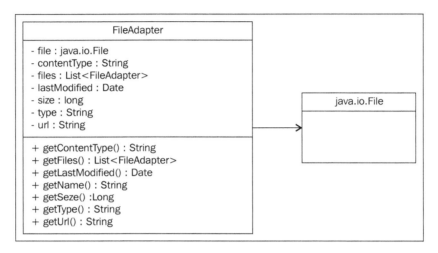

The `files` property has a `getter` method that constructs a list of `FileAdapter` objects for each of the files contained in the root directory.

```java
public List<FileAdapter> getFiles() {
    List<FileAdapter> list = null;
    File[] files = file.listFiles();
    if (files != null && files.length > 0) {
        list = new ArrayList<FileAdapter>();
        for (File file : files) {
            list.add(new FileAdapter(file));
        }
    }
    return list;
}
```

When the Trinidad tree component's renderer is processing the tree data, this method is invoked for each file in the root directory and for any subdirectories until there are no more files left to render. We can use this pattern whenever we need to model hierarchical data for the Trinidad tree and tree table components.

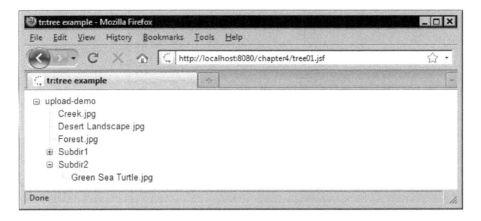

We will see an example of how to customize the Trinidad tree component's node icons later in this chapter.

Rendering a tree table

The Trinidad CoreTreeTable component is an equally powerful control to use when working with hierarchical data. This component is rendered by the <tr:treeTable> tag. One of the main advantages of this component over the CoreTree component is that it also supports rendering columns that can display arbitrary data about the elements in the tree.

In this example, we use the same TreeModel object used in the last example to render a tree table view of our uploaded files directory. Note that we declare additional <tr:column> tags for each column we wish to display in our table. We also set the row banding interval to one so that the rows are rendered with alternating shades of white and gray.

```
<tr:form>
    <tr:treeTable width="500px" var="file"
        value="#{backingBean.uploadedFilesTrinidadTreeModel}"
        rendered="true" summary="File Information"
        rowBandingInterval="1">
        <f:facet name="nodeStamp">
            <tr:column>
                <f:facet name="header">
                    <tr:outputText value="File Name" />
                </f:facet>
                <tr:outputText value="#{file.name}" />
            </tr:column>
        </f:facet>
        <tr:column inlineStyle="text-align:right">
            <f:facet name="header">
```

```
                    <tr:outputText value="File Size" />
            </f:facet>
                <tr:outputText value="#{file.size}">
                <tr:convertNumber type="number" />
            </tr:outputText>
        </tr:column>
        <tr:column inlineStyle="text-align:right">
            <f:facet name="header">
                <tr:outputText value="Last Modified" />
            </f:facet>
            <tr:outputText value="#{file.lastModified}">
                <tr:convertDateTime type="both" timeStyle="short" />
            </tr:outputText>
        </tr:column>
    </tr:treeTable>
</tr:form>
```

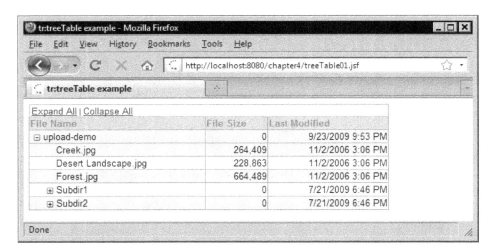

Creating navigation menus

One of the strengths of the Trinidad framework is the ease with which it enables us to implement complex navigation menus. Trinidad includes a number of useful components designed for this purpose.

Rendering a navigation tree

The `CoreNavigationTree` component is rendered by the `<tr:navigationTree>` tag and provides a hierarchical navigation menu that can be bound to a model object provided by a backing bean or to an XML file containing metadata about the navigation structure of the application.

Like the `CoreTree` component, this component can be bound to a model representing hierarchical data, however the `CoreNavigationTree` component expects a model of type `MenuModel`. The `MenuModel` interface extends the `TreeModel` interface and adds the ability to associate a view with an element in the tree structure.

This enables the navigation tree component to be aware of the various views in the application and to highlight, enable, disable, and otherwise manipulate the appearance of nodes in the tree according to the user's current location and browsing history within the network of views that make up the navigational structure of the site.

In this example, we bind the `<tr:navigationTree>` tag to a Trinidad `ProcessMenuModel` object that represents a categorized, hierarchical model of product information.

```
<tr:navigationTree inlineStyle="width:300px;"
    value="#{productBean.productCategoryModel}" var="node">
        <f:facet name="nodeStamp">
          <tr:commandNavigationItem text="#{node.label}"
              destination="#{node.viewId}" />
        </f:facet>
</tr:navigationTree>
```

Each product has a category, and categories can belong to other categories, so our model provides hierarchical data that can be visualized by this component. The Java code required to construct the `MenuModel` that provides a navigational representation of our product catalog is a bit more intricate than our previous example. This is due to the fact that we have to determine the view ID for each product and category so that they can be navigated by the user, and because our product model is a bit more complex than our file example.

```
public MenuModel getProductCategoryModel() {
    try {
        if (productCategoryModel == null) {
            String view = FacesContext.getCurrentInstance().
                        getViewRoot().getViewId();
            NavigationItem rootItem = new NavigationItem("Products",
                                                        view);
            List<ProductCategory> categories = getProductCategories();
            Collections.sort(categories);
```

```
        for (ProductCategory category : categories) {
            // include top-level categories only
            if (category.getParentCategory() != null) {
                continue;
            }
            String categoryViewId = view + "?category=" +
            URLEncoder.encode(category.getName(), "UTF-8");
            NavigationItem categoryItem = new
            NavigationItem(category.getName(), categoryViewId);
            rootItem.getChildren().add(categoryItem);
            for (ProductCategory subcategory : category.
                getSubcategories()) {
                String subcategoryViewId = categoryViewId +
                "&subcategory=" + URLEncoder.encode(subcategory.
                getName(), "UTF-8");
                NavigationItem subcategoryItem = new
                NavigationItem(subcategory.getName(),
                subcategoryViewId);
                categoryItem.getChildren().add(subcategoryItem);
                List<Product> products = new
                ArrayList<Product>(subcategory.getProducts());
                Collections.sort(products);
                for (Product product : products) {
                    String productViewId = view + "?product=" +
                    product.getId();
                    NavigationItem productItem = new
                    NavigationItem(product.getName(), productViewId);
                    subcategoryItem.getChildren().add(productItem);
                }
            }
        }
        ChildPropertyTreeModel treeModel = new
        ChildPropertyTreeModel(rootItem, "children");
        productCategoryModel = new ProcessMenuModel(treeModel,
                                                    "viewId");
    }
} catch (Exception e) {
    e.printStackTrace();
}
return productCategoryModel;
}
```

Once the tree is rendered, we have an attractive navigation element that provides a bookmarkable, search engine-friendly link structure for our product information.

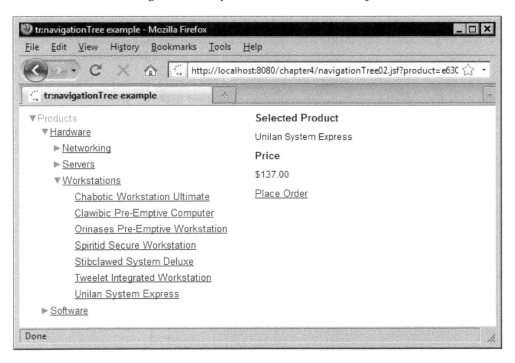

Rendering breadcrumbs

Implementing a breadcrumb-style navigation system for web applications is another common task that is easily solved with the Trinidad framework. To clarify, a breadcrumb navigation system is the one that provides users with a visual and informational cue about their current location within a site's information architecture.

As the name suggests, breadcrumbs can be used to retrace a user's steps back to the previous "landmark" within the information they are exploring. The Trinidad CoreBreadCrumbs component rendered by the `<tr:breadCrumbs>` tag provides a powerful and easy-to-use control for modeling a website's navigation structure and for tracking the user's current location within that structure.

In this example, we render a set of breadcrumbs horizontally using nested `CoreCommanNavigationItem` components rendered by the `<tr:commandNavigationItem>` tag. By using the `destination` attribute, we are able to render any standard hyperlink element on the page, that's improving our site's usability, bookmarkability, and navigability by using GET instead of POST. In other words, we are using Trinidad components here to implement the "pull-style" MVC pattern.

If we wanted to use the built-in JSF navigation system instead, we could simply use the `action` attribute of the `<tr:commandNavigationItem>` with an action method expression or a navigation outcome from `faces-config.xml`. Using the JSF navigation system for simple navigation use cases, however, is not recommended because it requires "push-style" MVC and therefore sends a POST instead of a GET request to the server when navigating from one view to the next.

Using POST for navigating between pages is not bookmarkable, suffers from the double-submit problem (unless using the Post-Redirect-Get pattern), and is not search engine friendly (search engine spiders do not typically POST). Therefore, although the JSF navigation system is convenient for transitioning between views that involve some kind of server-side state change, such as an order processing page flow, it is not always the best choice for implementing site navigation features such as menus and breadcrumbs.

```
<tr:breadCrumbs orientation="horizontal">
        <tr:commandNavigationItem text="Home"
            destination="/index.jsf" />
        <tr:commandNavigationItem text="About"
            destination="/about.jsf" />
        <tr:commandNavigationItem text="Company Information"
            destination="/company/index.jsf" />
        <tr:commandNavigationItem text="Investor Relations" />
</tr:breadCrumbs>
```

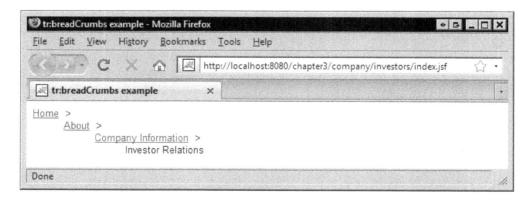

The `<tr:breadCrumbs>` tag can be used to create a navigation menu by declaring each of the menu items as a child element, or it or it can also be used to render navigation menu from a navigation structure declared in an external XML file. By externalizing the navigation structure from the view, we are also implementing best practices according to the MVC paradigm, which suggests that we should separate the model (our navigation structure) from its presentation.

Our first step in implementing this approach, is to declare a managed bean of type `XMLMenuModel`. The `XMLMenuModel` implements the `MenuModel` interface and so can be used wherever this type is expected. It also has a `source` property that defines the location of an XML file containing navigation metadata relative to the context root of the web application.

```
<managed-bean>
    <description>The XML menu model for a navigation menu.
    </description>
    <managed-bean-name>navigationMenuModel</managed-bean-name>
    <managed-bean-class>org.apache.myfaces.trinidad.model.
    XMLMenuModel</managed-bean-class>
    <managed-bean-scope>request</managed-bean-scope>
    <managed-property>
        <property-name>source</property-name>
        <property-class>java.lang.String</property-class>
        <value>/WEB-INF/menu-metadata.xml</value>
    </managed-property>
</managed-bean>
```

In this example, we create a file named `/WEB-INF/menu-metadata.xml` that contains an XML representation of our navigation structure. This file is made up of a `menu` root element that contains a number of arbitrarily nested `itemNode` child elements. Each `itemNode` represents a single element in our navigation tree, and has a number of attributes that correspond to the attributes of the `<tr:commandNavigationItem>` tag. We can also use EL expressions in this file to indicate dynamic values, such as the `disabled` attribute of the admin node in our navigation structure.

An important note about JSF View IDs

Notice in the following markup that the `focusViewId` attribute references the JSF page that the navigation menu node represents. For example, the **Company Information** node has a `focusViewId` of `/company/index.jsf`. We are following a convention throughout this book where the JSF FacesServlet is mapped to `*.jsf` and our Facelets XHTML pages are also named with `.jsf` suffix. This approach is primarily to make it easier to work with Facelets technology in Dreamweaver. The JSF specification reserves the .jsf file extension, but accepts that authoring tools may use this extension.

All the Facelets XHTML pages for the example applications discussed in this book were authored with Adobe Dreamweaver (`http://www.adobe.com/dreamweaver`) and JSFToolbox for Dreamweaver (`http://www.jsftoolbox.com`), therefore all the pages have a `.jsf` file extension (the same extension as the `FacesServlet` mapping). If we were using JSP pages as our view technology, our pages would have the `.jsp` file extension and we would reference the files using this extension in `menu-metadata.xml` and `faces-config.xml`. We would still use the `*.jsf` mapping when requesting the pages in the browser.

The following listing is from our `menu-metadata.xml` file. It declares the metadata used by the `<tr:breadCrumbs>` tag in this example:

```xml
<?xml version="1.0" encoding="iso-8859-1"?>
<menu xmlns="http://myfaces.apache.org/trinidad/menu">
    <itemNode id="home" label="Home" destination="/index.jsf"
        icon="/images/home.png" focusViewId="/index.jsf" />
    <itemNode id="about" label="About" destination="/about.jsf"
        focusViewId="/about.jsf" icon="/images/about.png">
        <itemNode id="company" label="Company Information"
            destination="/company/index.jsf"
            focusViewId="/company/index.jsf"
            icon="/images/company.png">
            <itemNode id="investors" label="Investor Relations"
                destination="/company/investors/index.jsf"
                focusViewId="/company/investors/index.jsf"
                icon="/images/investors.png" />
        </itemNode>
    </itemNode>
    <itemNode id="products" label="Products"
        destination="/products.jsf"
        focusViewId="/products.jsf" icon="/images/products.png" />
    <itemNode id="services" label="Services"
        destination="/services.jsf"
        focusViewId="/services.jsf" icon="/images/services.png" />
```

```
<itemNode id="contact" label="Contact Us"
    icon="/images/contact.png"
    destination="contact.jsf" focusViewId="/contact.jsf" />
<itemNode id="admin" label="Admin" icon="/images/admin.png"
    destination="admin.jsf" focusViewId="/admin.jsf"
    disabled="#{!backingBean.administrator}" />
</menu>
```

In our JSF page, we declare the `<tr:breadCrumbs>` tag and specify its value using an EL expression for the menu model expressed in `menu-metadata.xml`. The `navigationMenuModel` managed bean is a request-scoped `XMLMenuModel` instance.

```
<tr:breadCrumbs inlineStyle="margin-top:10px; height:100px"
    orientation="horizontal" value="#{navigationMenuModel}"
    var="node">
            <f:facet name="nodeStamp">
                <tr:commandNavigationItem text="#{node.label}"
                    destination="#{node.destination}" />
            </f:facet>
</tr:breadCrumbs>
```

Notice in the next screenshot that the current node in the breadcrumb navigation element is not hyperlinked. This behavior is built into the component; it "knows" that we are on the **Investor Relations** page and that the node should be rendered as text and not as a hyperlink. Also, we are able to specify icons to be rendered beside each navigation element.

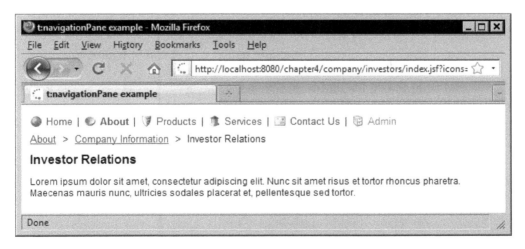

Rendering a multistep process (Train)

The Apache MyFaces Tomahawk `CoreTrain` component rendered by the `<tr:train>` tag is another useful component for implementing different navigation scenarios in our web applications. This particular component can be used whenever a multistep process is required. For example, we may have an insurance quote generator application that requires customer information to be entered over several screens before the form can be submitted.

To use this component effectively, we first need to create each of the screens that make up our page flow.

```
<tr:train styleClass="train" var="item"
    value="#{backingBean.trainModel}">
        <f:facet name="nodeStamp">
            <tr:commandNavigationItem text="#{item.label}"
                action="#{item.action}" />
        </f:facet>
</tr:train>
```

In this example, we construct a `ProcessMenuModel` from a list of `NavigationItem` objects. A `NavigationItem` is a custom class that we created to simplify the task of modeling navigation information for our train component. Each navigation item has a label, an outcome, and a view ID. Additionally, specific navigation rules have been created for this example in our `faces-config.xml` file.

```
public ProcessMenuModel getTrainModel() {
    if (trainModel == null) {
        trainModel = new ProcessMenuModel();
        List<NavigationItem> list = new ArrayList<NavigationItem>();
        list.add(new NavigationItem("Step 1", "/train01_1.jsf",
                                    "train_1"));
        list.add(new NavigationItem("Step 2", "/train02_1.jsf",
                                    "train_2"));
        list.add(new NavigationItem("Step 3", "/train03_1.jsf",
                                    "train_3"));
        list.add(new NavigationItem("Step 4", "/train04_1.jsf",
                                    "train_4"));
        list.add(new NavigationItem("Step 5", "/train05_1.jsf",
                                    "train_5"));
        trainModel.setViewIdProperty("viewId");
        trainModel.setWrappedData(list);
    }
    return trainModel;
}
```

The navigation rules that were added to `faces-config.xml` to support this navigation menu can be seen in the following XML fragment:

```xml
<navigation-rule>
    <display-name>*</display-name>
    <from-view-id>*</from-view-id>
    <navigation-case>
        <from-outcome>train_1</from-outcome>
        <to-view-id>/train01_1.jsf</to-view-id>
        <redirect />
    </navigation-case>
    <navigation-case>
        <from-outcome>train_2</from-outcome>
        <to-view-id>/train01_2.jsf</to-view-id>
        <redirect />
    </navigation-case>
    <navigation-case>
        <from-outcome>train_3</from-outcome>
        <to-view-id>/train01_3.jsf</to-view-id>
        <redirect />
    </navigation-case>
    <navigation-case>
        <from-outcome>train_4</from-outcome>
        <to-view-id>/train01_4.jsf</to-view-id>
        <redirect />
    </navigation-case>
    <navigation-case>
        <from-outcome>train_5</from-outcome>
        <to-view-id>/train01_5.jsf</to-view-id>
        <redirect />
    </navigation-case>
</navigation-rule>
```

When the component is rendered, it takes care of the details of navigating and highlighting the various steps in our navigation train.

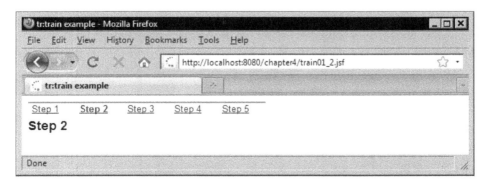

Rendering a process choice bar

The Trinidad `CoreProcessChoiceBar` component is rendered by the
`<tr:processChoiceBar>` tag and provides another useful navigational control.
In this example, we bind this component to a `ProcessMenuModel` instance in our
backing bean that defines the navigational data structure for the component.

```
<tr:processChoiceBar  var="node"
   value="#{backingBean.processMenuModel}" shortDesc="Select step">
      <f:facet name="nodeStamp">
         <tr:commandNavigationItem text="#{node.label}"
            action="#{node.outcome}" />
      </f:facet>
</tr:processChoiceBar>
```

The `ProcessMenuModel` object is also assembled from a list of `NavigationItem`
objects representing the different steps in the process.

```
public ProcessMenuModel getProcessMenuModel() {
    if (processMenuModel == null) {
        processMenuModel = new ProcessMenuModel();
        List<NavigationItem> list = new ArrayList<NavigationItem>();
        list.add(new NavigationItem("Step 1", "/processChoiceBar01_1.
                jsf", "processChoiceBar01"));
        list.add(new NavigationItem("Step 2", "/processChoiceBar01_2.
                jsf", "processChoiceBar02"));
        list.add(new NavigationItem("Step 3", "/processChoiceBar01_3.
                jsf", "processChoiceBar03"));
        list.add(new NavigationItem("Step 4", "/processChoiceBar01_4.
                jsf", "processChoiceBar04"));
        list.add(new NavigationItem("Step 5", "/processChoiceBar01_5.
                jsf", "processChoiceBar05"));
        processMenuModel.setViewIdProperty("viewId");
        processMenuModel.setWrappedData(list);
    }
    return processMenuModel;
}
```

Note that in this example too, specific navigation rules have been added to
`faces-config.xml`:

```
<navigation-rule>
    <display-name>*</display-name>
    <from-view-id>*</from-view-id>
    <navigation-case>
        <from-outcome>processChoiceBar01</from-outcome>
        <to-view-id>/processChoiceBar01_1.jsf</to-view-id>
        <redirect />
```

```
    </navigation-case>
    <navigation-case>
        <from-outcome>processChoiceBar02</from-outcome>
        <to-view-id>/processChoiceBar01_2.jsf</to-view-id>
        <redirect />
    </navigation-case>
    <navigation-case>
        <from-outcome>processChoiceBar03</from-outcome>
        <to-view-id>/processChoiceBar01_3.jsf</to-view-id>
        <redirect />
    </navigation-case>
    <navigation-case>
        <from-outcome>processChoiceBar04</from-outcome>
        <to-view-id>/processChoiceBar01_4.jsf</to-view-id>
        <redirect />
    </navigation-case>
    <navigation-case>
        <from-outcome>processChoiceBar05</from-outcome>
        <to-view-id>/processChoiceBar01_5.jsf</to-view-id>
        <redirect />
    </navigation-case>
</navigation-rule>
```

The `<tr:processChoiceBar>` tag renders a control similar in behavior but different in appearance to the component rendered by the `<tr:train>` tag.

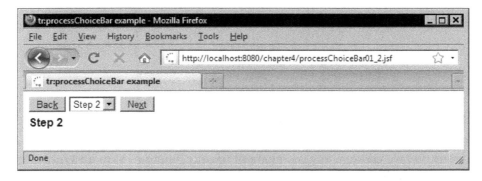

Skinning and theme selection

One of the most powerful and interesting features of the Trinidad framework is its support for customizing the appearance of a wide range of user interface elements through the use of a coordinated set of cascading style sheets, images, and other presentational resources.

Different themes can be created and declared as "skins" for the application in a centralized XML file named /WEB-INF/trinidad-skins.xml. The current skin for the application can be hardcoded in the /WEB-INF/trinidad-config.xml file, or it can be determined at runtime based on stored user preferences, a predefined schedule, or any other criteria. Additionally, custom Trinidad skins can be defined in a JAR file, enabling them to be reused more easily.

In our demonstration, we declare the skin family as an EL expression bound to a sessionScope variable named skinFamily. (This session variable has no special meaning in Trinidad and is not created by default; it is simply used here to demonstrate how to enable dynamic skin selection in a Trinidad application.) The skin-family value can be hardcoded or it can be obtained dynamically using an arbitrary EL expression. If the skin-family value is not specified, then the application will use Trinidad's default skin.

/WEB-INF/trinidad-config.xml

```
<?xml version="1.0"?>
<trinidad-config xmlns="http://myfaces.apache.org/trinidad/config">
  ...
  <skin-family>#{sessionScope.skinFamily}</skin-family>
  ...
</trinidad-config>
```

Creating a new Trinidad skin

The first step in creating a new Trinidad skin is to declare it in trinidad-skins.xml. In this example, we create a <skin> element for our "custom" skin and indicate that it supports the Trinidad desktop RenderKit. Trinidad also supports a PDA RenderKit; if we were implementing a skin for a PDA device, we would use the .pda suffix for our skin ID.

A common technique when implementing a new Trinidad skin is to extend the built-in "simple" skin and to customize it as desired. This is the approach we are demonstrating here using the `<extends>` element to indicate that our custom skin extends simple skin.

The last important detail here is the path to our skin's stylesheet. We will create this file next, in a subdirectory within our web application. A custom skin definition file also supports skinning component text values such as table column headers, tip expand/collapse links, and other built-in control labels. To override Trinidad's default component text values in our custom skin, we would include the `<bundle-name>` element that takes the fully qualified name of a Java class (for example, `com.example.MyResourceBundle`) that extends `java.util.ResourceBundle` or implements the `java.util.Map` interface and provides alternate text values for the standard Trinidad resource bundle keys (for example, `af_showDetail.DISCLOSED_TIP`). By overriding the default text messages in our custom skin, we can customize not only the appearance of Trinidad components but their built-in text values too.

```
<skins xmlns="http://myfaces.apache.org/trinidad/skin">
   <!--  Custom skin example -->
   <skin>
      <id>custom.desktop</id>
      <family>custom</family>
      <extends>
         simple.desktop
      </extends>
      <render-kit-id>
         org.apache.myfaces.trinidad.desktop</render-kit-id>
      <style-sheet-name>
         skins/custom/custom.css
      </style-sheet-name>
   </skin>
</skins>
```

Implementing the skin's cascading style sheet

The next step in implementing our custom skin is to create the cascading style sheet that we declared in the previous step. In this example, we will simply customize the appearance of the built-in Trinidad icons using our own custom images. This includes four built-in icons rendered by the `<tr:icon>` tag: the required icon, the warning icon, the error icon, and the information icon.

Additionally, we will introduce three new icons that can also be rendered with the `<tr:icon>` tag: an open folder icon, a closed folder icon, and a file icon. The naming convention for style selectors is important. For icons, the text after the `.AF` classname prefix and the `Icon` classname suffix, once the first letter has been converted to lowercase, is what defines the logical name of our icon. Once we understand this naming convention, it becomes easier to customize built-in icons as well as to introduce new ones.

```
.AFFolderOpenIcon:alias {
  content: url(/skins/custom/images/yellow-folder-open.png);
}
.AFFolderClosedIcon:alias {
  content: url(/skins/custom/images/yellow-folder-closed.png);
}
.AFFileIcon:alias {
  content: url(/skins/custom/images/document.png);
}
.AFInfoIcon:alias {
  content: url(/skins/custom/images/info.png);
}
.AFErrorIcon:alias {
  content: url(/skins/custom/images/error.png);
}
.AFWarningIcon:alias {
  content: url(/skins/custom/images/warning.png);
}
.AFRequiredIcon:alias {
  content: url(/skins/custom/images/required.png);
}
```

Now that we have customized and extended Trinidad's "simple" skin, let's look at an example of how we can apply this skin to our JSF pages at runtime. We created a page that allows the user to set a session-scoped variable with the name of the skin family they wish to use.

```
<tr:panelGroupLayout>
        <tr:selectOneChoice label="Choose a Skin:"
            value="#{sessionScope.skinFamily}" onchange="submit()">
            <tr:selectItem label="simple" value="simple" />
            <tr:selectItem label="minimal" value="minimal" />
            <tr:selectItem label="purple" value="purple" />
            <tr:selectItem label="purpleBigFont"
                value="purpleBigFont" />
            <tr:selectItem label="beach" value="beach" />
            <tr:selectItem label="custom" value="custom" />
        </tr:selectOneChoice>
</tr:panelGroupLayout>
```

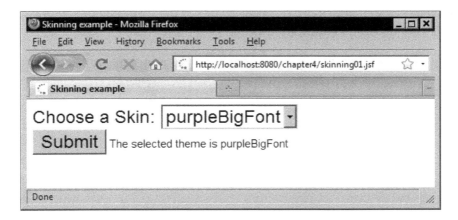

Rendering an icon

To see Trinidad skinning in action, let's examine a page that displays the standard set of icons in addition to the new icons if used by our custom skin. The `CoreIcon` component rendered by the `<tr:icon>` tag allows us to display an icon element on the screen as either an image or text. These icons typically appear beside input elements to indicate required fields or error messages, but they can also appear in other locations as well.

```
<trh:tableLayout width="20%" borderWidth="0" cellSpacing="5">
        <trh:rowLayout>
            <tr:icon name="required" />
            <tr:outputText value="Required" />
        </trh:rowLayout>
        <trh:rowLayout>
            <tr:icon name="info" />
            <tr:outputText value="Info" />
        </trh:rowLayout>
        <trh:rowLayout>
            <tr:icon name="warning" />
            <tr:outputText value="Warning" />
        </trh:rowLayout>
        <trh:rowLayout>
            <tr:icon name="error" />
            <tr:outputText value="Error" />
        </trh:rowLayout>
</trh:tableLayout>
```

Once we select our custom skin, the appearance of the icons changes to display the images that we specified in our stylesheet.

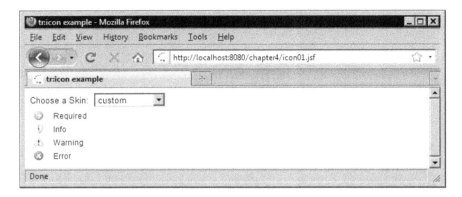

This also gives us access to our new custom icons which we can render by specifying the icon name in the name attribute of the <tr:icon> tag.

```
<trh:tableLayout width="20%" borderWidth="0" cellSpacing="5">
        <trh:rowLayout>
            <tr:icon name="file" />
            <tr:outputText value="File" />
        </trh:rowLayout>
        <trh:rowLayout>
            <tr:icon name="folderOpen" />
            <tr:outputText value="Folder Open" />
        </trh:rowLayout>
        <trh:rowLayout>
            <tr:icon name="folderClosed" />
            <tr:outputText value="Folder Closed" />
        </trh:rowLayout>
</trh:tableLayout>
```

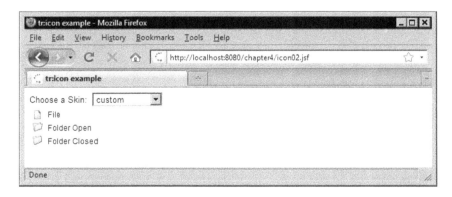

Customizing the Trinidad tree component's node icons

Earlier in this chapter we saw how to use the Trinidad tree component. We can customize the tree component's node icons in our custom skin by adding the following CSS pseudo-selectors to our custom skin's cascading style sheet (custom.css):

```
af|tree::node-icon:folder-expanded { content: url(/skins/custom/
images/yellow-folder-open.png); }
af|tree::node-icon:folder-collapsed { content: url(/skins/custom/
images/yellow-folder-closed.png); }
af|tree::node-icon:document { content: url(/skins/custom/images/
document.png); }
```

We also need to add a method to our FileAdapter class to support custom Trinidad tree node icons:

```
public String getNodeType() {
    return file.isDirectory() ? "folder" : "document";
}
```

The getNodeType() method is called by the Trinidad tree component's renderer to determine which icon to display. When we select our custom theme, the Trinidad skinning frame will display the icons declared in our stylesheet for the expanded, collapsed folder and document tree node states. The following screenshot demonstrates the result of customizing the Trinidad tree component's node icons in our custom Trinidad skin.

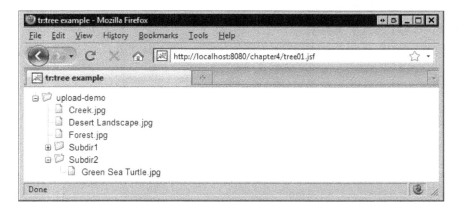

Implementing dialog windows

Traditional desktop applications have access to a richer set of dialog windows than available to typical web browsers. While alert and confirm dialogs can be launched using JavaScript, it is impossible to render a more complex dialog box; for example, a color chooser dialog, using these built-in windows.

A common solution to this problem is to implement dialogs using floating windows. The Trinidad framework includes built-in support for creating custom dialog windows using this technique. These dialogs are Ajax enabled, and support convenient features such as the ability to pass the selected value back to the page that originally launched the dialog.

Dialog window display options

The examples in this chapter use the default display mode for Trinidad dialog windows. An enhanced display mode that uses popup HTML `<iframe>` elements can be activated by adding the following to `web.xml`:

```
<context-param>

   <param-name>oorg.apache.myfaces.trinidad.renderkit.
ENABLE_LIGHTWEIGHT_DIALOGS</param-name>

   <param-value>true</param-value>

</context-param>
```

Declaring dialog navigation rules in faces-config.xml

To understand how to use Trinidad dialog windows, let's look at an example. First, we must configure our `faces-config.xml` file to include some special navigation rules that integrate with the Trinidad dialog framework. These rules have outcomes that are qualified using the `dialog:` prefix. The special prefix indicates to Trinidad that the action should display the view specified in the `<to-view-id>` element as a dialog window.

```
<navigation-rule>
    <display-name>*</display-name>
    <from-view-id>*</from-view-id>
      <navigation-case>
       <from-outcome>dialog:showProductSelectionDialog</from-outcome>
         <to-view-id>/inputListOfValues01_dialog.jsf</to-view-id>
      </navigation-case>
</navigation-rule>
```

Launching a dialog window

To launch a dialog window from another page, we need to specify the action of the dialog's navigation rule in the `action` attribute of the component that should launch the dialog.

```
<tr:form partialTriggers="inputListOfValues">
    <tr:inputListOfValues label="Select Product:"
        id="inputListOfValues"
        value="(Empty)" searchDesc="Pick an element" columns="50"
        action="dialog:showProductSelectionDialog" />
    <tr:panelGroupLayout rendered="#{productBean.selectedProduct ne
                                    null}"
        inlineStyle="display:block">
        <tr:outputText value="You Selected: " />
        <tr:outputText value="#{productBean.selectedProduct.name}" />
    </tr:panelGroupLayout>
</tr:form>
```

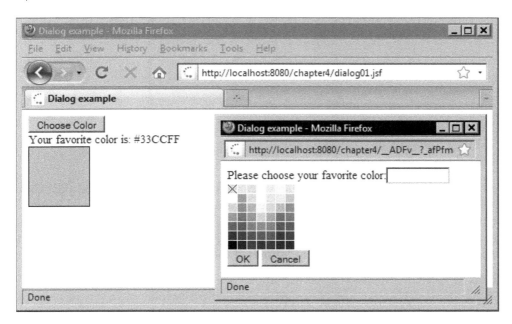

Returning a value from a dialog window

To return a value from the dialog window back to the page that launched it, we need to specify some method bindings in our dialog page markup. Notice that the **OK** and **Cancel** buttons both have `actionListener` attributes bound to methods in our `ProductBean` class.

Also notice that the `<tr:table>` tag used to render the list of products in this example specifies the `binding` attribute, which refers to an instance variable of type `UIXTable` in our backing bean. This is to facilitate extracting the selected value from the UI component when the user makes a selection our dialog window.

```
<tr:form>
    <tr:table summary="Product Table"
        value="#{productBean.products}"
        binding="#{productBean.productsTable}" var="product"
        rows="10" rowSelection="single">
        <f:facet name="footer">
            <h:panelGroup>
                <tr:commandButton text="OK"
                    actionListener="#{productBean.closeProductDialog}">
                    <f:param id="selectedProduct"
                        name="selectedProduct"
                        value="#{product}" />
                </tr:commandButton>
                <tr:commandButton text="Cancel"
                    actionListener="#{productBean.cancelDialog}" />
            </h:panelGroup>
        </f:facet>
        <tr:column>
            <f:facet name="header">
                <tr:outputText value="Products" />
            </f:facet>
            <tr:outputText value="#{product.name}" />
            <tr:outputText value="test1" />
        </tr:column>
    </tr:table>
</tr:form>
```

If we study the code in those methods, we can see the technique used to pass data between application windows. First, let's examine the code for the **Cancel** button. Here, we make a call to the Trinidad `RequestContext` API to indicate that a null value, specified as the first argument in the `returnFromDialog` method, should be returned back to the component that launched the dialog.

```
public void cancelDialog(ActionEvent event) {
    RequestContext.getCurrentInstance().returnFromDialog(null, null);
}
```

When the user clicks **OK**, the `closeProductDialog` method is called. In this method, we extract the row key representing the selected rows in the products table. This technique can be used when there is more than one row selected in the table.

Next, we obtain a reference to the selected product from the `UIParameter` object associated with the `UIComponent` that fired the event. We then pass the `Product` object to the Trinidad `RequestContext` API as the return value of the dialog that will be sent to the page that invoked it. When the dialog closes, the calling page is re-rendered and our product selection is displayed in the text field as well as the text message below it.

```java
public void closeProductDialog(ActionEvent event) {
    Iterator<Object> iterator = productsTable.getSelectedRowKeys().
                                iterator();
    Object rowKey = iterator.next();
    Object oldRowKey = productsTable.getRowKey();
    productsTable.setRowKey(rowKey);
    Product product = null;
    UIComponent component = event.getComponent();
    UIParameter param = (UIParameter) component.
                        findComponent("selectedProduct");
    if (param != null) {
        product = (Product) param.getValue();
    }
    if (param != null) {
        setSelectedProduct(product);
            RequestContext.getCurrentInstance().
            returnFromDialog(product.getName(), null);
    }
    productsTable.setRowKey(oldRowKey);
}
```

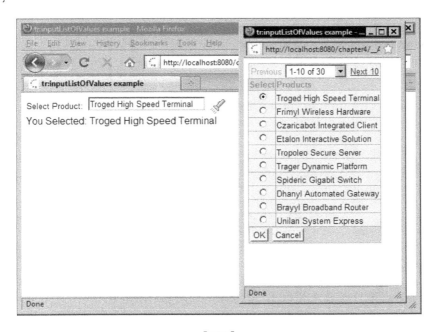

Summary

The Trinidad framework and component library represents a significant step forward in the evolution of rich user interface development on the JSF platform. With over 100 powerful UI components, Trinidad simplifies a wide range of challenging tasks faced by web application developers today.

Trinidad supports Ajax, or partial page rendering (PPR), and includes rich UI components with built-in Ajax capabilities that developers can use without having to learn Ajax APIs or write JavaScript code. Many Trinidad components support the `partialSubmit` and `partialTriggers` attributes to control which components submit an Ajax request and which components are updated after the Ajax request. Trinidad includes Ajax-enabled components to poll the server periodically, to render a customizable status indicator, to display a progress bar, and more.

Trinidad supports accepting color, number, date/time, and predefined lists of values from the user. Trinidad also support client-side validation in Trinidad using JavaScript `alert` messages and onblur/onchange event-based field validation. The Trinidad framework also includes powerful layout tags for rendering components individually as rows in a single-column table, in a complex layout table that defines row and column spans, in a form layout that includes labels and messages, and as `<div>` elements in a panel layout, for example.

Trinidad's shuttle controls can be used to render multiple selection lists that support shuttling items between two lists and arranging items in an arbitrary order. Trinidad also supports rendering hierarchical data using the tree and tree table components, and enables developers to create bookmarkable and search engine-friendly dynamic navigation menus and breadcrumb navigation systems. Trinidad provides components for implementing multistep processes using the `<tr:train>` and `<tr:processChoiceBar>` tags.

Trinidad includes a skinning framework to simplify the customization of the look and feel of a JSF application. Trinidad supports dynamic skin selection by binding the `<skin-family>` element in `/WEB-INF/trinidad-config.xml` to a session-scoped EL variable. Trinidad also supports creating custom skins that can extend its simple desktop theme. Custom skins can define new icons and developers can render these icons using the `<tr:icon>` tag.

The Trinidad dialog framework extends the JSF navigation system to support opening new JSF pages in a pop-up dialog window. Navigation rules for dialog windows have outcomes that are prefixed with `dialog:` and are referenced in the action attributes of components to launch a new dialog window. To return a value to the calling page and to close the dialog window, managed beans can call the Trinidad RequestContext API method `returnFromDialog()`.

5
ICEfaces Components

The ICEfaces component library is a robust and feature-rich Ajax component library for the JSF framework. ICEfaces boasts a collection of over 50 truly impressive JSF components that are fully Ajax enabled, giving developers all the advantages of asynchronous UI behavior with none of the overhead of writing cross-browser compatible JavaScript.

In this chapter, we will examine a number of common use cases in web application development and how to implement them using the ICEfaces component library. The topics we will cover include:

- Receiving input from users
- Creating navigation and pop-up menus
- Using tree components
- Displaying data in tables
- Rendering charts
- Laying out components with panels
- Creating a tabbed user interface
- Working with modal dialogs

Receiving input from users

The ICEfaces component library includes Ajax-enabled versions of the standard JSF HTML components. These components exhibit more sophisticated rendering behavior, allowing developers to implement more advanced and more responsive user interfaces.

ICEfaces includes a text input component as well as specialized components for receiving date selections, files, and rich text from users. ICEfaces components also support a rich variety of rendering effects to make the user interface more interesting and more informative for users by providing visual feedback in response to different events, such as validation, selections, and form submissions.

Rendering validation messages and text with effects

Let's look at a simple example of capturing text input from the user. In this example, we will ask for the user's name and will render a validation message with an effect as soon as the user clicks on the submit button.

This is accomplished by setting the effect attribute of the <ice:message> tag to a value expression that evaluates an Effect object returned by the backing bean. This effect will be rendered when the validation message is displayed beside the text field, whenever input validation fails.

```
<ice:form>
    <ice:outputLabel for="name" value="Enter your name: " />
    <ice:inputText id="name" value="#{backingBeanname}"
        required="#{true}" />
    <ice:commandButton value="Submit" />
<ice:message effect="#{backingBean.valueChangeEffect}"
    showDetail="#{true}" for="name" />
<ice:panelGroup rendered="#{backingBean.name ne null}">
    <ice:outputText value="Hello, #{backingBean.name}"
        effect="#{backingBean.valueChangeEffect}" />
</ice:panelGroup>
</ice:form>
```

In our backing bean's constructor, we create a new Highlight object and initialize it with a hexadecimal color code.

```
public BackingBean() {
    valueChangeEffect = new Highlight("#fda505");
}
```

When the form is rendered on the screen, the JSF framework calls our backing bean property accessor method, which resets the fired state of the Effect object. When the fired state of the object is set to false, ICEfaces renders a dynamic HTML effect in the browser. Once the fired state is set to true, the effect will no longer be rendered.

```
public Effect getValueChangeEffect() {
    return valueChangeEffect;
```

```
}
public String getName() {
    valueChangeEffect.setFired(false);
    return name;
}
```

Therefore, we reset it in the `getter` method of our `bean` property during each request, causing the validation message to reappear whenever the validation message has to be shown.

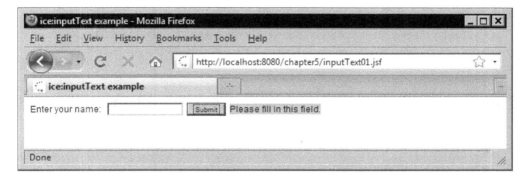

The same effect can also be applied to output text components. The same principle applies; the `Effect` object's `fired` state must be reset for the effect to be rendered. In this case, the message entered by the user is rendered dynamically below the text field once the button is clicked. This produces a very smooth effect in the browser since the page was updated incrementally using Ajax, avoiding the somewhat disorienting effect of a full-page refresh.

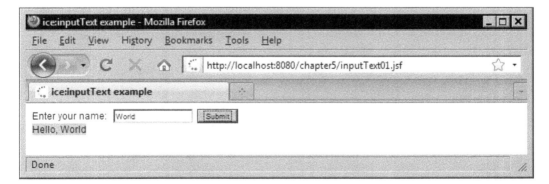

Receiving HTML input from users

Sometimes, it is desirable to enable users to enter rich text in the browser to simulate a word processor-like experience while entering descriptive text. This can be achieved using the ICEfaces `InputRichText` component, rendered by the `<ice:inputRichText>` tag. This tag provides a JSF component for the popular **FCKeditor**—a browser-based text editor. This component enables us to bind the editor to a `String` property in our backing bean while giving users a powerful and flexible interface for text entry. This tag also supports flexible parameters for width, height, skinning, and toolbar customization.

```
<ice:inputRichText id="iceInpRchTxt" height="200" width="600"
toolbar="#{inputRichText.toolbarMode}" value="#{inputRichText.value}"
language="en" skin="silver" />
```

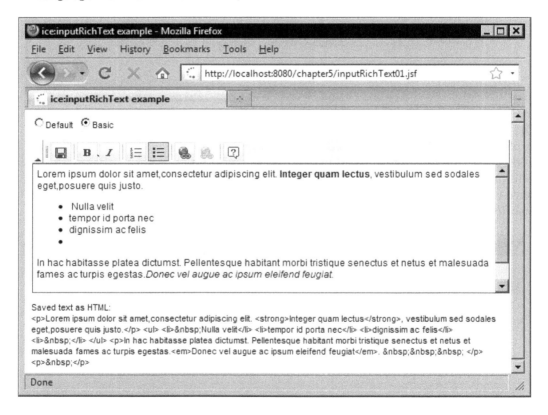

Handling file uploads with ICEfaces

ICEfaces also includes a useful component for handling file uploads. The InputFile component is rendered by the `<ice:inputFile>` tag as an HTML input element of type file. It can be combined with a progress bar component to provide continuous feedback to the user about the status of the file upload.

```
<ice:form>
      <ice:inputFile id="inputFileName" width="600"
          progressListener="#{backingBean.fileUploadProgress}"
          actionListener="#{backingBean.uploadFile}" />
      <ice:outputProgress value="#{backingBean.fileProgress}"
styleClass="uploadProgressBar" />
</ice:form>
```

The backing bean code required to process the file upload is as follows. We check the `status` property of the `FileInfo` to determine if the file has been saved or not.

```
public void uploadFile(ActionEvent event) {
      InputFile inputFile = (InputFile) event.getSource();
      FileInfo fileInfo = inputFile.getFileInfo();
      if (fileInfo.getStatus() == FileInfo.SAVED) {
         System.out.println("Saved file: " + fileInfo.getFile().
                             getPath());
         currentFile = new InputFileData(fileInfo);
         synchronized (fileList) {
            fileList.add(currentFile);
         }
      }
   }
```

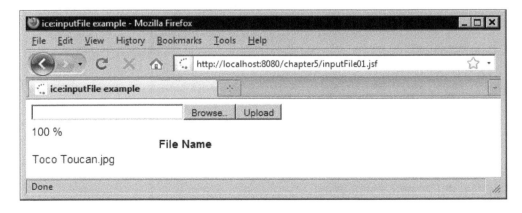

Rendering a calendar component

ICEfaces also includes an attractive calendar component that can be used to handle date selections by the user. The SelectInputDate component is rendered by the <ice:selectInputDate> tag as an interactive calendar with a customizable look and feel. The calendar supports a number of options, such as rendering the month and year as drop-down lists, the format of the selected date, and whether to render the calendar as a pop up or not.

```
...
<head>
<ice:outputStyle href="/xmlhttp/css/xp/xp.css" />
</head>
...
<ice:form>
      <ice:outputLabel for="calendar1"
          value="Enter your birth date: " />
      <ice:selectInputDate id="calendar1" renderMonthAsDropdown="true"
          renderYearAsDropdown="true"
          popupDateFormat="EEE, MMM d, yyyy"
          value="#{backingBean.date}"
          rendered="#{backingBean.pattern eq 'date'}"
          renderAsPopup="true"
          valueChangeListener="#{dateSelect.effect2ChangeListener}" />
      <h:message style="color: red" for="calendar1" />
      <ice:outputText value="Your birth date is: #{backingBean.date}"
          rendered="#{backingBean.date ne null}" />
</ice:form>
```

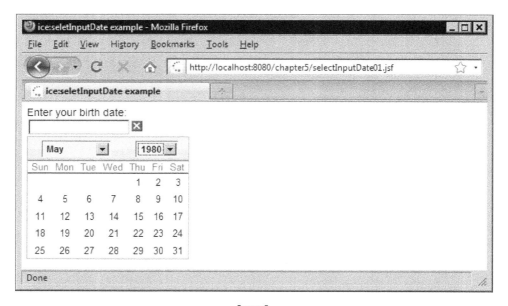

In the next example, we render a similar calendar using the built-in **Rime** theme for ICEfaces. By simply changing the stylesheet attached to the document, we can completely redefine the appearance of the calendar component. Also notice in this example that we do not render the month and year as a drop down, but rather with navigable arrow buttons.

```
<ice:outputStyle href="/xmlhttp/css/rime/rime.css" />
```

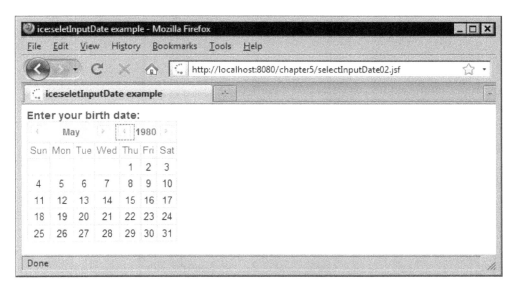

Creating navigation and pop-up menus

In **Human Machine Interface (HMI)** design, navigation menus present a useful "affordance" by which users can interact with a system, much like door handles allow access to rooms in a building in the real world.

ICEfaces includes a useful set of navigation menu components that can be combined to create simple but effective navigation menus, both statically and dynamically. In our first example, we will look at how to create a navigation menu with submenus in our JSF page.

Creating a horizontal navigation menu with submenus

The ICEfaces menu components support both a horizontal and a vertical orientation. Menus can be nested to create submenus, and menu items can be statically declared or dynamically bound to a backing bean property. In the following example, the product's menu item and its submenus are dynamically bound to a collection in our backing bean.

```
<ice:menuBar orientation="horizontal">
        <ice:menuItem value="Home" />
        <ice:menuItem value="About">
           <ice:menuItem value="Company Information" />
           <ice:menuItem value="Investor Relations" />
        </ice:menuItem>
        <ice:menuItem value="Products">
           <ice:menuItems value="#{productBean.productMenuItems}" />
        </ice:menuItem>
        <ice:menuItem value="Services" />
        <ice:menuItem value="Contact" />
</ice:menuBar>
```

To create the navigation menu programmatically, we construct a List of `MenuItem` objects as shown in the following code example:

```
public List<MenuItem> getProductMenuItems() {
      List<MenuItem> model = null;
      try {
         model = new ArrayList<MenuItem>();
         List<ProductCategory> categories = getProductCategories();
         String view = FacesContext.getCurrentInstance().
                      getViewRoot().getViewId();
         String context = FacesContext.getCurrentInstance().
                       getExternalContext().getRequestContextPath();
         if (!context.equals("/")) {
            view = context + view;
         }
         Collections.sort(categories);
         for (ProductCategory category : categories) {
            MenuItem categoryItem = new MenuItem();
            String categoryViewId = view + "?category=" + URLEncoder.
                              encode(category.getName(),
                              "UTF-8");
            categoryItem.setLink(categoryViewId);
            categoryItem.setValue(category.getName());
            categoryItem.setId("item" + category.getId());
            model.add(categoryItem);
```

```
        for (ProductCategory subcategory :
            category.getSubcategories()) {
          String subcategoryViewId = categoryViewId +
          "&subcategory=" + URLEncoder.encode(subcategory.
                              getName(), "UTF-8");
          MenuItem subcategoryItem = new MenuItem();
          subcategoryItem.setLink(subcategoryViewId);
          subcategoryItem.setValue(subcategory.getName());
          subcategoryItem.setId("item" + subcategory.getId());

          categoryItem.getChildren().add(subcategoryItem);
          List<Product> products = new
          ArrayList<Product>(subcategory.getProducts());
          Collections.sort(products);
          for (Product product : products) {
            String productViewId = view + "?product=" + product.
                              getId();
            MenuItem productItem = new MenuItem();
            productItem.setLink(productViewId);
            productItem.setValue(product.getName());
            productItem.setId("item" + product.getId());
          subcategoryItem.getChildren().add(productItem);
          }
        }
      }
    } catch (Exception e) {
      e.printStackTrace();
    }
    return model;
}
```

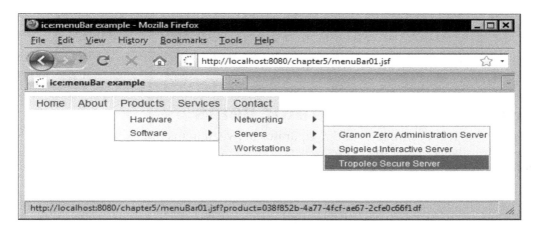

Rendering a vertical navigation menu with submenus

The same menu can be rendered vertically by changing the `orientation` attribute from `horizontal` to `vertical`.

```
<ice:menuBar orientation="vertical">
        <ice:menuItem value="Home" />
        <ice:menuItem value="About">
            <ice:menuItem value="Company Information" />
            <ice:menuItem value="Investor Relations" />
        </ice:menuItem>
        <ice:menuItem value="Products">
            <ice:menuItems value="#{productBean.productMenuItems}" />
        </ice:menuItem>
        <ice:menuItem value="Services" />
        <ice:menuItem value="Contact" />
</ice:menuBar>
```

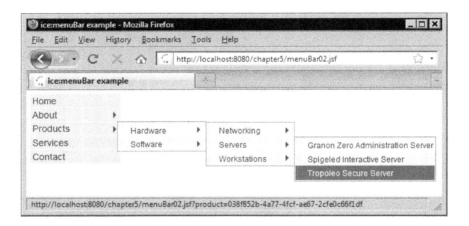

Adding menu separator items

Sometimes, it is desirable to add a separator between items in the menu. This can be accomplished using the `<ice:menuItemSeparator>` tag as shown in the following example:

```
<ice:menuBar orientation="horizontal">
        <ice:menuItem value="File">
          <ice:menuItem value="New" />
        <ice:menuItem value="Open" />
        <ice:menuItem value="Save" />
            <ice:menuItemSeparator />
        <ice:menuItem value="Exit" />
```

```
    </ice:menuItem>
        <ice:menuItem value="Edit" />
        <ice:menuItem value="View" />
        <ice:menuItem value="Help" />
</ice:menuBar>
```

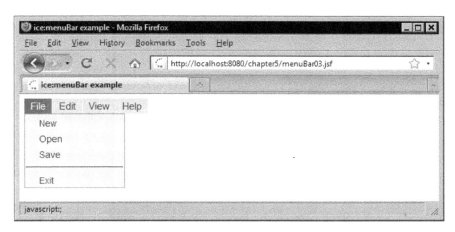

Using context menus

Desktop applications often provide context menus for users to make selections from a pop-up menu that presents options relevant to the task at hand. ICEfaces includes a contextual menu component rendered by the `<ice:menuPopup>` tag that can also be used to produce this type of menu. It also takes `<ice:menuItem>` tags as its children, and therefore supports submenus as well.

The context menu rendered by the `<ice:MenuPopup>` tag can be reused by other components in the view. The `<ice:panelGroup>` tag has a `menuPopup` attribute that specifies the ID of a `MenuPopup` component to support sharing a pop-up menu between multiple parts of the page.

```
<ice:panelGroup styleClass="componentBox">
        <ice:panelGroup styleClass="exampleBox
            menuPopupContainer menuPopupContainer"
            style="width:362px;height:122px;">
          <ice:panelGroup style="padding:5px;" id="menuBarImage"
              menuPopup="menuPopupEffects">
            <ice:graphicImage value="/images/Toco Toucan.jpg"
                width="200" height="110" />
          </ice:panelGroup>
        </ice:panelGroup>
        <ice:menuPopup id="menuPopupEffects" imageDir="/images">
```

```
            <ice:menuItem id="effects" onclick="return false;"
               value="Effects">
              <ice:menuItem id="shake" value="Shake"
                 actionListener="#{menuPopupBean.executeMenuEffect}">
                <f:param name="effectType" value="shake" />
              </ice:menuItem>
              <ice:menuItem id="highlight" value="Highlight"
                 actionListener="#{menuPopupBean.executeMenuEffect}">
                <f:param name="effectType" value="hightlight" />
              </ice:menuItem>
              <ice:menuItem id="pulsate" value="Pulsate"
                 actionListener="#{menuPopupBean.executeMenuEffect}">
                <f:param name="effectType" value="pulsate" />
              </ice:menuItem>
            </ice:menuItem>
          </ice:menuPopup>
</ice:panelGroup>
```

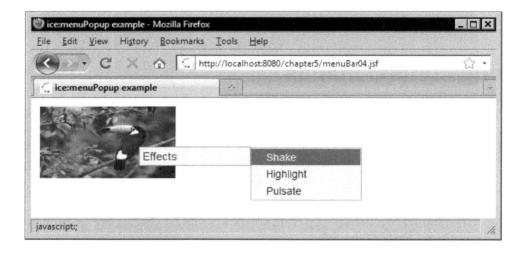

Using tree components

The ICEfaces component library provides a robust tree component that can be used to render hierarchical data. By default, the `<ice:tree>` tag renders a tree component without any node icons, however, custom node icons can also be defined.

Using the default tree node icons

In this example, we bind the ICEfaces tree component to a model property in our backing bean that represents a set of files and folders on the file system.

```
<ice:form>
  <ice:tree value="#{backingBean.treeModel}" var="item"
      hideRootNode="#{false}" hideNavigation="#{false}">
    <ice:treeNode>
      <f:facet name="content">
        <ice:panelGroup style="display: inline">
          <ice:outputText value="#{item.userObject.text}" />
        </ice:panelGroup>
      </f:facet>
    </ice:treeNode>
  </ice:tree>
</ice:form>
```

The ICEfaces tree component expects the same `javax.swing.tree.TreeModel` interface as the `Swing` tree component. The nodes of the tree model must be `DefaultMutableTreeNode` instances, and the user object property of each node must be an `IceUserObject` instance.

```
public TreeModel getTreeModel() {
      if (treeModel == null) {
          File dir = getUploadDirectory();
          DefaultMutableTreeNode rootTreeNode = new
          DefaultMutableTreeNode();
          buildTreeModel(dir, rootTreeNode);
          ((IceUserObject) rootTreeNode.getUserObject()).
            setExpanded(true);
          treeModel = new DefaultTreeModel(rootTreeNode);
      }
      return treeModel;
  }
```

To construct the `TreeModel`, we use a recursive method that takes a `File` and a `DefaultMutableTreeNode` object.

```
private void buildTreeModel(File file, DefaultMutableTreeNode node) {
      IceUserObject object = new IceUserObject(node);
      object.setText(file.getName());
      object.setLeaf(!file.isDirectory());
      node.setAllowsChildren(file.isDirectory());
      node.setUserObject(object);
      File[] files = file.listFiles();
```

```
     if (files != null) {
        for (File f : files) {
           DefaultMutableTreeNode child = new
           DefaultMutableTreeNode();
           node.add(child);
           buildTreeModel(f, child);
        }
     }
  }
```

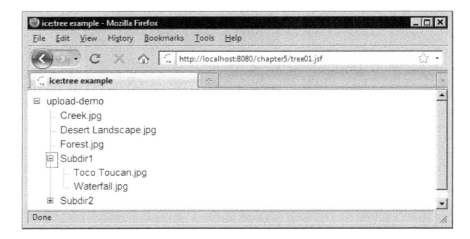

Using custom tree node icons

The ICEfaces tree component has the ability to display customized tree node icons.
This is accomplished by using the `icon` facet of the tag. In this example, we use an
`<ice:graphicImage>` tag to render an icon appropriate to each node in the tree. The
`IceUserObject` class has an `icon` property that allows us to specify a filename to be
used as the icon for that node.

```
<ice:form>
  <ice:tree value="#{backingBean.treeModel2}" var="item"
      hideRootNode="#{false}" hideNavigation="#{false}">
    <ice:treeNode>
     <f:facet name="icon">
        <ice:graphicImage value="/images/#{item.userObject.icon}"/>
     </f:facet>
     <f:facet name="content">
        <ice:panelGroup style="display: inline">
          <ice:outputText value="#{item.userObject.text}" />
```

```
        </ice:panelGroup>
      </f:facet>
    </ice:treeNode>
  </ice:tree>
</ice:form>
```

To support custom tree node icons, we use a similar recursive method that also sets the icons of the user object while it is constructing the tree model. Each `IceUserObject` instance contains information about the icons to render for expanded, contracted, and leaf icons in the tree.

```
private void buildTreeModelWithIcons(File file,
                                    DefaultMutableTreeNode node)
{
    IceUserObject object = new IceUserObject(node);
    object.setText(file.getName());
    object.setLeaf(!file.isDirectory());
    object.setLeafIcon("document.png");
    object.setBranchContractedIcon("yellow-folder-closed.png");
    object.setBranchExpandedIcon("yellow-folder-open.png");
    node.setAllowsChildren(file.isDirectory());
    node.setUserObject(object);
    File[] files = file.listFiles();
    if (files != null) {
        for (File f : files) {
            DefaultMutableTreeNode child = new
            DefaultMutableTreeNode();
            node.add(child);
            buildTreeModelWithIcons(f, child);
        }
    }
}
```

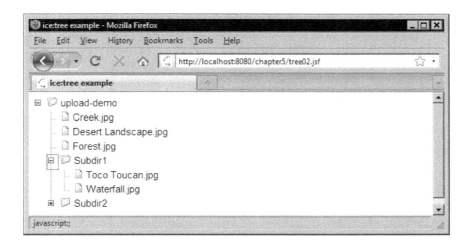

Displaying data in tables

ICEfaces includes a powerful data table component that provides many advanced features out of the box without requiring much additional coding. This component supports sorting by clicking on column headers, dragging to resize column headers, row selection, pagination, and more.

The ICEfaces data table component

To construct an ICEfaces data table, we use the `<ice:dataTable>` tag in combination with the `<ice:column>` tag, similar to the way the standard JSF HTML data tables are assembled. Each column can have a header facet, and the table supports row banding as well.

```
<ice:dataTable value="#{customerBean.customerList}" var="customer"
rows="5">
        <ice:column>
            <f:facet name="header">
                <ice:outputText value="Full Name" />
            </f:facet>
            <ice:outputText value="#{customer.fullName}" />
        </ice:column>
        <ice:column>
            <f:facet name="header">
                <ice:outputText value="Birth Date" />
            </f:facet>
            <ice:outputText value="#{customer.birthDate}">
                <f:convertDateTime type="date" dateStyle="medium" />
            </ice:outputText>
        </ice:column>
        <ice:column>
            <f:facet name="header">
                <ice:outputText value="Phone Number" />
            </f:facet>
            <ice:outputText value="#{customer.phoneNumber}" />
        </ice:column>
        <ice:column>
            <f:facet name="header">
                <ice:outputText value="Country of Origin" />
            </f:facet>
            <ice:outputText value="#{customer.countryOfOrigin.name}" />
        </ice:column>
</ice:dataTable>
```

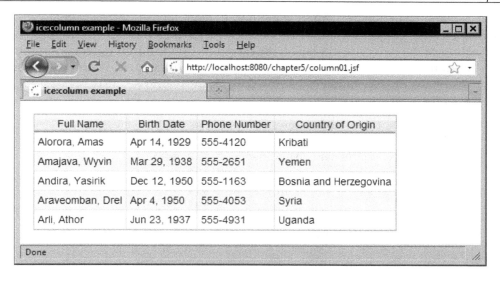

Rendering dynamic columns

The ICEfaces component library also includes a dynamic columns component that allows us to render columns as well as rows from a data model. We provide two data models in this example, one for the rows and one for the columns.

```
<ice:dataTable var="customer" value="#{customerBean.rowDataModel}"
    rows="5" columnClasses="column-odd,column-even">
  <ice:columns value="#{customerBean.columnDataModel}"
        var="column">
      <f:facet name="header">
      <ice:panelGroup>
            <ice:outputText value="#{column}" />
      </ice:panelGroup>
        </f:facet>
        <ice:outputText value="#{customerBean.cellValue}" />
    </ice:columns>
</ice:dataTable>
```

In our backing bean, we implement a method named `getCellValue()` that determines which object should be rendered for a particular cell by examining the intersection of the two data models. In this example, the column model is simply a series of numbers, so we obtain the current column number and we use that as an index to look up the cell value in the row data model.

```
@SuppressWarnings("unchecked")
public Object getCellValue() {
    Object value = null;
    DataModel rowDataModel = getRowDataModel();
    if (rowDataModel.isRowAvailable()) {
        List<Object> rowData = (List<Object>) rowDataModel.
                                getRowData();
        DataModel columnDataModel = getColumnDataModel();
        if (columnDataModel.isRowAvailable()) {
            Object columnData = columnDataModel.getRowData();
            int column = Integer.parseInt(columnData.toString());
            value = rowData.get(column - 1);
        }
    }
    return value;
}
```

The row data model contains heterogeneous lists of objects representing different properties of the customer object. Each row has a list of objects that represent a particular customer.

```
public DataModel getRowDataModel() {
    if (rowDataModel == null) {
        List<List<Object>> rowData = new ArrayList<List<Object>>();
        List<Customer> customers = getCustomerList();
        List<Object> customerData = null;
        for (Customer customer : customers) {
            customerData = new ArrayList<Object>();
            customerData.add(customer.getFullName());
            customerData.add(customer.getBirthDate());
            customerData.add(customer.getPhoneNumber());
            customerData.add(customer.getCountryOfOrigin());
            rowData.add(customerData);
        }
        rowDataModel = new ListDataModel(rowData);
    }
    return rowDataModel;
}
```

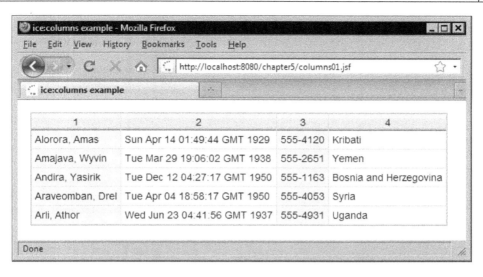

Implementing sortable column headers

The ICEfaces data table also supports sortable column headers. To implement sorting in our data table, first we need to set the `sortAscending` and `sortColumn` attributes. The `sortAscending` attribute refers to a Boolean property in our backing bean that indicates whether to sort in ascending or descending order. The `sortColumn` attribute refers to a `String` property in our backing bean that keeps track of which column is currently being sorted.

```
<ice:dataTable value="#{customerBean.sortableCustomerModel.list}"
    var="customer" id="cs" rows="5"
    sortAscending="#{customerBean.sortableCustomerModel.ascending}"
    sortColumn="#{customerBean.sortableCustomerModel.columnName}">
        <ice:column>
            <f:facet name="header">
                <ice:commandSortHeader id="nameHeader"
                                        columnName="fullName">
                    <ice:outputText value="Full Name" />
                </ice:commandSortHeader>
            </f:facet>
            <ice:outputText value="#{customer.fullName}" />
        </ice:column>
        <ice:column>
            <f:facet name="header">
                <ice:commandSortHeader id="birthDateHeader"
                                        columnName="birthDate">
```

```
                    <ice:outputText value="Birth Date" />
                </ice:commandSortHeader>
            </f:facet>
            <ice:commandSortHeader id="birthDateHeader"
                                   columnName="birthDate">
                <ice:outputText value="#{customer.birthDate}">
                    <f:convertDateTime type="date" dateStyle="medium" />
                </ice:outputText>
            </ice:commandSortHeader>
        </ice:column>
        <ice:column>
            <f:facet name="header">
                <ice:commandSortHeader id="phoneNumberHeader"
                    columnName="phoneNumber">
                    <ice:outputText value="Phone Number" />
                </ice:commandSortHeader>
            </f:facet>
            <ice:outputText value="#{customer.phoneNumber}" />
        </ice:column>
        <ice:column>
            <f:facet name="header">
                <ice:commandSortHeader id="countryHeader"
                                       columnName="countryOfOrigin">
                    <ice:outputText value="Country of Origin" />
                </ice:commandSortHeader>
            </f:facet>
            <ice:outputText value="#{customer.countryOfOrigin.name}" />
        </ice:column>
    </ice:dataTable>
```

To implement sorting in our backing bean requires a bit more work. First, we provide a special model class named SortableDataModel to handle sorting of the customer objects when the user clicks on a column. This class also has additional responsibilities, such as handling row selection. These will be covered later. For now, let's examine how the SortableDataModel class manages column sort ordering for our data table.

```
┌─────────────────────────────────────────────────────────┐
│         SortableDatamodel<Textends Selectable>            │
├─────────────────────────────────────────────────────────┤
│ - ascending : boolean                                     │
│ - columnName : String                                     │
│ - enhancedMultiple : boolean                              │
│ - lastAscending : String                                  │
│ - lastColumnName : String                                 │
│ - list : List<T>                                          │
│ - mode : String                                           │
│ - multiple : boolean                                      │
│ - selectedValues : List<T>                                │
├─────────────────────────────────────────────────────────┤
│ + checkState()                                            │
│ + getColumnName() : String                                │
│ + getList() : List<T>                                     │
│ + getMode() : String                                      │
│ + getSelectedValues() : List<T>                           │
│ + isAscending() : boolean                                 │
│ + isMultiple() : boolean                                  │
│ + rowSelectionListener(listener : RowSelectionListener)   │
│ + setAscending(ascending : boolean)                       │
│ + setColumnName(columnName : String)                      │
│ + setEnhancedMultiple(enhancedMultiple : boolean)         │
│ + setList(list : List<T>)                                 │
│ + setMode(mode : String)                                  │
│ + setMultiple(multiple : boolean)                         │
└─────────────────────────────────────────────────────────┘
```

When the ICEfaces data table is rendered, the data is displayed in a default sort order. In our implementation, we initially sort the data by the customer's name.

```
public SortableDataModel<Customer> getSortableCustomerModel() {
    if (sortableCustomerModel == null) {
        List<Customer> customers = getCustomerList();
        sortableCustomerModel = new
        SortableDataModel<Customer>(customers, "fullName");
        sortableCustomerModel.setColumnName("fullName");
    }
    return sortableCustomerModel;
}
```

The constructor of our `SortableDataModel` class takes a List of `Selectable` objects and a string identifying the property name to sort by. It stores these arguments in instance variables, and then calls the `checkState()` method to initially sort the list.

```
public SortableDataModel(List<T> list, String initialSortColumn) {
    this.list = list;
    this.columnName = initialSortColumn;
    checkState();
}
```

When the user clicks on a column, the selected column name and the ascending or descending direction of the column are stored in properties of our SortableDataModel object. The ICEfaces data table component does not sort the data model for us, it simply passes the user's column selection to our backing bean.

Therefore, we have to make sure that the data model is properly sorted before the view is rendered. This can be accomplished using a JSF PhaseListener class that is invoked just before the RENDER_RESPONSE phase of the request processing lifecycle.

In this example, we write a new class named CustomerSortListener that implements the PhaseListener interface. It obtains a reference to our SortableDataModel object and invokes the checkState() method before the view is rendered.

```
public class CustomerSortListener implements PhaseListener {
    private static final long serialVersionUID = 1L;
    public void afterPhase(PhaseEvent arg0) {
    }
    public void beforePhase(PhaseEvent arg0) {
        FacesContext context = arg0.getFacesContext();
        ELContext el = context.getELContext();
        ExpressionFactory factory = context.getApplication().
                                    getExpressionFactory();
        ValueExpression expr =
        factory.createValueExpression(el,
        "#{customerBean.sortableCustomerModel}",
        SortableDataModel.class);
        SortableDataModel<?> model = (SortableDataModel<?>) expr.
                                    getValue(el);
        model.checkState();
    }
    public PhaseId getPhaseId() {
        return PhaseId.RENDER_RESPONSE;
    }
}
```

Next, we must register this PhaseListener class in the faces-config.xml file.

```
<lifecycle>
    <phase-listener>chapter4.phase.CustomerSortListener
    </phase-listener>
</lifecycle>
```

Now, when the user clicks on a column in our data table, ICEfaces sends an Ajax request to our backing bean and stores the sort column name and direction in our SortableDataModel object. Just before the response is sent back to the browser, our PhaseListener is invoked and the table data is sorted accordingly.

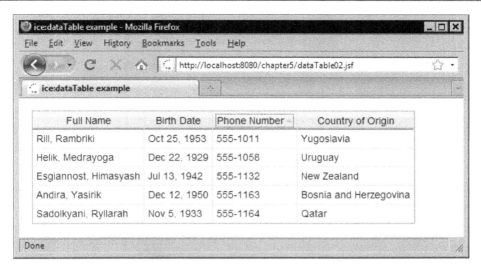

A more efficient alternative to implementing a sortable data table with ICEfaces is to set the `actionListener` attribute in the `<ice:commandSortHeader>` tag. This attribute expects a method expression that is responsible for sorting the data by a particular column. The following example demonstrates this approach:

```
<h:form>
    <ice:dataTable
        value="#{customerBean.sortableCustomerModel.list}"
        var="customer" id="cs" rows="5"
        sortAscending="#{customerBean.sortableCustomerModel.
                        ascending}"
        sortColumn="#{customerBean.sortableCustomerModel.
                    columnName}" resizable="true">
    <ice:column>
        <f:facet name="header">
            <ice:commandSortHeader id="nameHeader"
                columnName="fullName"
                actionListener="#{customerBean.
                                sortCustomersByName}">
                <ice:outputText value="Full Name" />
            </ice:commandSortHeader>
        </f:facet>
        <ice:outputText value="#{customer.fullName}" />
    </ice:column>
    <ice:column>
        <f:facet name="header">
            <ice:commandSortHeader id="birthDateHeader"
                columnName="birthDate"
                actionListener="#{customerBean.
                                sortCustomersByBirthDate}">
```

```
                   <ice:outputText value="Birth Date" />
              </ice:commandSortHeader>
          </f:facet>
          <ice:commandSortHeader id="birthDateHeader"
                                 columnName="birthDate">
              <ice:outputText value="#{customer.birthDate}">
                  <f:convertDateTime type="date" dateStyle="medium" />
              </ice:outputText>
          </ice:commandSortHeader>.
      </ice:column>
      <ice:column>
          <f:facet name="header">
              <ice:commandSortHeader id="phoneNumberHeader"
                 columnName="phoneNumber"
                 actionListener="#{customerBean.
                                   sortCustomersByPhoneNumber}">
                 <ice:outputText value="Phone Number" />
              </ice:commandSortHeader>
          </f:facet>
          <ice:outputText value="#{customer.phoneNumber}" />
      </ice:column>
      <ice:column>
          <f:facet name="header">
              <ice:commandSortHeader id="countryHeader"
                 columnName="countryOfOrigin"
                 actionListener="#{customerBean.
                                   sortCustomersByCountry}">
                 <ice:outputText value="Country of Origin" />
              </ice:commandSortHeader>
          </f:facet>
          <ice:outputText value="#{customer.countryOfOrigin.name}"
           />
      </ice:column>
   </ice:dataTable>
</h:form>
```

The backing bean methods needed to support this behavior are listed below:

```
public void sortCustomersByBirthDate(ActionEvent event) {
    sortableCustomerModel.setColumnName("birthDate");
    sortableCustomerModel.checkState();
}
public void sortCustomersByCountry(ActionEvent event) {
    sortableCustomerModel.setColumnName("countryOfOrigin");
    sortableCustomerModel.checkState();
}
```

```
public void sortCustomersByName(ActionEvent event) {
    sortableCustomerModel.setColumnName("fullName");
    sortableCustomerModel.checkState();
}
public void sortCustomersByPhoneNumber(ActionEvent event) {
    sortableCustomerModel.setColumnName("phoneNumber");
    sortableCustomerModel.checkState();
}
```

Supporting resizable columns

One of the nice features about the ICEfaces data table is that it supports resizable columns simply by setting the `resizable` attribute to true. This enables users to resize columns by clicking and dragging the edges of the column headers in our table.

```
<ice:dataTable value="#{customerBean.sortableCustomerModel.list}"
    var="customer" id="cs" rows="5"
    sortAscending="#{customerBean.sortableCustomerModel.ascending}"
    sortColumn="#{customerBean.sortableCustomerModel.columnName}"
    resizable="true">
    <ice:column>
        <f:facet name="header">
            <ice:commandSortHeader id="nameHeader"
                                    columnName="fullName">
                <ice:outputText value="Full Name" />
            </ice:commandSortHeader>
        </f:facet>
        <ice:outputText value="#{customer.fullName}" />
    </ice:column>
    <ice:column>
        <f:facet name="header">
            <ice:commandSortHeader id="birthDateHeader"
                                    columnName="birthDate">
                <ice:outputText value="Birth Date" />
            </ice:commandSortHeader>
        </f:facet>
        <ice:commandSortHeader id="birthDateHeader"
                                columnName="birthDate">
            <ice:outputText value="#{customer.birthDate}">
                <f:convertDateTime type="date" dateStyle="medium" />
            </ice:outputText>
        </ice:commandSortHeader>
    </ice:column>
    <ice:column>
        <f:facet name="header">
```

```
                     <ice:commandSortHeader id="phoneNumberHeader"
                        columnName="phoneNumber">
                        <ice:outputText value="Phone Number" />
                     </ice:commandSortHeader>
                 </f:facet>
                 <ice:outputText value="#{customer.phoneNumber}" />
             </ice:column>
             <ice:column>
                 <f:facet name="header">
                     <ice:commandSortHeader id="countryHeader"
                                            columnName="countryOfOrigin">
                        <ice:outputText value="Country of Origin" />
                     </ice:commandSortHeader>
                 </f:facet>
                 <ice:outputText value="#{customer.countryOfOrigin.name}"
                     />
             </ice:column>
</ice:dataTable>
```

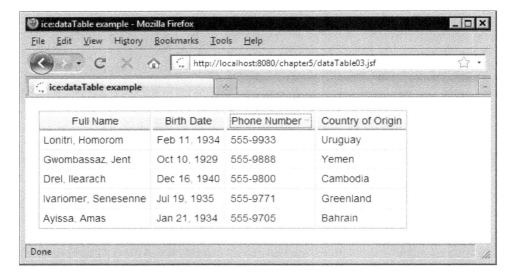

Data table single row selection mode

One of the more advanced features of the ICEfaces data table component is the
ability for users to select rows in the table. This is accomplished by nesting the
`<ice:rowSelector>` tag inside the first `<ice:column>` tag within the data table.

This tag is bound to the Boolean selected property of each customer object being rendered in the table. Therefore, when the user selects rows, they are effectively setting the selected property to true in the customer object represented by that row. After the customer model object is updated, a selection event is sent to the rowSelectionListener method in our SortableDataModel object.

The multiple and enhancedMultiple attributes of the <ice:rowSelector> tag support three possible selection modes. By default, the row selector supports a single row selection mode. In this mode, the user can click on a row to select it.

```
<ice:selectOneRadio value="#{customerBean.sortableCustomerModel.mode}"
        onchange="submit()" immediate="#{true}">
    <f:selectItem itemLabel="Single" itemValue="single" />
    <f:selectItem itemLabel="Multiple" itemValue="multiple" />
    <f:selectItem itemLabel="Enhanced Multiple"
                itemValue="enhanced" />
</ice:selectOneRadio>
    <ice:panelGrid columns="2">
        <ice:panelGroup style="text-align:left; vertical-align:top;">
            <ice:outputText value="Customer Table" />
            <ice:dataTable
                value="#{customerBean.sortableCustomerModel.list}"
                var="customer" id="cs" rows="5" resizable="#{true}"
                sortAscending="#{customerBean.sortableCustomerModel.
                            ascending}"
                sortColumn="#{customerBean.sortableCustomerModel.
                        columnName}">
            <ice:column>
                <ice:rowSelector id="selected"
                    value="#{customer.selected}"
                    multiple="#{customerBean.sortableCustomerModel.
                            multiple}"
                    enhancedMultiple="#{customerBean.
                    sortableCustomerModel.enhancedMultiple}"
                    selectionListener="#{customerBean.
                    sortableCustomerModel.rowSelectionListener}"
                    preStyleOnSelection="#{true}" />
                <f:facet name="header">
                    <ice:commandSortHeader id="nameHeader"
                                        columnName="fullName">
                        <ice:outputText value="Full Name" />
                    </ice:commandSortHeader>
                </f:facet>
                <ice:outputText value="#{customer.fullName}" />
            </ice:column>
```

```
            <ice:column>
                <f:facet name="header">
                    <ice:commandSortHeader id="phoneNumberHeader"
                        columnName="phoneNumber">
                        <ice:outputText value="Phone Number" />
                    </ice:commandSortHeader>
                </f:facet>
                <ice:outputText value="#{customer.phoneNumber}" />
            </ice:column>
            <ice:column>
                <f:facet name="header">
                    <ice:commandSortHeader id="countryHeader"
                        columnName="countryOfOrigin">
                        <ice:outputText value="Country of Origin" />
                    </ice:commandSortHeader>
                </f:facet>
                <ice:outputText
                    value="#{customer.countryOfOrigin.name}" />
            </ice:column>
        </ice:dataTable>
    </ice:panelGroup>
    <ice:panelGroup style="text-align:left; vertical-align:top;">
        <ice:outputText value="Selected Customers" />
        <ice:dataTable
            value="#{customerBean.sortableCustomerModel.
                    selectedValues}"
            var="customer">
            <ice:column>
                <f:facet name="header">
                    <ice:outputText value="Customer Name" />
                </f:facet>
                <ice:outputText value="#{customer.fullName}" />
            </ice:column>
        </ice:dataTable>
    </ice:panelGroup>
</ice:panelGrid>
```

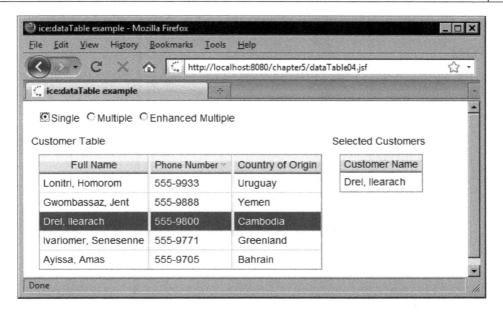

Data table multiple row selection mode

When the `multiple` attribute is set to true, it allows multiple row selections. This mode allows the user to click on rows in sequence to make a multiple row selection.

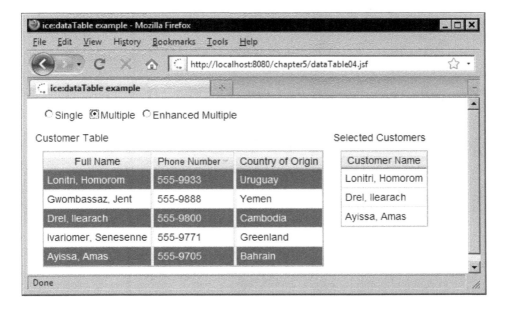

Data table enhanced multiple row selection mode

When the `enhancedMultiple` attribute is set to true, the table supports a more advanced selection mode where:

- Clicking selects a row and deselects other rows.

- Pressing the *Ctrl* key while clicking toggles a row while preserving other selected rows.

- Pressing the *Shift* key while clicking selects all contiguous rows from the previous selected row to the current row, and deselects all other selected rows.

- Pressing the *Ctrl+Shift* keys while clicking selects all contiguous rows from the previous selected row to the current row, while preserving other selected rows.

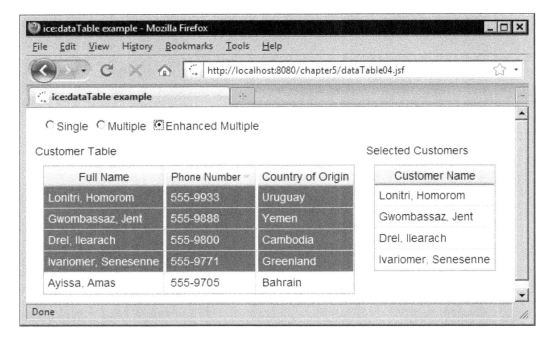

Implementing data set paging

The ICEfaces data table component also supports data set paging. This is implemented using the `<ice:dataPaginator>` tag. This tag has a `for` attribute that specifies the identifier of the data table for which it is providing pagination. The `<ice:dataPaginator>` tag is very easy to use and renders an attractive and customizable data set pagination control that allows the user to navigate between pages in the data set.

```
<ice:dataTable value="#{customerBean.customerList}" var="customer"
    id="customerTable" rows="5">
        <ice:column>
            <f:facet name="header">
                <ice:outputText value="Full Name" />
            </f:facet>
            <ice:outputText value="#{customer.fullName}" />
        </ice:column>
        <ice:column>
            <f:facet name="header">
                <ice:outputText value="Birth Date" />
            </f:facet>
            <ice:outputText value="#{customer.birthDate}">
                <f:convertDateTime type="date" dateStyle="medium" />
            </ice:outputText>
        </ice:column>
        <ice:column>
            <f:facet name="header">
                <ice:outputText value="Phone Number" />
            </f:facet>
            <ice:outputText value="#{customer.phoneNumber}" />
        </ice:column>
        <ice:column>
            <f:facet name="header">
                <ice:outputText value="Country of Origin" />
            </f:facet>
            <ice:outputText value="#{customer.countryOfOrigin.name}"
                />
        </ice:column>
    </ice:dataTable>
        <ice:dataPaginator for="customerTable" paginatorMaxPages="10"
            id="scroll" vertical="#{false}" paginator="#{true}"
            styleClass="carNumber">
        <f:facet name="first">
            <ice:outputText value="First" />
        </f:facet>
```

```
              <f:facet name="last">
                 <ice:outputText value="Last" />
              </f:facet>
              <f:facet name="previous">
                 <ice:outputText value="Previous" />
              </f:facet>
              <f:facet name="next">
                 <ice:outputText value="Next" />
              </f:facet>
          </ice:dataPaginator>
```

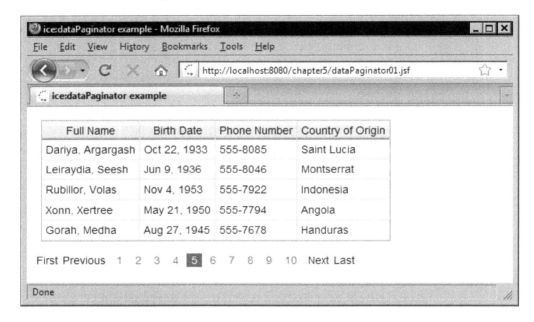

Rendering charts

The ICEfaces component library includes support for the open source **jCharts** project. This project provides a wide variety of chart objects that are rendered as JPEG images in the browser. We will look at how to render some of these charts using the ICEfaces `<ice:outputChart>` tag.

Rendering a stacked bar chart

Our first example demonstrates how to render a stacked bar chart using a static data set declared in our JSF page. This example renders a chart that displays unit test results for a series of test suites. The data is hardcoded in the data attribute of the tag. The values in a series are separated by commas, while the series themselves are separated by a colon. It is important that the number of labels and the number of series are equal.

```
<ice:outputChart type="barstacked" chartTitle="Unit Test Results"
xaxisLabels="Suite 1, Suite 2, Suite 3" yaxisTitle="Test Methods"
xaxisTitle="Test Suites" labels="pass, fail" data="70, 30, 10 : 10,
50, 70" colors="green, red" />
```

Rendering a 3-D pie chart

In our next example, we will see how to render a three-dimensional pie chart dynamically using data provided by our backing bean. This time, instead of using hardcoded values in the data attribute, we bind it to a List of Double objects representing the distribution of male and female customers. Once again, it is important that the number of labels and the number of series are equal. We have two labels, one for male and one for female, so our list has two double values: the number of men and the number of women.

```
<ice:outputChart type="pie3D" chartTitle="Customer Gender"
    height="400" labels="male,female"
    data="#{customerBean.customerGenderData}" colors="blue, green" />
```

The Java code in our CustomerBean class is as follows:

```
public List<Double> getCustomerGenderData() {
    if (customerGenderData == null) {
        customerGenderData = new ArrayList<Double>();
        List<Customer> customers = getCustomerList();
        double male = 0;
        double female = 0;
        for (Customer customer : customers) {
            if (customer.getMale() != null && customer.getMale()) {
                male++;
            } else {
                female++;
            }
        }
        customerGenderData.add(male);
        customerGenderData.add(female);
    }
    return customerGenderData;
}
```

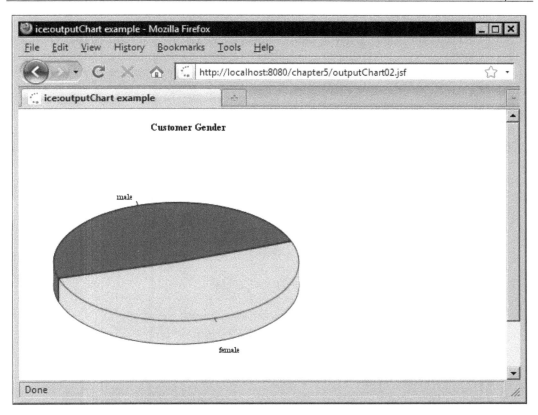

Rendering a bar chart

Let's look at how to render a bar chart that displays more customer demographic information. In this case, our chart displays the number of customers in different age groups. Once again, the data attribute of the tag is bound to the backing bean property, but in this case we use a two-dimensional array of double values instead of a list.

```
<ice:outputChart type="bar" labels="Customers" chartTitle="Customer
Demographics"  xaxisLabels="#{customerBean.ageGroupLabels}"
data="#{customerBean.customerAgeBarChartData}" xaxisTitle="Age Groups"
yaxisTitle="Number of Customers" />
```

The Java code required to construct the data for this chart is a bit more complicated. The first dimension in our array of doubles has a size of one, indicating that we have only one series of values to display the chart (we only have one group of customers). The second dimension in our array of doubles has a size of six, one element for each age group.

To construct the data, first we iterate an array of AgeGroup enums. For each age group, we iterate our collection of Customer objects and increment a counter for each customer within that age group.

```
public double[][] getCustomerAgeBarChartData() {
    if (customerAgeBarChartData == null) {
        customerAgeBarChartData = new double[1][6];
        List<Customer> customers = getCustomerList();
        int customerCount = customers.size();
        AgeGroup[] ageGroups = AgeGroup.values();
        for (int i = 0; i < ageGroups.length; i++) {
            customerAgeBarChartData[0][i] = 0;
            AgeGroup ageGroup = ageGroups[i];
            for (int j = 0; j < customerCount; j++) {
                Customer customer = customers.get(j);
                int age = customer.getAge();
                int[] range = ageGroup.getRange();
                int min = range[0];
                int max = range[1];
                if (age < max && age >= min) {
                    customerAgeBarChartData[0][i]++;
                }
            }
        }
    }
    return customerAgeBarChartData;
}
```

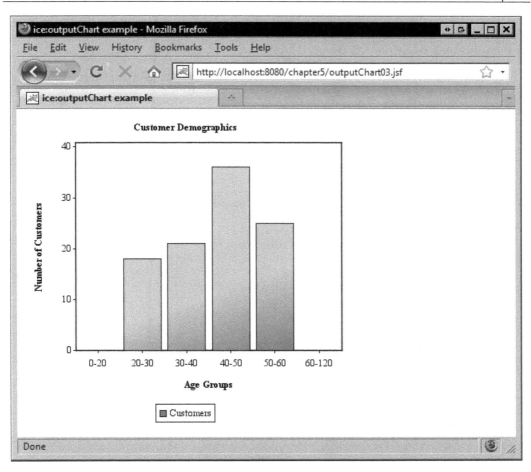

Laying out components with panels

The ICEfaces component library also includes a set of panels that support a wide range of user interface layouts. Let's look at a few of these panel components to gain a better appreciation of the power of ICEfaces' layout capabilities.

Working with a border layout

Swing/AWT programmers will be familiar with the `BorderLayout` class. This class provides an interesting layout manager for the Java GUI toolkit that subdivides a panel into five distinct regions. These regions are known as the North, South, East, West, and Center regions.

The `<ice:panelBorder>` tag supports the `BorderLayout` layout algorithm within a JSF application. Each region is represented by a facet with the same name as shown in the following example.

```
<ice:panelBorder cellspacing="2" cellpadding="2" align="center"
    height="200px" width="400px">
        <f:facet name="north">
           <ice:outputText value="North" />
        </f:facet>
        <f:facet name="west">
           <ice:outputText value="West" />
        </f:facet>
        <f:facet name="center">
           <ice:outputText value="Center" />
        </f:facet>
        <f:facet name="east">
           <ice:outputText value="East" />
        </f:facet>
        <f:facet name="south">
           <ice:outputText value="South" />
        </f:facet>
</ice:panelBorder>
```

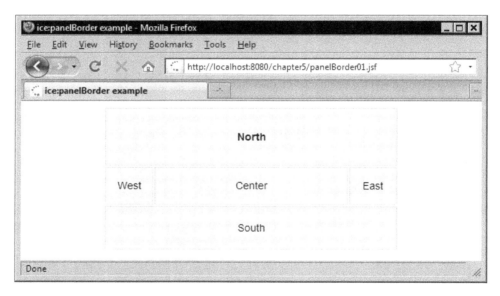

Rearranging elements in a list

Sometimes, it is desirable to enable users to rearrange elements in a list. The ICEfaces `<ice:panelPositioned>` tag is an excellent choice for this use case. In the following example, we use the `<ice:panelPositioned>` tag to render a list of products that can be re-positioned by the user by dragging and dropping elements in the list.

```
<ice:form>
    <ice:panelGrid columns="2" cellpadding="10">
     <ice:panelGroup>
      <ice:outputText value="Modifiable Product List"
                    style="font-weight:bold; padding:5px" />
      <ice:panelPositioned id="products" var="product"
          value="#{productBean.rankedProducts}" styleClass="
          positionPanelContainer"
          listener="#{productBean.rankChanged}"
          constraint="vertical">
        <ice:panelGroup style="cursor:move;" styleClass="container">
          <ice:panelGroup styleClass="moveLabel"
                        style="border: 4px red">
              <ice:graphicImage url="/images/#{product.icon}"
                  width="16px" style="vertical-align:middle;
                  padding-right:5px" />
            <ice:outputText id="name" value="#{product.name}" />
          </ice:panelGroup>
        </ice:panelGroup>
      </ice:panelPositioned>
     </ice:panelGroup>
     <ice:panelGroup>
        <ice:outputText value="Ranked Products"
                      style="font-weight:bold; padding:5px" />
        <ice:panelSeries id="rankedProducts" var="product"
            styleClass="rankPanelContainer"
            value="#{productBean.rankedProducts}">
          <ice:panelGroup effect="#{product.effect}"
                        styleClass="container">
            <ice:outputText id="nameWithRank"
                          value="#{product.nameWithRank}" />
          </ice:panelGroup>
        </ice:panelSeries>
     </ice:panelGroup>
    </ice:panelGrid>
</ice:form>
```

The following screenshot demonstrates the `<ice:panelPositioned>` component in action. The product items shown in the list on the left are draggable. The selected item is currently being dragged and dropped to another position in the list.

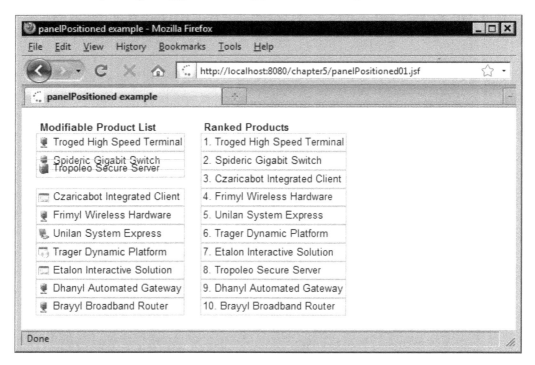

Once the mouse button is released, the drop operation is completed and the rank of the positioned item is reflected in the list on the right. A highlight effect briefly flashes on the page to indicate the change in position before fading out.

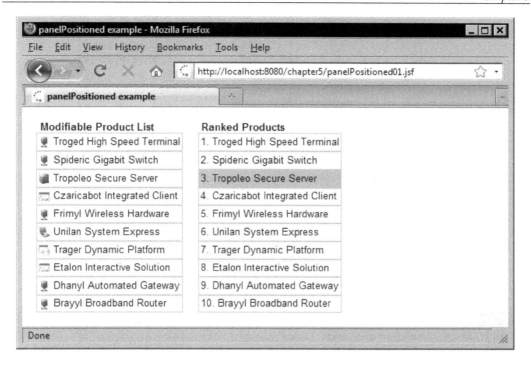

Rendering a series of components

The ICEfaces component library includes a number of components that support data iteration. The PanelSeries component is a simple but powerful component for iterating dynamic data from a backing bean. This component renders its data using any arbitrary set of child components. In this example, we bind the `<ice:panelSeries>` tag's `value` attribute to a collection of products from our backing bean as a series of floating `<div>` elements. The `var` attribute specifies the name of the iterator variable to use, similar to the `dataTable` tag.

```
<ice:panelSeries value="#{productBean.randomProducts}" var="product"
          rows="9">
      <ice:panelGroup styleClass="productBox">
          <ice:graphicImage url="/images/#{product.icon}" />
          <ice:panelGroup styleClass="iceDatTblColHdr">
              <ice:outputText value="#{product.name}"
                             style="font-weight:bold;" />
          </ice:panelGroup>
```

```
<ice:panelGroup style="padding:10px;">
    <ice:outputText value="Category: "
                    style="font-weight:bold;" />
    <ice:outputText value="#{product.productCategory.
                            name}" />
    <br />
    <ice:outputText value="Price: "
                    style="font-weight:bold;" />
    <ice:outputText value="#{product.price}">
        <f:convertNumber type="currency"
          currencySymbol="$" maxFractionDigits="0" />
    </ice:outputText>
    <br />
    <ice:outputText value="In Stock: "
                    style="font-weight:bold;" />
    <ice:outputText value="#{product.quantityInStock}"
        />
</ice:panelGroup>
        </ice:panelGroup>
    </ice:panelSeries>
```

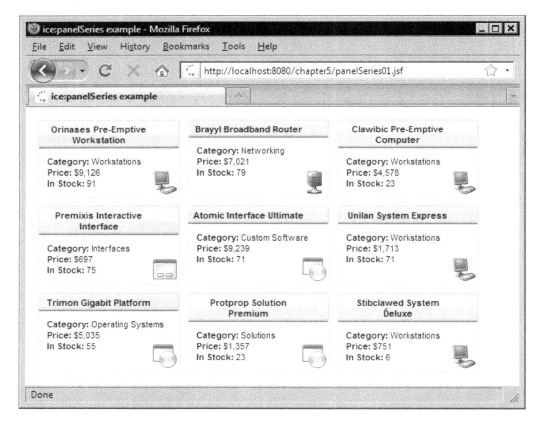

Rendering collapsible panels

Another interesting layout component in the ICEfaces component library
is PanelCollapsible component. This component is rendered by the
`<ice:panelCollapsible>` tag as a `<div>` element that responds to mouse click
events by expanding and collapsing to reveal or hide its child content. Other
components such as forms, images, and text can be nested inside this component.
In this example, we combine the `<ice:panelCollapsible>` tag with the
`<ice:panelSeries>` tag to produce a series of panels to display groups of products.

```
<ice:panelCollapsible expanded="true">
    <f:facet name="header">
        <ice:panelGroup>
            <ice:outputText value="Recommended" />
        </ice:panelGroup>
    </f:facet>
    <ice:panelGrid width="100%">
        <ice:panelSeries value="#{productBean.randomProducts}"
                    var="product" rows="3">
            <ice:panelGroup styleClass="productBox">
                <ice:graphicImage url="/images/#{product.icon}"/>
                <ice:panelGroup styleClass="iceDatTblColHdr">
                    <ice:outputText value="#{product.name}"
                                style="font-weight:bold;" />
                </ice:panelGroup>
                <ice:panelGroup style="padding:10px;">
                    <ice:outputText value="Category: "
                                style="font-weight:bold;" />
                    <ice:outputText value="#{product.
                                    productCategory.name}" />
                    <br />
                    <ice:outputText value="Price: "
                                style="font-weight:bold;" />
                    <ice:outputText value="#{product.price}">
                        <f:convertNumber type="currency"
                                    currencySymbol="$"
                                    maxFractionDigits="0" />
                    </ice:outputText>
                    <br />
                    <ice:outputText value="In Stock: "
                                style="font-weight:bold;" />
                    <ice:outputText value="#{product.quantityInStock}"
                        />
```

```
            </ice:panelGroup>
          </ice:panelGroup>
        </ice:panelSeries>
      </ice:panelGrid>
  </ice:panelCollapsible>
```

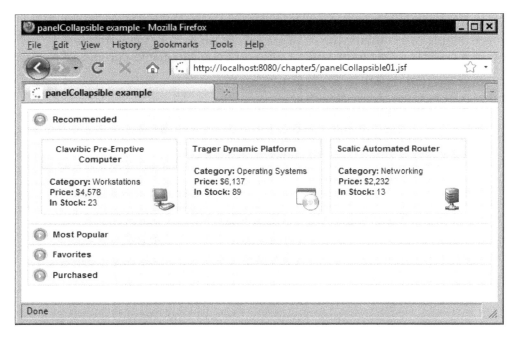

```
<ice:panelTabSet tabPlacement="top">
      <ice:panelTab label="Recommended">
        <ice:panelSeries value="#{productBean.randomProducts}"
                         var="product" rows="6">
        <ice:panelGroup styleClass="productBox">
          <ice:graphicImage url="/images/#{product.icon}" />
          <ice:panelGroup styleClass="iceDatTblColHdr">
            <ice:outputText value="#{product.name}"
                            style="font-weight:bold;" />
          </ice:panelGroup>
          <ice:panelGroup style="padding:10px;">
            <ice:outputText value="Category: "
                            style="font-weight:bold;" />
            <ice:outputText value="#{product.productCategory.
                                     name}" />
            <br />
            <ice:outputText value="Price: "
                            style="font-weight:bold;" />
            <ice:outputText value="#{product.price}">
```

```
                        <f:convertNumber type="currency"
                                    currencySymbol="$"
                                    maxFractionDigits="0" />
                </ice:outputText>
                <br />
                <ice:outputText value="In Stock: "
                                style="font-weight:bold;" />
                <ice:outputText value="#{product.quantityInStock}" />
            </ice:panelGroup>
        </ice:panelGroup>
    </ice:panelSeries>
    </ice:panelTab>
    <ice:panelTab label="Most Popular">
    </ice:panelTab>
    <ice:panelTab label="Favorites">
    </ice:panelTab>
    <ice:panelTab label="Purchases" disabled="#{true}">
    </ice:panelTab>
</ice:panelTabSet>
```

Creating a tabbed user interface

ICEfaces also includes a panel component that supports tabbed user interface
layouts. The `<ice:panelTabSet>` tag renders a set of child `<ice:panelTab>` tags
in a series of tabs that the user can interact with to display the contents of the
series of panels on the screen. The following example demonstrates how to use the
`<ice:panelTab>` tag. Only the first tab has been implemented; the remaining three
tabs are simply included for illustration purposes.

```
<ice:form>
    <ice:panelTabSet tabPlacement="top">
        <ice:panelTab label="Recommended">
            <ice:panelSeries value="#{productBean.randomProducts}"
                            var="product" rows="6">
            <ice:panelGroup styleClass="productBox">
                <ice:graphicImage url="/images/#{product.icon}" />
                <ice:panelGroup styleClass="iceDatTblColHdr">
                    <ice:outputText value="#{product.name}"
                                    style="font-weight:bold;" />
                </ice:panelGroup>
                <ice:panelGroup style="padding:10px;">
                    <ice:outputText value="Category: "
                                    style="font-weight:bold;" />
                    <ice:outputText value="#{product.productCategory.
                                                name}" />
                    <br />
```

```
                      <ice:outputText value="Price: "
                                      style="font-weight:bold;" />
                      <ice:outputText value="#{product.price}">
                         <f:convertNumber type="currency"
                                          currencySymbol="$"
                                          maxFractionDigits="0" />
                      </ice:outputText>
                      <br />
                      <ice:outputText value="In Stock: "
                                      style="font-weight:bold;" />
                      <ice:outputText value="#{product.quantityInStock}" />
                   </ice:panelGroup>
                 </ice:panelGroup>
              </ice:panelSeries>
            </ice:panelTab>
            <ice:panelTab label="Most Popular">
            </ice:panelTab>
            <ice:panelTab label="Favorites">
            </ice:panelTab>
            <ice:panelTab label="Purchases" disabled="#{true}">
            </ice:panelTab>
         </ice:panelTabSet>
   </ice:form>
```

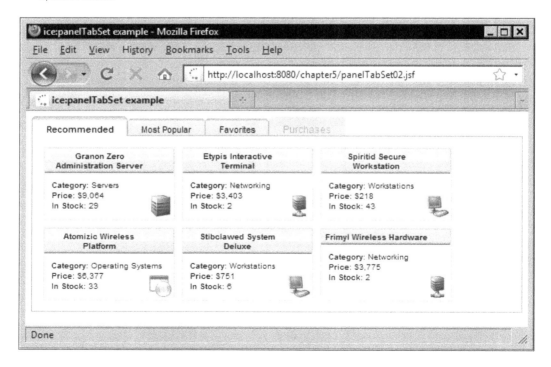

Working with modal dialogs

Web browser support for modal dialogs is quite limited. To date, there is no standard browser support for rendering a complex modal dialog window. Fortunately, the ICEfaces library includes such a component.

Rendering a simple modal dialog

To render a simple modal dialog with ICEfaces, we can use the `<ice:panelPopup>` tag. This tag has a "header" and "body" facet to render the dialog title and message content, respectively.

The `modal` attribute of the tag expects a Boolean value that determines whether the dialog is modal or not. When this attribute is set to true, the dialog appears centered over a transparent gray background that covers the entire screen. When this attribute is set to false, the dialog is displayed next to the button and the background is not modified.

```
<ice:panelGroup style="height: 75px;">
    <ice:panelGroup style="float:left">
        <ice:outputLabel value="Modal Popup Message"
            for="modalMessageInput" />
    </ice:panelGroup>
    <ice:panelGroup styleClass="clearer" />
    <ice:panelGroup style="float:left">
        <ice:inputText id="modalMessageInput"
            value="#{popup.modalMessage}"
            disabled="#{popup.modalRendered}" size="30"
            maxlength="90" style="font-size:12px" />
        <ice:commandButton id="toggleModal"
            value="#{popup.determineModalButtonText}"
            disabled="#{popup.modalRendered}"
            style="margin-right: 2px;font-size:12px"
            actionListener="#{popup.toggleModal}" />
    </ice:panelGroup>
</ice:panelGroup>
<ice:panelPopup id="modalPnlPop" draggable="false"
    modal="true" visible="#{popup.modalRendered}"
    autoCentre="#{popup.autoCentre}" styleClass="corePopup">
    <f:facet name="header">
        <ice:panelGroup styleClass="popupHeaderWrapper">
            <ice:outputText value="Modal Popup Dialog"
                styleClass="popupHeaderText" />
            <ice:commandButton id="modalPnlCloseBtn"
                type="button" image="/images/close.gif"
                actionListener="#{popup.toggleModal}"
                styleClass="popupHeaderImage"
                title="Close Popup" alt="Close" />
```

```
        </ice:panelGroup>
    </f:facet>
  <f:facet name="body">
      <ice:panelGroup styleClass="popupBody">
          <ice:outputText value="#{popup.modalMessage}" />
          <br />
          <ice:commandButton id="modalPnlCloseButton"
              type="submit" value="Close"
              actionListener="#{popup.toggleModal}" />
      </ice:panelGroup>
  </f:facet>
</ice:panelPopup>
```

The following screenshot demonstrates the `<ice:panelPopup>` tag in action. First, we render a text input field and a button on the screen.

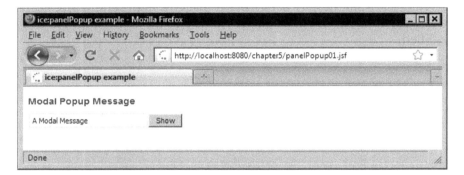

When the user clicks on the **Show** button, our modal dialog is displayed in the foreground and a semi-transparent layer is rendered over the background. The dialog can be closed by clicking the **Close** button, or by clicking our custom close icon in the top-right corner.

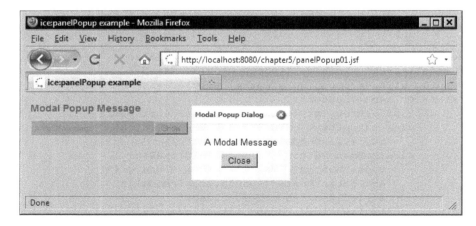

Rendering a draggable dialog box

The `<ice:panelPopup>` tag also has a `draggable` attribute. This attribute controls
whether or not the user can drag the modal dialog box around on the screen. When
the `autoCenter` attribute is set to true, the dialog will automatically return to the
center of the screen when the drag operation is completed.

```
<ice:panelGroup styleClass="exampleBox panelPopupExampleContainer"
        style="height: 75px;">
    <ice:panelGroup style="float:left">
        <ice:outputLabel value="Draggable Popup Message"
        for="draggableMessageInput" />
    </ice:panelGroup>
    <ice:panelGroup styleClass="clearer" />
    <ice:panelGroup style="float:left">
        <ice:inputText id="draggableMessageInput"
            value="#{popup.draggableMessage}"
            disabled="#{popup.draggableRendered}" size="30"
            maxlength="90"
            style="font-size:12px" />
        <ice:commandButton id="toggleDraggable"
            value="#{popup.determineDraggableButtonText}"
            disabled="#{popup.draggableRendered}"
            style="font-size:12px"
            actionListener="#{popup.toggleDraggable}" />
    </ice:panelGroup>
    <ice:panelGroup styleClass="clearer" />
        <ice:panelGrid style="float:left" columns="2" cellspacing="2"
            cellpadding="3">
            <ice:outputLabel value="Auto Center"
                            for="autoCentreCheck" />
            <ice:selectBooleanCheckbox id="autoCentreCheck"
                value="#{popup.autoCentre}"
                disabled="#{popup.draggableRendered or popup.
                        modalRendered}" />
        </ice:panelGrid>
</ice:panelGroup>

<!-- Draggable Panel Popup -->
<ice:panelPopup id="draggablePnlPop" draggable="true" modal="false"
        rendered="#{popup.draggableRendered}"
        visible="#{popup.draggableRendered}"
        autoCentre="#{popup.autoCentre}" styleClass="corePopup">
    <f:facet name="header">
        <ice:panelGroup styleClass="popupHeaderWrapper">
            <ice:outputText value="Draggable Popup Dialog"
                styleClass="popupHeaderText" />
```

```
            <ice:commandButton id="draggablePnlCloseBtn" type="button"
              image="/images/close.gif"
               actionListener="#{popup.toggleDraggable}"
               styleClass="popupHeaderImage" title="Close Popup"
               alt="Close" />
         </ice:panelGroup>
      </f:facet>
      <f:facet name="body">
         <ice:panelGroup styleClass="popupBody">
         <ice:outputText value="#{popup.draggableMessage}" />
         <br />
            <ice:commandButton id="draggablePnlCloseButton"
                       type="submit" value="Close"
                       actionListener="#{popup.toggleDraggable}" />
         </ice:panelGroup>
      </f:facet>
   </ice:panelPopup>
```

Rendering a draggable modal dialog

The following screenshot demonstrates two more features of the `<ice:panelPopup>` tag: draggable and auto-centering modal dialogs. In this example, we render a checkbox to enable the "auto-center" behavior of the ICEfaces modal dialog component. When it is checked, the modal dialog will always be displayed in the center of the screen.

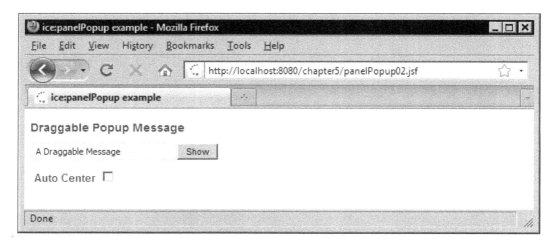

When the user clicks the **Show** button, a draggable modal dialog box is displayed. The user can drag the title bar of the dialog to re-position it on the screen. If the **Auto Center** checkbox is checked, the dialog will return to a centered position.

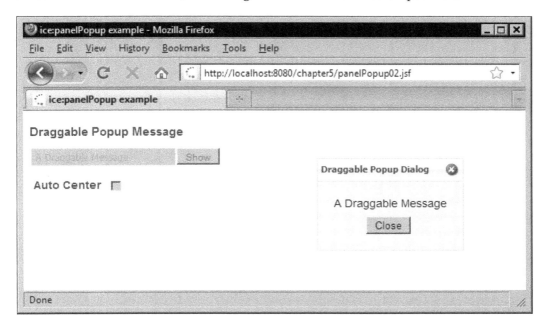

Summary

In this chapter, we looked at a number of common use cases for web developers and how these could be implemented using the ICEfaces component library. In particular, we looked at how to receive input from users, how to create navigation pop-up menus, working with tree components, displaying tabular data, rendering charts, laying out components on the screen with panels, creating tabbed user interfaces, and using modal dialogs.

ICEfaces is a truly impressive Ajax component library for the JSF framework. With over 50 powerful and feature-rich UI components, ICEfaces enables JSF developers to quickly and easily develop advanced user interfaces that significantly improve the Web user experience.

6
JBoss Seam Components

In this chapter, we will explore the JBoss Seam framework and the Seam JSF component library. Seam is one of the most exciting technologies available today for JSF developers. This powerful framework significantly enhances web development on the Java EE platform, and provides a much needed bridge between many important and complementary technologies. In addition to discussing the Seam framework, we will also set the stage for a more in-depth discussion of two other important JBoss technologies covered in the next chapter: the JBoss RichFaces and Ajax4jsf component libraries.

Introducing the JBoss Seam framework

The JBoss Seam framework sets out to bridge the gap between JSF managed beans and EJB3 components. It introduces a flexible set of Java annotations that provide a nice alternative to XML for JSF managed bean configuration and that significantly enhances the **Dependency Injection (DI)** capabilities of the JSF framework.

Additionally, Seam introduces a new conversation scope to the JSF environment, enabling developers to support more fine-grained interaction between users and components in the Java Web tier. Seam conversations solve a number of common issues for Java web applications, gracefully handling the "back button" problem and allowing users to interact with the same JSF page concurrently in multiple tabs without any side effects.

The Seam framework also includes a powerful set of JSF controls that greatly simplify JSF application development. With the Seam JSF tag library, developers can implement sophisticated validation schemes with minimal coding effort. In particular, the `<s:validateAll>` tag delegates JSF validation duties to the **Hibernate Validator** framework, enabling developers to apply a rich set of annotations to JPA domain model classes to declare validation constraints that can be verified automatically during the JSF request processing lifecycle. By providing tight integration with the Java Persistence API and support for the Hibernate Validator framework, Seam encourages developers to follow the "DRY" principle ("Don't Repeat Yourself") when implementing domain model validation.

Seam also provides a convenient JSF tag for automatically converting lists of JPA entities to lists of JSF `SelectItem` objects, saving the developer, the extra work of preparing JSF-specific data structures for selection-oriented UI components. When combined with the `<s:convertEntity>` tag, the Seam framework can also perform automatic type conversion for JSF of any JPA domain model object. This also saves the developer a lot of work in implementing custom converters for different domain model classes.

Generating Java EE Applications with seam-gen

The JBoss Seam framework includes a useful command-line utility program named "seam-gen" that can be used to create a simple but fully functional Java web application with CRUD screens (Create-Read-Update-Delete) from an existing relational database. Please see the Setup Guide for the code bundle accompanying this book for details on how to use the seam-gen utility to create and deploy a Java EE application based on the relational database included with this book.

Our examples will highlight key features of the JBoss Seam framework and will feature Java source code, JSF markup, and configuration files to demonstrate how to leverage the power of Java EE in a Seam-enabled JSF application.

Java Enterprise Edition (Java EE) technology

Let's consider some of the benefits of using the full Java EE technology stack in our JSF applications. Since you are reading this book, it's a safe bet that you have an interest in Java Web frameworks, you most likely have some experience working with both **Java Standard Edition (Java SE)** and **Java Enterprise Edition (Java EE)** middleware APIs such as JDBC and Servlets/JSP, and you are probably familiar with the JavaBeans programming model. (If you do not have experience with these APIs, you may want to pick up a book or two on the subject. The more familiar you are with these and other enterprise Java technologies, the easier it will be to understand how they can be integrated together in the context of a JSF application and the more you will appreciate their value from a development point of view.)

Over the past few years there has been a growing trend in the Enterprise Java community towards simpler, lighter, and more elegant programming paradigms and design patterns, such as Model-View-Controller, Dependency Injection, and annotation-based configuration. The surging success of open source frameworks such as Spring, Hibernate, and Struts were like catalysts that help to refine dramatically the Java EE architecture in general and the Enterprise JavaBeans™ (EJB) component model in particular.

Before MVC Web frameworks such as JSF, typical *n*-tier Java web applications consisted of Java Servlets and JSP pages that communicated with a database using JDBC directly or via references to local or remote EJB session beans obtained from the **Java Naming and Directory Interface (JNDI)**. With the emergence of the Struts framework (the predecessor to JavaServer Faces) in the year 2000, Java developers had new tools for building web applications. The success of Struts and its custom tag libraries led to the emergence of the Java Standard Tag Library (JSTL), a set of JSP tags that provided common functionality needed by many web applications, such as conditional logic and iteration.

With the release of Java EE 5, developers now have a much simpler programming model to deal with when implementing an EJB-based business tier for a Java web application. If you are unfamiliar with the benefits of EJB, please read on. If you are already a seasoned Java EE developer with significant EJB programming experience, you may want to skip ahead to the next section.

Understanding Java SE and Java EE

Under the stewardship of Sun Microsystems, the Java platform evolved into two separate editions: Java Standard Edition (Java SE) and Java Enterprise Edition (Java EE). Java SE defines a set of standardized application program interfaces (APIs) for everyday development, such as file handling, multithreading, networking, database programming, GUI development, **Remote Method Invocation** (**RMI**), and more.

Real-world enterprise applications have to deal with a much broader set of concerns than addressed by Java SE. Therefore, the Java EE specification was designed to address these concerns. It defines APIs for a wide range of enterprise programming tasks, such as developing web applications with Servlets and JSPs, writing XML-based web services, building transactional business-tier components using EJBs, **Object/Relational Mapping** (**ORM**) with the Java Persistence API (JPA), container-managed security with the Java Authentication and Authorization Service (JAAS), container-managed transactions with the **Java Transaction API** (**JTA**), asynchronous messaging with the **Java Message Service** (**JMS**), and much more.

Introducing Enterprise JavaBeans (EJB3) technology

One of the most compelling reasons for using the JBoss Seam framework is how easy it makes to use EJB3 components in our JSF applications. EJB components are transactional by default, which means that any public method calls on our EJBs are automatically wrapped in a database transaction that is managed by the Java EE application server. Additionally, the application server's EJB container provides a number of key services to improve the performance and scalability of our EJB objects, such as passivation and activation, object pooling, asynchronous messaging, and much more.

The Java EE 5 specification defines four types of EJB components: session beans, message-driven beans (MDBs), timer beans, and entity beans. **Session beans** come in two varieties: **Stateful Session Beans** (**SFSBs**) and **Stateless Session Beans** (**SLSBs**). Stateful session beans make excellent controllers for JSF views, as by design they are able to store per-client conversational state between requests.

Stateless session beans are useful for implementing application services that do not manage conversational state. **Message-driven beans** (**MDBs**) can also be used as infrastructural components because they can run asynchronously and support a loosely-coupled architecture where communication between objects does not require direct references. **Timer beans** can also be useful infrastructural components as they can be scheduled to perform recurring background tasks.

Introducing the Java Persistence API (JPA)

The **Java Persistence API (JPA)** is the standard persistence technology for the Java platform. Although JPA is a subset of the EJB3 specification, it can be used in both Java SE and Java EE environments. JPA entity beans support object/relational mapping and can have their state persisted to and restored from a relational database. As such they are excellent candidates for implementing an application domain model and can also be used as **Data Transfer Objects (DTOs)** to transfer data between the different tiers of the application.

JPA entities can also be annotated to express an application's validation constraints in an efficient way. For example, JPA supports a basic set of object/relational mapping annotations such as @Table, @Column, @JoinColumn, @ManyToOne, and @OneToMany to map our domain model to a relational database schema. JPA also includes more advanced annotations such as @Inheritance and @MappedSuperclass that enable us to apply **Object-Oriented Programming (OOP)** concepts to our persistence layer. For example, we can map a class hierarchy to one or more tables using different inheritance mapping strategies.

The @Transient annotation in JPA enables us to add transient (non-persistent) properties to our entity classes. Transient in this sense is not the same as the "transient" keyword in the Java language that excludes fields during object serialization; rather, transient in the JPA context generally means "state which is not saved to the database".

What is a property?

A "property" is another name for an object attribute, more specifically an instance variable with a getter and a setter method. Getter methods are also known as "accessor" methods, as they provide access to the instance variable. Setter methods are also called "mutators" because they enable callers to modify (mutate) the value of the instance variable. A property can be read-write (getter and setter), read-only (getter only), and write-only (setter only). Properties do not need an instance variable, but their signatures must conform to the JavaBeans programming guidelines to be recognized properly using the Java Reflection API.

For example, our Customer class has a transient getAge() method that simply calculates the customer's current age in years:

```
@Transient
public int getAge() {
    Date today = new Date();
    double millis = today.getTime() - birthDate.getTime();
    double seconds = millis / 1000d;
```

```
        double minutes = seconds / 60d;
        double hours = minutes / 60d;
        double days = hours / 24d;
        double years = days / 365d;
        int age = new Double(Math.floor(years)).intValue();
        return age;
    }
```

This is a good example of a transient property because storing volatile data such as a customer's age in the database would not be efficient. There are many possible examples of good candidates for transient properties, such as a `getTotal()` method in an Invoice class that calculates the current value of the invoice (plus sales tax, minus discounts).

Implementing transient properties in a JPA domain model is an excellent practice because it encapsulates business logic and data in a portable way. Applications that use JPA but do not take advantage of transient properties are at risk of falling into the **Anemic Domain Model anti-pattern** (`http://martinfowler.com/bliki/ AnemicDomainModel.html`).

We will see a number of examples of how to use JPA entities in Seam-enabled JSF applications throughout this chapter.

Container Managed Transactions (CMT)

The Java EE specification requires that EJB containers support **Container Managed Transactions** (**CMT**). EJB components are transactional by default, so any public methods invoked on an EJB instance are automatically executed in a database transaction. EJB components support transaction propagation and declarative transaction demarcation. By default, any method called by the original method is also executed in the same transaction, unless the other method specifies a different transaction attribute type. Container managed transactions are one of the most compelling reasons to use EJB technology.

Activation and passivation for Stateful Session Beans (SFSBs)

EJB technology is designed to handle the high performance requirements of enterprise Java applications, so it provides some useful features to improve application efficiency. As stateful session beans are more memory-intensive than stateless session beans, the EJB container supports a sophisticated memory management feature that is similar to virtual memory in a modern operating system.

When our computer's physical memory (RAM) has been used up by running processes, the operating system attempts to make more memory available by "swapping" data for inactivate programs out of physical memory and onto the hard disk. When an inactive program becomes active again, the operating system swaps the application's data back into physical memory from the hard disk, possibly swapping another inactive program's data to the hard disk to make more RAM available.

The EJB container manages the memory available to a Java EE application in a similar way. When a stateful session bean becomes inactive (that is, its methods have not been invoked for a certain period of time), the EJB container can make more physical memory available by "passivating" (serializing) the stateful session bean instance to disk and releasing any object references. If the bean's client attempts to invoke one of the bean methods, the EJB container will "activate" (deserialize) the bean back into memory from the hard disk.

Object pooling for Stateless Session Beans (SLSBs)

Similarly, the EJB container provides some performance optimizations for stateless session beans. Stateless session beans do not hold per-client conversational state in their instance variables like stateful session beans do. As a consequence, stateless session beans consume less memory than stateful session beans; however the creation of a stateless session bean can still be expensive.

A stateless session bean may depend on external resources such as a JPA persistence context, a JMS destination, or other stateless session beans, so creating and injecting these dependencies is an expensive task for the EJB container. Furthermore, as stateless session beans are stateless by definition, one instance is interchangeable with another. This means the EJB container can manage a pool of stateless session beans from which clients (servlets, JSF managed beans, other session beans, and so on) can obtain "method ready" references that have already been initialized.

Integrating EJB3 and JSF with Seam

The Seam framework includes Java annotations that enable EJB components to be integrated easily into a JSF application. We will see the use of the Seam framework's @In, @Name, and @Scope annotations in this chapter to annotate an EJB stateful session bean class so that it can be used "seamlessly" as a JSF managed bean.

Throughout this chapter, we will see examples of key Java EE middleware APIs in action. The example application for this chapter is a full featured Enterprise Application that is deployed to a Java EE 5 compatible application server as an **Enterprise ARchive** or **EAR** file for short. This EAR file consists of one EJB JAR file that contains the EJB components for our JSF application, as well as our JPA domain model implementation. The EAR file also consists of a **Web Application Archive** or **WAR** file that contains a set of managed beans, Facelets pages, and configuration files for our web application. The web application module is a "client" of the EJB session bean components in the EJB module, and both the Web and EJB modules share a common set of Java library dependencies that are packaged and deployed within the EAR file.

To run the examples in this chapter, you will also need to install the sample database included with the application. The simplest way to get started is to download and install the open source MySQL database and run the SQL script provided with the application. This script will create the necessary database and populate it with the sample data shown in the screenshots throughout this book. A preconfigured JBoss Application Server (version 4.2.3) is also available for download from the publisher's website that includes the necessary data source and database driver JAR to run the example application for this chapter. Please refer to the instructions included with the application for more detailed information.

In this chapter, we will examine how to solve a number of common web application development problems using the JBoss Seam framework in combination with the JBoss RichFaces and Ajax4jsf component libraries. We will look at several examples of how to develop next generation web user interfaces using RichFaces, Ajax4jsf, Seam, EJB3 components, and JPA persistence. Our example application will be a full featured Java EE 5 application that is deployed to the JBoss Application Server. This example application can be used as a prototype or starting point for real-world JSF applications based on JBoss Seam, EJB3 and JPA technogies.

A powerful trio: JBoss Seam, RichFaces, and Ajax4jsf

The combination of the JBoss RichFaces library, the JBoss Seam framework, and the Ajax4jsf library enables us to build rich, compelling, and powerful user interfaces for our JSF application.

JBoss RichFaces provides a very useful set of input components, while Ajax4jsf adds the Ajax capabilities, and the Seam framework provides the glue that bridges JSF and EJB and simplifies a number of common JSF development tasks.

The examples in this chapter include components from the Seam, RichFaces, and Ajax4jsf libraries, but the focus of this chapter is primarily on the Seam framework itself. JBoss RichFaces and Ajax4jsf will be covered in more detail in the next chapter. Therefore, when studying the example code, try to concentrate on the Seam markup and remember the overall goal of the chapter.

Introducing Seam components

The JBoss Seam framework is one of the most powerful tools available for JSF developers today. Not surprisingly, this power comes with some complexity. While Seam includes a small set of JSF UI components, its main value proposition is as a technology integration framework and Dependency Injection (DI) container. Therefore, the term "component" is overloaded in Seam, as the framework includes a number of infrastructural components as well. Many of these framework-level components are exposed to JSF applications as managed beans and configured through properties files and XML files such as `seam.properties` and `META-INF/components.xml`.

Introducing REST

The Seam framework supports building RESTful Web Services using the JBoss RESTEasy implementation of the **Java API for RESTful Web Services (JAX-RS)**. JAX-RS is a popular Java specification (JSR-311) for building RESTful Web Services on the Java platform.

REST is an architectural approach to build distributed applications and web services articulated by Roy Fielding in 2000. **REST** is an acronym for **Representational State Transfer** and emphasizes "nouns" (resources) over "verbs" (service methods) when building web services.

In fact, REST is based on the concept of the "uniform interface" in which all service methods are specified in advanced, and clients and services exchange "representations" of resources across the network. In practice, RESTful Web Services and their clients are HTTP based and use HTTP methods to communicate (GET, PUT, POST, DELETE, and HEAD). The Seam framework supports injecting Seam-managed components into JAX-RS resources and providers, making it easier to build RESTful Web Services based on EJB3 technology.

Next steps

Now that we have introduced some important Java EE concepts such as EJB3, JPA, and JAX-RS, we can begin to discuss the JBoss Seam framework in more detail.

The topics we will cover in this chapter include:

- Validating user input with the Seam framework
- Implementing JSF validation with Seam
- JPA and the Hibernate Validator framework
- Decorating the UI to improve form validation
- Seam validation messages
- Adding cutting-edge Ajax technology with Ajax4jsf
- Displaying success messages in JSF
- Seam conversation management
- Temporary conversations
- Starting a long-running conversation
- Concurrent conversations

Validating user input with the Seam framework

In many ways, the JSF validation framework follows the example of previous MVC frameworks, such as Struts. The Struts framework introduced an XML-based validation layer that enabled developers to declare validation rules in an XML file, which the framework would then apply to form bean properties during form submission. Struts includes a number of built-in validators to support common scenarios, such as checking for required fields, verifying a numeric value, and validating a credit card number format.

The JSF validation framework also includes a number of built-in validators that can be registered on components in the view, such as the `<f:validateLongRange>` and `<f:validateLength>` tags. It is important to note that JSF validators are not components themselves, but rather they are classes that implement the `javax.faces.validator.Validator` interface that are invoked during the conversion/validation phase of the JSF request processing lifecycle. UI components that subclass `javax.faces.component.UIInput` also inherit a `required` property, reflected in the fact that so many JSF tags have a `required` attribute. Therefore, many JSF components have built-in support for required field validation.

As we saw in previous chapters, JSF component libraries sometimes include custom validators, such as the `<t:validateEqual>` tag in the Apache MyFaces Tomahawk library. We can always write our own custom validators simply by implementing the `javax.faces.validator.Validator` interface, declaring our custom validator in `faces-config.xml`, and registering it on a UI component in our view using the `<f:validator>` tag.

All of these approaches are perfectly acceptable ways to implement form validation. However, they all have the same limitation: the validation constraints are limited to our presentation layer. For simple web applications, the downside of this reality may not be immediately apparent, but for more complex *n*-tier applications that have multiple interfaces, duplicating validation constraints both vertically and horizontally becomes a problem.

Take for example a Java EE application with a presentation layer based on JSF, a business tier implemented using EJB3 components, and a data access layer based on the Java Persistence API and a relational database. It is good practice to ensure that validation constraints are enforced at each tier in the application architecture. For example, in our presentation layer we should ensure that the user cannot submit a form without completing all required fields.

In our business tier, we should ensure that a `Customer` object has a valid `Address` object before attempting to save the Customer in our database. In our data access tier, we should ensure that the address record actually exists in the `address` table before inserting or updating a row in the customer table using foreign key constraints. Validation rules should be consistent from the top tier to the bottom tier of our application.

Now to complicate things a bit, let's consider that our Java EE application also provides a RESTful Web Service API based on the Java API for RESTful Web Services (JAX-RS). If we implemented validation only in our JSF presentation layer, we would not be able to reuse the validation logic for REST clients accessing our application over HTTP. So the challenge of implementing validation in our application now includes a horizontal axis as well as a vertical one.

By defining our validation constraints in our domain model, we can reuse this code more effectively as the Model of an MVC application is separate from a particular View, or presentation layer. Therefore, a JSF application could use the validation logic expressed in the domain model at the same time that a RESTful Web Service reuses the same logic by sharing the domain model. Ideally, we should be able to declare our validation constraints in one place, and to reuse them across all the tiers and interfaces of our application. This is where the JBoss Seam framework can greatly simplify our jobs as developers.

Implementing JSF validation with Seam

The Seam framework can simplify the process of implementing JSF validation. Firstly, Seam encourages us to follow the "DRY" principle ("Don't Repeat Yourself") popularized in *The Pragmatic Programmer* and advises us to try to avoid repetition when writing code. We can apply the DRY principle to JSF by declaring our validation constraints once and only once in our domain model. This can be accomplished using Seam's built-in support for the Hibernate Validator framework.

Secondly, Seam removes the need to declare additional validators in our user interface. Registering validators such as the `<f:validateLongRange>` or `<t:validateEmail>` with our components and declaring custom validators in `faces-config.xml` becomes a thing of the past. As an additional benefit, Seam JSF validation includes enhancements such as highlighting invalid input fields that are not possible using basic JSF validation mechanisms.

In short, JSF validation is a significant improvement over previous frameworks, but still provides only a subset of the functionality needed to fully implement validation constraints in a Java EE application. Fortunately, the JBoss Seam framework greatly reduces the burden of implementing validation across the tiers of our application and provides excellent support for using cutting-edge Ajax technologies in our views.

JPA and the Hibernate Validator framework

Hibernate Validator is an annotation-based validation framework that provides a set of annotations that implement a number of common validation scenarios, such as checking for nulls, verifying that a date is in the past or in the future, ensuring that a number is greater than or less than a particular value, checking that an e-mail address is well formed, and so on. Hibernate Validator annotations are used in the domain model, and the Hibernate Validator framework is activated in the view by surrounding form fields with the Seam `<s:validateAll>` tag.

The Hibernate Validator framework also supports custom validation annotations, enabling developers to express validation constraints that may be unique to an application or that are not supported by the framework.

Once we have added the necessary Hibernate Validator annotations to our domain model, we will use a Seam JSF control in our view to automatically validate user input according to the validation constraints we defined.

Let's review the updated `Customer` class to see what refinements have been made to support this approach. First, we added the `@Entity` JPA annotation at the class level to indicate that our `Customer` class is a JPA entity. JPA enables us to store and retrieve the state of a `Customer` object in a relational database.

We also added the `@Table` annotation to indicate to the JPA implementation that our class is mapped to a table in a particular database schema. Next, we add the necessary JPA annotations such as `@ManyToOne`, `@JoinColumn`, and `@Transient` to the getter methods of our `Customer` class. Additionally, Hibernate Validator annotations have been added to the getters to indicate validation constraints (highlighted in the following example).

```
@Entity
@Table(catalog = "jsfbook")
public class Customer extends AbstractEntity implements
Comparable<Customer>, Serializable {
    private static final long serialVersionUID = 1L;
    private Date birthDate;
    private Country countryOfOrigin;
    private String emailAddress;
    private String firstName;
    private Color favoriteColor;
    private Set<String> interests = new HashSet<String>(0);
    private String lastName;
    private Boolean male;
    private String phoneNumber;
    private SatisfactionLevel satisfactionLevel;
```

```java
public int compareTo(Customer o) {
    String lastFirst1 = getFullName();
    String lastFirst2 = o.getFullName();
    return lastFirst1.compareTo(lastFirst2);
}

@Past
public Date getBirthDate() {
    return birthDate;
}

@ManyToOne(cascade = {}, fetch = FetchType.LAZY, optional = true)
@JoinColumn(name = "country_id", insertable = true,
            updatable = true, nullable = true)
public Country getCountryOfOrigin() {
    return countryOfOrigin;
}

@Email
public String getEmailAddress() {
    return emailAddress;
}

@NotNull
public String getFirstName() {
    return firstName;
}

@Transient
public String getFullName() {
    return this.lastName + ", " + this.firstName;
}

@Transient
public Set<String> getInterests() {
    return interests;
}

@NotNull
public String getLastName() {
    return lastName;
}

public Boolean getMale() {
    return male;
}

public String getPhoneNumber() {
    return phoneNumber;
}
```

```java
public Color getFavoriteColor() {
    return favoriteColor;
}
public void setFavoriteColor(Color favoriteColor) {
    this.favoriteColor = favoriteColor;
}

@Transient
public SatisfactionLevel getSatisfactionLevel() {
    return satisfactionLevel;
}
public void setBirthDate(Date birthDate) {
    this.birthDate = birthDate;
}
public void setCountryOfOrigin(Country countryOfOrigin) {
    this.countryOfOrigin = countryOfOrigin;
}
public void setEmailAddress(String emailAddress) {
    this.emailAddress = emailAddress;
}
public void setFirstName(String firstName) {
    this.firstName = firstName;
}
public void setInterests(Set<String> interests) {
    this.interests = interests;
}
public void setLastName(String lastName) {
    this.lastName = lastName;
}
public void setMale(Boolean male) {
    this.male = male;
}
public void setPhoneNumber(String phoneNumber) {
    this.phoneNumber = phoneNumber;
}
public void setSatisfactionLevel(SatisfactionLevel
                                 satisfactionLevel) {
    this.satisfactionLevel = satisfactionLevel;
}
@Transient
public int getAge() {
    Date today = new Date();
    double millis = today.getTime() - birthDate.getTime();
    double seconds = millis / 1000d;
```

```
        double minutes = seconds / 60d;
        double hours = minutes / 60d;
        double days = hours / 24d;
        double years = days / 365d;
        int age = new Double(Math.floor(years)).intValue();
        return age;
    }
}
```

Now that the `Customer` class in our domain model is properly configured with JPA and Hibernate Validator annotations, we can implement our JSF form to take advantage of Seam's validation support.

First, we define some facets inside our form that will be picked up by Seam's `<s:validateAll>` tag. These facets can be declared on any parent component of the Seam validation control. In particular, in the `beforeInvalidField` facet we declare an `<h:graphicImage>` tag to render an error icon before the invalid field when a validation error occurs.

We define the `afterInvalidField` facet to render the `<s:message>` tag with the `error` CSS class applied to it. This tag will render the Hibernate Validator error message associated with each invalid field.

JSF required="true" and Hibernate Validator @NotNull

Although we have annotated the properties in our model class with the Hibernate Validator `@NotNull` annotation, we still have to use the JSF `required="true"` attribute on any required fields, otherwise JSF validation will not detect invalid input if the user does not provide input for those fields.

In our example, as we have overridden some JSF validation messages in our message bundle, a customized "required field" message will be rendered beside any incomplete fields.

The `aroundInvalidField` facet will be used to define the decoration that is applied to the input component for any invalid fields. We will wrap any invalid fields with Seam's `<s:span>` tag to render a span with the `invalid` CSS class applied to it. This will surround the field with a yellow box containing the error message.

```
<a4j:form id="customerForm" styleClass="customer-form">
    <f:facet name="beforeInvalidField">
        <h:graphicImage src="images/error.gif" />
```

```
    </f:facet>
    <f:facet name="afterInvalidField">
        <s:message errorClass="error" showSummary="#{true}"
          showDetail="#{false}" />
    </f:facet>
    <f:facet name="aroundInvalidField">
        <s:span styleClass="invalid" />
    </f:facet>
```

The next step in implementing our JSF form is to surround all the input components with the Seam framework's `<s:validateAll>` tag. This will instruct Seam to validate all the nested components using the Hibernate Validator annotations we have applied to our domain model. Note that we wrap each input component with Seam's `<s:decorate>` tag so that Seam can apply the facets we defined earlier to each invalid field.

Decorating the UI to improve form validation

The Seam framework, as the name suggests, is an excellent tool for integrating different technologies together. One of the technologies that Seam supports very well is Facelets. We saw how to use the Facelets `<ui:decorate>` tag to markup a section of our JSF page to be "decorated" by a template defined in another page. For example, we can define a simple template that surrounds our content with an HTML `<div>` element that has a particular style applied to it. The benefit of this approach is that common UI structures can be defined in one place and reused more easily.

Seam provides the `<s:decorate>` tag to surround user interface fields for validation purposes in the same way. In fact, the `<s:decorate>` tag also supports the template attribute, so an external Facelets template can be used to provide the markup for styling the form fields during validation.

For example, the following file could define a Facelets decoration template for validation. Notice in the following example that we combine several Seam tags with Facelets tags. The `<s:label>` tag renders an HTML `<label>` element with the appropriate CSS class applied to it.

Seam provides two Boolean variables named `invalid` and `required` within the scope of the `<s:decorate>` tag that can be used in EL expressions to determine if the field was validated successfully and whether or not it was required. The following example demonstrates the use of the `invalid` variable in a ternary EL expression to determine which CSS style class to apply to the label. This way, we can give the label a different appearance (such as making it red) when the user enters an invalid value. Additionally, an asterisk will be rendered beside the label if the field was required, demonstrating the use of the `required` variable in the scope of the `<s:decorate>` tag.

Notice that we are using the Facelets `<ui:insert>` tag to specify where to insert both the label and the UI component when the validation result is rendered. This approach combines the power of Facelets templating with Seam's UI validation capabilities.

validation.jsf

```
<!DOCTYPE html PUBLIC "-//W3C//DTD XHTML 1.0 Transitional//EN"
"http://www.w3.org/TR/xhtml1/DTD/xhtml1-transitional.dtd">
<html xmlns="http://www.w3.org/1999/xhtml"
      xmlns:f="http://java.sun.com/jsf/core"
      xmlns:h="http://java.sun.com/jsf/html"
      xmlns:s="http://jboss.com/products/seam/taglib"
      xmlns:ui="http://java.sun.com/jsf/facelets">
<head>
<meta http-equiv="Content-Type" content="text/html; charset=utf-8" />
<title>s:decorate example</title>
</head>
<body>
<ui:composition>
   <div>
     <s:label styleClass="#{invalid ? 'error' : ''}">
       <ui:insert name="label" />
       <s:span styleClass="required" rendered="#{required}">*</s:span>
     </s:label>
     <span styleClass="#{invalid ? 'error' : ''}">
       <h:graphicImage value="/images/error.gif"
         rendered="#{invalid}" />
       <s:validateAll>
         <ui:insert />
       </s:validateAll>
     </span>
     <s:message styleClass="error" />
   </div>
</ui:composition>
</body>
</html>
```

A JSF form with input fields could be decorated as follows. Notice that both the first name and last name fields are surrounded with Seam's `<s:decorate>` tag and our validation template is referenced using the `template` attribute. This makes it possible to reuse the validation markup and to pass the field label directly to the template so that it appears in the right place when the form is validated.

Seam validation messages

Seam provides a built-in JSF managed bean named "messages" that extends JSF's internationalization support. Notice in the following example that we are using the Seam message bundle component named "messages" in our EL expressions to obtain field labels.

This component loads a message bundle named "messages.properties" from the class path, following the usual naming convention for Java internationalization support. The benefit of this component is that we no longer have to register our message bundles in `faces-config.xml` (and load them on a page-by-page basis with the `<f:loadBundle>` tag if we are using JSF 1.1).

We can also declare per-page message bundles in `pages.xml`, one of Seam's configuration files, and access them via this component. These are more examples of how Seam can simplify JSF development by making a lot of tasks easier and more convenient for developers.

decorate01.jsf

```
<!DOCTYPE html PUBLIC "-//W3C//DTD XHTML 1.0 Transitional//EN"
"http://www.w3.org/TR/xhtml1/DTD/xhtml1-transitional.dtd">
<html xmlns="http://www.w3.org/1999/xhtml"
      xmlns:f="http://java.sun.com/jsf/core"
      xmlns:h="http://java.sun.com/jsf/html"
      xmlns:s="http://jboss.com/products/seam/taglib"
      xmlns:ui="http://java.sun.com/jsf/facelets">
<head>
<meta http-equiv="Content-Type" content="text/html; charset=utf-8" />
<title>s:decorate example</title>
<link rel="stylesheet" type="text/css" href="/chapter6/css/style.css"
/>
</head>
<body>
<h:form>
  <s:decorate template="validation.jsf">
   <ui:define name="label">#{messages.firstNameLabel}</ui:define>
   <h:inputText label="#{messages.firstNameLabel}" id="firstName"
     value="#{customerBean.customer.firstName}" required="#{true}" />
```

```
      </s:decorate>
      <s:decorate template="validation.jsf">
        <ui:define name="label">#{messages.lastNameLabel} </ui:define>
        <h:inputText label="#{messages.lastNameLabel}" id="lastName"
          value="#{customerBean.customer.lastName}" required="#{true}" />
      </s:decorate>
        <h:commandButton value="Sign Up" />
    </h:form>
    </body>
    </html>
```

The next screenshot demonstrates the use of the `<s:decorate>` tag and an external validation template to render form labels and validation messages in a consistent and intuitive way. JSF does not provide a simple mechanism to indicate required fields; with this approach, Seam makes it easy to indicate to users which fields are required using any arbitrary convention. In the following example, required fields are indicated with a red asterisk. Also, the field labels are obtained from a message bundle using the built-in Seam "messages" component in our EL expressions.

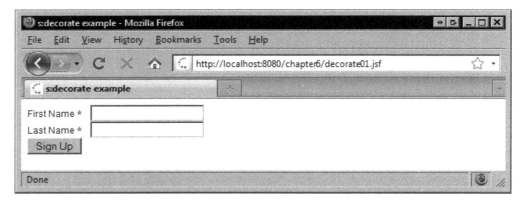

Once the form is submitted, our validation template is applied to the page. We can see in the next screenshot that an **X** icon is rendered beside each invalid field, and the default JSF required validation message is rendered next to each field.

Notice that we are not overriding the default required message. Instead, we are setting the `label` attribute on the `<h:inputText>` tags to provide a localized label for each field (**First Name** and **Last Name**). This label is inserted into the default JSF validation message instead of using the component's ID as is the default behavior, resulting in a far more readable error message for the user. Also notice that the `invalid` CSS style class is applied to the error messages and to the field labels as per our `validation.jsf` template.

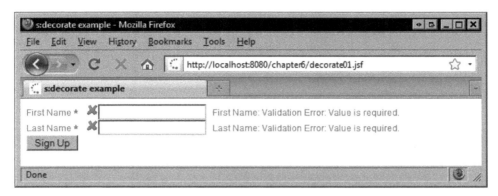

Adding cutting-edge Ajax technology with Ajax4jsf

We also add the `<a4j:support>` tag as a child of each input component tag to add Ajax capabilities to the standard JSF components. We indicate that the `onblur` event of the component should trigger an Ajax request that will submit the form and re-render the component that fired the event. The effect of this technique is that invalid fields will be instantly highlighted when the user tabs through the fields in the form.

We also set the `ajaxSingle` attribute to true to indicate that Ajax4jsf should only include the active component in the Ajax request when it submits the JSF form on the `onblur` event. This is an important technique for Ajax performance optimization as it limits the volume of form data that is sent to the server on each Ajax request, sending only the data that is necessary to validate the active component. This technique will be covered in more detail in the next chapter.

```
<s:validateAll>
   <h:panelGrid columns="2">
      <h:outputLabel for="firstName"
        value="#{bundle.firstNameLabel}" />
      <s:decorate id="firstNameDecoration">
         <h:inputText id="firstName"
           value="#{customerBean.customer.firstName}"
```

```
                    required="#{true}">
        <a4j:support ajaxSingle="true" event="onblur"
            reRender="firstNameDecoration" />
          </h:inputText>
      </s:decorate>
      <h:outputLabel value="#{messages.lastNameLabel}"
        for="lastName" />
      <s:decorate id="lastNameDecoration">
          <h:inputText id="lastName"
            value="#{customerBean.customer.lastName}"
            required="#{true}">
        <a4j:support ajaxSingle="true" event="onblur"
            reRender="lastNameDecoration" />
          </h:inputText>
      </s:decorate>
      <h:outputLabel for="dateOfBirth"
        value="#{messages.dateOfBirthLabel}" />
      <s:decorate id="dateOfBirthDecoration">
          <rich:calendar id="dateOfBirth"
              value="#{customerBean.customer.birthDate}"
              required="#{true}">
       <a4j:support ajaxSingle="true" event="onchanged"
            reRender="dateOfBirthDecoration" />
          </rich:calendar>
      </s:decorate>
<h:outputLabel for="gender" value="#{messages.genderLabel}" />
<s:decorate id="genderDecoration">
      <h:selectOneRadio id="gender"
        value="#{customerBean.customer.male}"
        required="#{true}">
          <f:selectItem itemLabel="Male" itemValue="#{true}" />
          <f:selectItem itemLabel="Female" itemValue="#{false}" />
        <a4j:support ajaxSingle="true" event="onchange"
            reRender="genderDecoration" />
          </h:selectOneRadio>
</s:decorate>
      <h:outputLabel for="phoneNumber"
        value="#{messages.phoneNumberLabel}" />
      <s:decorate id="phoneNumberDecoration">
          <h:inputText id="phoneNumber"
            value="#{customerBean.customer.phoneNumber}">
        <a4j:support ajaxSingle="true" event="onblur"
            reRender="phoneNumberDecoration" />
   </h:inputText>
      </s:decorate>
      <h:outputLabel for="emailAddress"
        value="#{messages.emailAddressLabel}" />
      <s:decorate id="emailAddressDecoration">
```

```
            <h:inputText id="emailAddress"
              value="#{customerBean.customer.emailAddress}"
              required="#{true}">
            <a4j:support ajaxSingle="true" event="onblur"
                reRender="emailAddressDecoration" />
        </h:inputText>
        </s:decorate>
        <h:outputLabel for="emailAddress"
          value="#{messages.emailAddressConfirmLabel}" />
        <s:decorate id="emailAddress2Decoration">
            <h:inputText id="emailAddress2" required="#{true}">
            <a4j:support event="onblur"
                reRender="emailAddress2Decoration" />
          <s:validateEquality for="emailAddress"
            message="Email addresses do not match." />
        </h:inputText>
        </s:decorate>
        <h:outputLabel value="#{messages.countryLabel}"
          for="country" required="#{true}" />
        <s:decorate id="countryDecoration">
            <h:selectOneMenu id="country"
              value="#{customerBean.customer.countryOfOrigin}"
              required="#{true}">
              <s:selectItems noSelectionLabel="Select"
                value="#{customerBean.countries}" var="country"
                label="#{country.name}" />
            <s:convertEntity />
        <a4j:support event="onchange" reRender="countryDecoration" />
            </h:selectOneMenu>
        </s:decorate>
    </h:panelGrid>
```

Finally, we use the `<a4j:commandButton>` tag to render an Ajax-enabled command button component that will submit the form.

```
        <a4j:commandButton value="Save"
            actionListener="#{customerBean.saveCustomer}"
            reRender="customerForm" />
    </s:validateAll>
    </a4j:form>
```

To demonstrate, we partially complete the form and click the **Save** button. The three remaining required fields are instantly highlighted after the Ajax request.

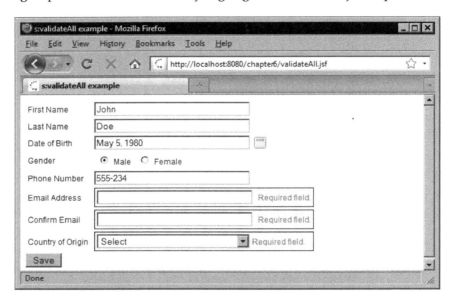

Next, we enter an invalid e-mail address and press the *Tab* key to cycle to the next field. The e-mail address field is instantly highlighted and a Hibernate Validation error message is displayed next to the field.

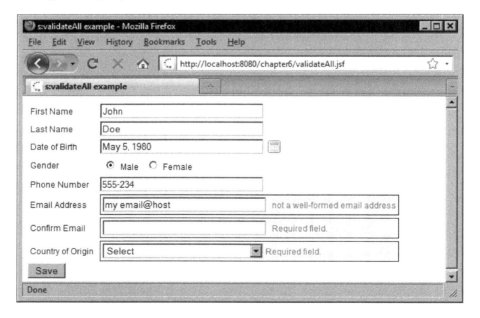

We correct the e-mail address and tab to the next field. The e-mail address validation message disappears.

Finally, all validation messages have been cleared.

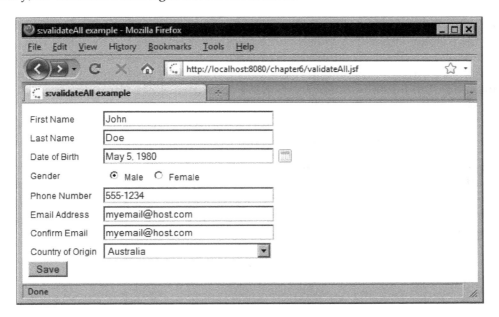

Displaying success messages in JSF

The JSF framework includes built-in support for rendering validation error messages when form validation fails. These messages are typically rendered using the `<h:message>` or `<h:messages>` tags. When a JSF form is posted to the server, the JSF framework's request processing lifecycle includes the following phases:

1. Restore the UI component tree for the view.
2. Apply the incoming form data to the UI components in the tree.
3. Attempt to convert and validate the data.
4. If the conversion/validation is successful, update the application's model.
5. Invoke the backing bean method associated with the component that submitted the form.
6. Send the response back to the client.

When a conversion or validation error causes the conversion and validation phase to fail, the JSF framework sends back a response containing request-scoped `FacesMessage` objects containing the validation messages for the invalid fields. As these message objects are request scoped, they cannot be displayed to the user if a redirect response is issued. If a redirect was sent by the server (as is commonly the case for success outcomes), the browser would send a new request and the validation messages scoped to the previous request would be lost.

In a successful scenario, the navigation rules defined by the application are executed after the Invoke Application phase and a response is sent back to the client that may involve a redirect. Therefore, it is impossible to send "success" messages to the user after a form submission that results in a redirect: any request-scoped messages would be lost in the subsequent request. We can forward or redirect the user to a success page that displays a static success message or obtains a success message from a backing bean, but there is no reliable way to send success messages to a JSF page after a redirect using the standard JSF `FacesMessage` API.

The Seam framework includes a mechanism for sending success messages to the user after a redirect. This mechanism involves storing the success message in session scope for a single request, and then removing it once the message has been rendered. We will see an example of this later on in this chapter when we discuss Seam conversation management.

Seam conversation management

The JBoss Seam framework provides elegant solutions to a number of problems. One of these problems is the concept of conversation management. Traditional web applications have a limited number of scopes (or container-managed memory regions) in which they can store data needed by the application at runtime.

In a typical Java web application, these scopes are the application scope, the session scope, and the request scope. JSP-based Java web applications also have a page scope. *Application scope* is typically used to store stateless components or long-term read-only application data. *Session scope* provides a convenient, medium-term storage for per-user application state, such as user credentials, application preferences, and the contents of a shopping cart. *Request scope* is short-term storage for per-request information, such as search keywords, data table sort direction, and so on.

Seam introduces another scope for JSF applications: the conversation scope. The *conversation scope* can be as short-term as the request scope, or as long-term as the session scope. Seam conversations come in two types: temporary conversations and long-running conversations. A temporary Seam conversation typically lasts as long as a single HTTP request. A long-running Seam conversation typically spans several screens and can be tied to more elaborate use cases and workflows within the application, for example, booking a hotel, renting a car, or placing an order for computer hardware.

There are some important implications for Seam's conversation management when using Ajax capabilities of RichFaces and Ajax4jsf. As an Ajax-enabled JSF form may involve many Ajax requests before the form is "submitted" by the user at the end of a use case, some subtle side effects can impact our application if we are not careful.

Let's look at an example of how to use Seam conversations effectively with Ajax.

Temporary conversations

When a Seam-enabled conversation-scoped JSF backing bean is accessed for the first time, through a value expression or method expression from the JSF page for instance, the Seam framework creates a temporary conversation if a conversation does not already exist and stores the component instance in that scope.

If a long-running conversation already exists, and the component invocation requires a long-running conversation, for example by associating the view with a long-running conversation in `pages.xml`, by annotating the bean class or method with Seam's `@Conversational` annotation, by annotating a method with Seam's `@Begin` annotation, or by using the `conversationPropagation` request parameter, then Seam stores the component instance in the existing long-running conversation.

ShippingCalculatorBean.java

The following source code demonstrates how to declare a conversation-scoped backing being using Seam annotations. In this example, we declare the `ShippingCalculatorBean` as a Seam-managed conversation-scoped component named `shippingCalculatorBeanSeam`.

```java
@Name("shippingCalculatorBeanSeam")
@Scope(ScopeType.CONVERSATION)
public class ShippingCalculatorBean implements Serializable {
    /**
     *
     */
    private static final long serialVersionUID = 1L;

    private Country country;

    private Product product;

    public Country getCountry() {
        return country;
    }

    public Product getProduct() {
        return product;
    }

    public Double getTotal() {
        Double total = 0d;
        if (country != null && product != null) {
            total = product.getPrice();
            if (country.getName().equals("USA")) {
                total = +5d;
            } else {
                total = +10d;
            }
        }
        return total;
    }

    public void setCountry(Country country) {
        this.country = country;
    }

    public void setProduct(Product product) {
        this.product = product;
    }
}
```

faces-config.xml

We also declare the same `ShippingCalculatorBean` class as a request-scoped backing bean named `shippingCalculaorBean` in `faces-config.xml`. Keep in mind that the JSF framework manages this instance of the class, so none of the Seam annotations are effective for instances of this managed bean.

```
<managed-bean>
    <description>Shipping calculator bean.</description>
    <managed-bean-name>shippingCalculatorBean</managed-bean-name>
    <managed-bean-class>chapter5.bean.ShippingCalculatorBean
    </managed-bean-class>
    <managed-bean-scope>request</managed-bean-scope>
</managed-bean>
```

pages.xml

The `pages.xml` file is an important Seam configuration file. When a Seam-enabled web application is deployed, the Seam framework looks for and processes a file in the `WEB-INF` directory named `pages.xml`.

This file contains important information about the pages in the JSF application, and enables us to indicate if a long-running conversation should be started automatically when a view is first accessed.

In this example, we declare two pages in `pages.xml`, one that does not start a long-running conversation, and one that does.

```
<?xml version="1.0" encoding="utf-8"?>
<pages xmlns="http://jboss.com/products/seam/pages"
       xmlns:xsi="http://www.w3.org/2001/XMLSchema-instance"
       xsi:schemaLocation="http://jboss.com/products/seam/pages
       http://jboss.com/products/seam/pages-2.1.xsd">
<page view-id="/conversation01.jsf" />
<page view-id="/conversation02.jsf">
  <begin-conversation join="true"/>
</page>
...
</pages>
```

conversation01.jsf

Let's look at the source code for our first Seam conversation test page. In this page, we render two forms side-by-side in an HTML panel grid. The first form is bound to the JSF-managed request-scoped `ShippingCalculatorBean`, and the second form is bound to the Seam-managed conversation-scoped `ShippingCalculatorBean`. The form allows the user to select a product and a shipping destination, and then calculates the shipping cost when the command button is clicked.

When the user tabs through the fields in a form, an Ajax request is sent, submitting the form data and re-rendering the button. The button is in a disabled state until the user has selected a value in both the fields. The Ajax request creates a new HTTP request on the server, so for the first form JSF creates a new request-scoped instance of our `ShippingCalculatorBean` for every Ajax request.

As the view is not configured to use a long-running conversation, Seam creates a new temporary conversation and stores a new instance of our `ShippingCalculatorBean` class in that scope for each Ajax request.

Therefore, the behavior that can be observed when running this page in the browser is that the calculation simply does not work. The value is always zero. This is because the model state is being lost due to the incorrect scoping of our backing beans.

```
<h:panelGrid columns="2" cellpadding="10">
    <h:form>
        <rich:panel>
            <f:facet name="header">
                <h:outputText value="Shipping Calculator (No
                                     Conversation)" />
            </f:facet>
            <h:panelGrid columns="1" width="100%">
                <h:outputLabel value="Select Product: " for="product" />
                <h:selectOneMenu id="product"
                  value="#{shippingCalculatorBean.product}">
                    <s:selectItems var="product"
                       value="#{productBean.products}"
                       label="#{product.name}" noSelectionLabel="Select" />
                      <a4j:support event="onchange" reRender="button" />
                  <s:convertEntity />
                </h:selectOneMenu>
                <h:outputLabel value="Select Shipping Destination: "
                   for="country" />
                <h:selectOneMenu id="country"
                  value="#{shippingCalculatorBean.country}">
                    <s:selectItems var="country"
                      value="#{customerBean.countries}"
                      label="#{country.name}" noSelectionLabel="Select" />
                    <a4j:support event="onchange"
                    reRender="button"/>
                  <s:convertEntity />
                </h:selectOneMenu>
            <h:panelGrid columns="1" columnClasses="centered"
              width="100%">
                <a4j:commandButton id="button" value="Calculate"
                    disabled="#{shippingCalculatorBean.country eq null or
                    shippingCalculatorBean.product eq null}"
                    reRender="total" />
```

```
            <h:panelGroup>
                <h:outputText value="Total Shipping Cost: " />
                <h:outputText id="total"
                  value="#{shippingCalculatorBean.total}">
                    <f:convertNumber type="currency" currencySymbol="$"
                      maxFractionDigits="0" />
                </h:outputText>
            </h:panelGroup>
        </h:panelGrid>
        </h:panelGrid>
    </rich:panel>
</h:form>
<h:form>
 <rich:panel>
    <f:facet name="header">
        <h:outputText value="Shipping Calculator (with Temporary
                             Conversation)" />
    </f:facet>
    <h:panelGrid columns="1">
        <h:outputLabel value="Select Product: " for="product" />
        <h:selectOneMenu id="product"
          value="#{shippingCalculatorBeanSeam.product}">
            <s:selectItems var="product"
              value="#{productBean.products}"
              label="#{product.name}" noSelectionLabel="Select" />
        <a4j:support event="onchange"
            reRender="button" />
      <s:convertEntity />
        </h:selectOneMenu>
        <h:outputLabel value="Select Shipping Destination: "
          for="country" />
        <h:selectOneMenu id="country"
          value="#{shippingCalculatorBeanSeam.country}">
            <s:selectItems var="country"
              value="#{customerBean.countries}"
              label="#{country.name}" noSelectionLabel="Select" />
            <a4j:support event="onchange"
                reRender="button" />
        <s:convertEntity />
        </h:selectOneMenu>
        <h:panelGrid columns="1" columnClasses="centered"
          width="100%">
      <a4j:commandButton id="button" value="Calculate"
          disabled="#{shippingCalculatorBeanSeam.country eq null
          or shippingCalculatorBeanSeam.product eq null}"
          reRender="total" />
        <h:panelGroup>
```

```
                <h:outputText value="Total Shipping Cost: " />
                <h:outputText id="total"
                  value="#{shippingCalculatorBeanSeam.total}">
                  <f:convertNumber type="currency" currencySymbol="$"
                    maxFractionDigits="0" />
                </h:outputText>
              </h:panelGroup>
            </h:panelGrid>
            </h:panelGrid>
          </rich:panel>
        </h:form>
</h:panelGrid>
```

The following screenshot demonstrates the problem of using request-scoped or temporary conversation-scoped backing beans in an Ajax-enabled JSF application. As an Ajax request is simply an asynchronous HTTP request marshalled by client-side code executed by the browser's JavaScript interpreter, the request-scoped backing beans are recreated with every Ajax request. The model state is lost and the behavior of the components in the view is incorrect. (We will take a more in-depth look at the Ajax behavior of these components in the next chapter; for now, let's try to understand this example in terms of Seam's conversation management.)

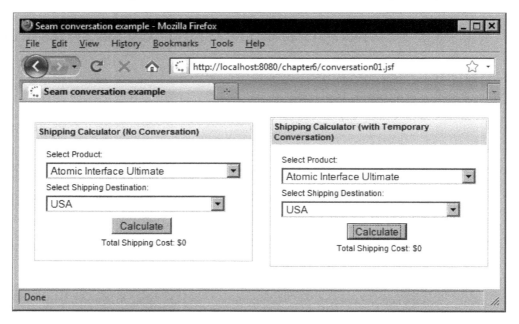

conversation02.jsf

Let's look at an example of how to implement this form correctly. First of all, we declare that the view should start a long-running conversation in `pages.xml` (rmentioned above). Then, we bind the form to the conversation-scoped `ShippingCalculatorBean`.

Now every Ajax request obtains a reference to the same conversation-scoped backing bean. Seam serializes the Ajax requests within a long-running conversation on the server side to control concurrency and to ensure our backing bean is handling at most one request at a time.

```
<h:form>
    <rich:panel style="width:50%">
        <f:facet name="header">
            <h:outputText value="Shipping Calculator (with Long-Running
                                  Conversation)" />
        </f:facet>
        <h:panelGrid columns="1">
            <h:outputLabel value="Select Product: " for="product" />
            <h:selectOneMenu id="product"
              value="#{shippingCalculatorBeanSeam.product}">
                <s:selectItems var="product"
                  value="#{productBean.products}" label="#{product.name}"
                  noSelectionLabel="Select" />
                <a4j:support event="onchange"
                    reRender="button" /><s:convertEntity />
            </h:selectOneMenu>
            <h:outputLabel value="Select Shipping Destination: "
              for="country" />
            <h:selectOneMenu id="country"
              value="#{shippingCalculatorBeanSeam.country}">
                <s:selectItems var="country"
                  value="#{customerBean.countries}"
                  label="#{country.name}" noSelectionLabel="Select" />
                <a4j:support event="onchange"
                    reRender="button" /><s:convertEntity />
            </h:selectOneMenu>
            <h:panelGrid columns="1" columnClasses="centered"
            width="100%">
            <a4j:commandButton id="button" value="Calculate"
                disabled="#{shippingCalculatorBeanSeam.country eq null
                or shippingCalculatorBeanSeam.product eq null}"
                reRender="total" />
            <h:panelGroup>
                <h:outputText value="Total Shipping Cost: " />
```

```
        <h:outputText id="total"
          value="#{shippingCalculatorBeanSeam.total}">
          <f:convertNumber type="currency" currencySymbol="$"
            maxFractionDigits="0" />
        </h:outputText>
      </h:panelGroup>
    </h:panelGrid>
  </h:panelGrid>
  </rich:panel>
</h:form>
```

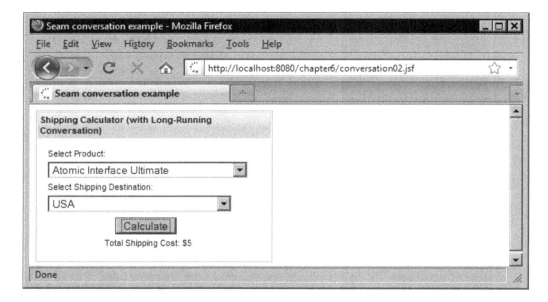

Starting a long-running conversation

There are several ways to start a long-running conversation in Seam. We can declare that a view should automatically start a long-running conversation in `pages.xml`; we can set the `conversationPropagation` request parameter to `begin` using the Seam `<s:conversationPropagation>` tag, or we can annotate a backing bean method with the Seam framework's `@Begin` annotation. Let's look at an example of defining and executing a long-running conversation based on an online product ordering use case.

Declaring navigation rules in faces-config.xml

In this example, we design a JSF page flow in our `faces-config.xml` file that ties together all the necessary screens that make up this use case. The first screen in the page flow is the customer registration step. The second screen is the shipping and product information step. The third screen is the order details confirmation step. Our navigation flow branches after the third step. If we are out of stock, we redirect the user to an error page. Otherwise, we redirect the user to the order processed page.

The following screenshot shows a visual representation of the navigation rules that make up our page flow.

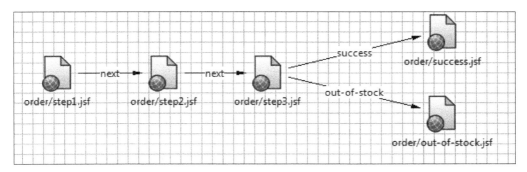

The navigation rules are declared in `faces-config.xml` as follows:

```
<navigation-rule>
    <display-name>order/step1.jsf</display-name>
    <from-view-id>/order/step1.jsf</from-view-id>
    <navigation-case>
        <from-outcome>next</from-outcome>
        <to-view-id>/order/step2.jsf</to-view-id>
        <redirect />
    </navigation-case>
</navigation-rule>
<navigation-rule>
    <display-name>order/step2.jsf</display-name>
    <from-view-id>/order/step2.jsf</from-view-id>
    <navigation-case>
        <from-outcome>next</from-outcome>
        <to-view-id>/order/step3.jsf</to-view-id>
        <redirect />
    </navigation-case>
</navigation-rule>
<navigation-rule>
    <display-name>order/step3.jsf</display-name>
```

```
        <from-view-id>/order/step3.jsf</from-view-id>
        <navigation-case>
            <from-outcome>success</from-outcome>
            <to-view-id>/order/success.jsf</to-view-id>
            <redirect />
        </navigation-case>
    </navigation-rule>

    <navigation-rule>
        <display-name>order/step3.jsf</display-name>
        <from-view-id>/order/step3.jsf</from-view-id>
        <navigation-case>
            <from-outcome>out-of-stock</from-outcome>
            <to-view-id>/order/out-of-stock.jsf</to-view-id>
            <redirect />
        </navigation-case>
    </navigation-rule>
    <navigation-rule>
        <display-name>order/step3.jsf</display-name>
        <from-view-id>/order/step3.jsf</from-view-id>
        <navigation-case>
            <from-outcome>back</from-outcome>
            <to-view-id>/order/step2.jsf</to-view-id>
            <redirect />
        </navigation-case>
    </navigation-rule>
    <navigation-rule>
        <display-name>order/step2.jsf</display-name>
        <from-view-id>/order/step2.jsf</from-view-id>
        <navigation-case>
            <from-outcome>back</from-outcome>
            <to-view-id>/order/step1.jsf</to-view-id>
            <redirect />
        </navigation-case>
    </navigation-rule>
    <navigation-rule>
        <display-name>order/out-of-stock.jsf</display-name>
        <from-view-id>/order/out-of-stock.jsf</from-view-id>
        <navigation-case>
            <from-outcome>back</from-outcome>
            <to-view-id>/order/step3.jsf</to-view-id>
            <redirect />
        </navigation-case>
    </navigation-rule>
```

Defining a long-running conversation in pages.xml

We have grouped all the views for this use case in one directory named "order". Conveniently, we can declare in `pages.xml` that all the pages in this directory should be associated with a long-running conversation as follows:

```
<page view-id="/order/*">
    <begin-conversation join="true"/>
</page>
```

Implementing OrderBeanImpl.java

Next, we implement a long-running conversation-scoped stateful session bean. We use the EJB3 `@Stateful` annotation to indicate to the EJB container that this component should be managed as a stateful session bean. This includes automatic, JTA-enabled transactions for all methods, activation/passivation for efficient memory management, declarative security, and more.

We use the Seam framework's `@Conversational` annotation to indicate that this component should only be invoked within the context of a long-running conversation. If a view attempts to access this bean outside a long-running conversation, Seam will throw an exception.

We use the `@Name` annotation to indicate that the bean should be available as a JSF managed bean with the name `orderBean`, and we use the `@Scope` annotation to indicate that the bean should be stored in conversation scope.

We also use several Seam annotations within the class to declare some dependencies which will be injected by the Seam framework. As we are using a Seam-managed persistence context, we can annotate our `EntityManager` instance variable with the Seam framework's `@In` annotation and Seam will inject the appropriate object at runtime. Notice that we use the Seam `@End` annotation on our `submitOrder` method to indicate that the long-running conversation should be concluded after the method is invoked.

OrderBeanImpl.java

```
@Stateful
@Conversational
@Name("orderBean")
@Scope(ScopeType.CONVERSATION)
public class OrderBeanImpl implements OrderBean {

    private LineItem lineItem;

    @In
    private EntityManager em;
```

```java
@In
private FacesMessages facesMessages;

@Logger
private Log logger;

private Order order;

private List<Order> orders;

public LineItem getLineItem() {
    if (lineItem == null) {
        lineItem = new LineItem();
        lineItem.setQuantity(1);
        Order order = getOrder();
        lineItem.setOrder(order);
        order.getLineItems().add(lineItem);
    }
    return lineItem;
}

public Order getOrder() {
    if (order == null) {
        order = new Order();
        order.setCustomer(new Customer());
    }
    return order;
}

private Integer getUniqueOrderNumber() {
    Integer value = null;
    Query query = em.createNamedQuery(Queries.UNIQUE_ORDER_NUMBER);
    value = (Integer) query.getSingleResult();
    return value;
}

@SuppressWarnings("unchecked")
public List<Order> getOrders() {
    if (orders == null) {
     orders =
            em.createNamedQuery(Queries.ALL_ORDERS).getResultList();
    }
    return orders;
}

public void setOrder(Order order) {
    this.order = order;
}

@End
```

```java
public String submitOrder() {
    String outcome = null;
    try {
        if (lineItem.getProduct().getQuantityInStock() > 0) {
            order.setOrderNumber(getUniqueOrderNumber());
            em.persist(order);
            facesMessages.add("Thank you. Your order has been
                              received.");
            outcome = "success";
        } else {
            outcome = "out-of-stock";
        }
    } catch (Exception e) {
        logger.error("Failed to submit order:", e);
        facesMessages.add(Severity.ERROR, "Sorry, we were unable to
                          process your order.");
    }
    return outcome;
}

@Remove
@Destroy
public void remove() {
}
}
```

In the preceding example, we use the JPA `EntityManager` API to execute named queries. A **named query** is a **Java Persistence Query Language (JPQL)** query named and declared in an external configuration file or in an annotation. As we are using Hibernate as our JPA provider, we externalize our named queries in a file named `Queries.hbm.xml`. When our application is initialized, Hibernate will scan this file and validate our named queries, reporting issues such as invalid syntax, missing columns, invalid object paths, and so on. Our JPA named queries are declared as follows:

Queries.hbm.xml

```xml
<?xml version="1.0" encoding='UTF-8'?>
<!DOCTYPE hibernate-mapping PUBLIC
  "-//Hibernate/Hibernate Mapping DTD 3.0//EN"
  "http://hibernate.sourceforge.net/hibernate-mapping-3.0.dtd" >
<hibernate-mapping>
  <query name="Product.findAll">
    <![CDATA[
    select distinct product
    from Product product
```

```
        inner join fetch product.category
        order by product.name
        ]]>
</query>
<query name="ProductCategory.findAll">
    <![CDATA[
        select category
        from ProductCategory category
        order by category.name
        ]]>
</query>
<query name="Customer.findAll">
    <![CDATA[
        select customer
        from Customer customer
        order by customer.lastName, customer.firstName
        ]]>
</query>
<query name="Country.findAll">
    <![CDATA[
        select country
        from Country country
        order by country.name
        ]]>
</query>
<query name="Order.findAll">
    <![CDATA[
        select o
        from Order o
        order by o.orderNumber
        ]]>
</query>
<query name="ProductCategory.findByName">
    <![CDATA[
        select category
        from ProductCategory category
        where category.name = ?
        order by category.name
        ]]>
</query>
<query name="ProductCategory.findSubCategoryByName">
    <![CDATA[
```

```
        select category
        from ProductCategory category
        inner join fetch category.parentCategory parent
        where parent = ?
        and category.name = ?
        order by category.name
        ]]>
    </query>
    <query name="Product.findByPrice">
        <![CDATA[
        select product
        from Product product
        where product.price <= ?
        ]]>
    </query>
    <query name="Order.findUniqueOrderNumber">
        <![CDATA[
        select (max(o.orderNumber) + 1)
        from Order o
        ]]>
    </query>
</hibernate-mapping>
```

Notice in the `OrderBeanImpl` source code listing that we called the `EntityManager` API by passing a `String` constant as follows:

```
em.createNamedQuery(Queries.UNIQUE_ORDER_NUMBER)
```

Instead of hardcoding the query name in our code, we also externalize this information in a constant interface. By using a constant we avoid the risk of typos in our code as the Java compiler will ensure that our constant reference is valid. Also, we can reuse the query more easily. This indirection has an additional benefit: if we decide to rename the query, we can do so in one place (the constant interface) and we do not have to hunt through code to find and replace string literals.

Queries.java

```
package chapter6.model;

public class Queries {

    public static final String ALL_COUNTRIES = "Country.findAll";

    public static final String ALL_CUSTOMERS = "Customer.findAll";

    public static final String ALL_ORDERS = "Order.findAll";

    public static final String ALL_PRODUCT_CATEGORIES =
                            "ProductCategory.findAll";
```

```
public static final String ALL_PRODUCTS = "Product.findAll";

public static final String PRODUCT_CATEGORY_BY_NAME =
                    "ProductCategory.findByName";

public static final String PRODUCT_SUBCATEGORY_BY_NAME =
                    "ProductCategory.findSubCategoryByName";

public static final String PRODUCTS_BY_PRICE =
                    "Product.findByPrice";

public static final String UNIQUE_ORDER_NUMBER =
                    "Order.findUniqueOrderNumber";

}
```

The introductory page of the order process

The first view in our page flow is an introductory page that simply navigates to the first step in our ordering process. Notice that we use the Seam `<s:link>` tag to render a hyperlink that includes the conversation ID as a query string parameter. This is called conversation propagation.

Seam conversation propagation using hyperlinks

Seam automatically propagates the conversation during JSF form submissions using the HTTP POST method. For any GET requests (for instance, clicking on a hyperlink), we are responsible for including the current conversation ID as a request parameter to ensure that the request is handled properly. Seam provides a hyperlink control rendered by the `<s:link>` tag that automatically includes the current conversation ID on the query string. We can also include the conversation ID as a query string parameter by nesting the Seam `<s:conversationId>` tag inside the standard JSF `<h:outputLink>` tag. Conversation ID propagation is automatic when a JSF form is submitted using POST.

The markup for the introductory screen in our order process is as follows:

```
<h1>Product Order Form</h1>
<a4j:form>
<rich:panel>
<f:facet name="header">
   <h:outputText value="Welcome to our Store" />
</f:facet>
<p>Welcome to our store. Our step-by-step forms will guide you through
the ordering process.</p>
<s:link view="/order/step1.jsf" value="Place an order" />
</rich:panel>
</a4j:form>
```

The following screenshot shows the introductory screen of our ordering process. Notice in the status bar of the browser window that the URL generated by the Seam JSF hyperlink control contains a query string parameter named `cid` with a value of one. As long as we pass this parameter from page to page, all the requests will be handled as a part of the same conversation. The conversation ID is automatically submitted during JSF postback requests. When a new conversation is started, Seam will increment the conversation ID automatically.

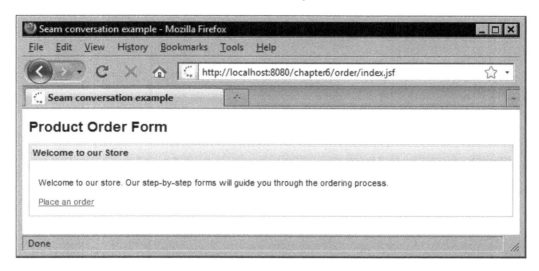

The customer registration screen (Step 1)

The first screen, our page flow, requires the user to provide customer information before placing an order. This view is basically identical to the example used in the Seam validation section of this chapter. Therefore, much of the JSF markup has been removed for simplification purposes.

Notice that the action has been hardcoded in the `<a4j:commandButton>` tag and corresponds to a navigation rule declaration in `faces-config.xml`. No additional work is required for the Seam conversation ID to be propagated to the server when the form is submitted; this happens automatically.

```
<h1>Step 1. Customer Registration</h1>
<a4j:form id="customerForm" styleClass="customer-form">
    ...
     <a4j:commandButton value="Next Step" action="next"
        reRender="customerForm" />
    ...
</a4j:form>
```

The following screenshot shows the customer registration step in the online ordering page flow of our application.

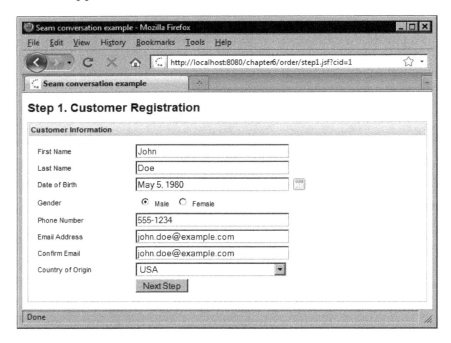

The shipping information screen (Step 2)

The following screen requires the user to select a product and a shipping destination before clicking on the **Next Step** button. Once again, Seam conversation propagation happens automatically when the form is submitted.

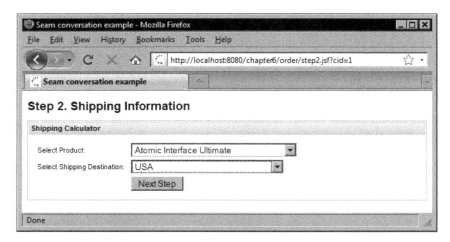

The order details confirmation screen (Step 3)

The next screen requires the user to confirm the order details before submitting the order for processing. Once again, the JSF markup has been omitted for brevity. Notice that the command button invokes the `submitOrder` backing bean method to submit the order.

As noted earlier, this method is annotated with the Seam framework `@End` annotation, indicating that the long-running conversation ends after the method is invoked. When the method returns, Seam demotes the long-running conversation to a temporary conversation and destroys it after the view is rendered. Any references to conversation-scoped beans are released when the Seam conversation is destroyed, efficiently freeing up server resources in a more fine-grained way than by invalidating the session.

```
<h:form>
    . . .
    <a4j:commandButton action="#{orderBean.submitOrder}"
        value="Submit Order" />
    . . .
</h:form>
```

The following screenshot shows the order details confirmation screen.

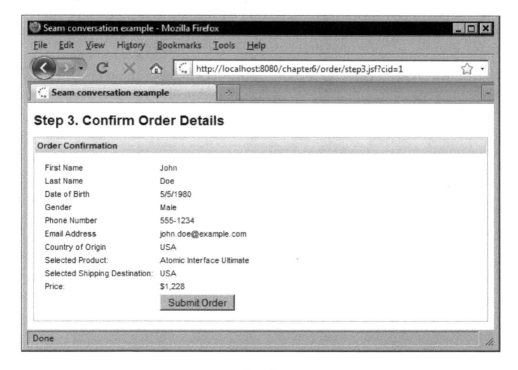

Concurrent conversations

The JBoss Seam framework supports the concept of concurrent conversations. An individual user may choose to open multiple browser tabs to access the same page. This scenario is not as uncommon as we might think. The user might, for example, try to rent a car for two separate trips, or place two separate orders, or book two different hotels, within the same browser session.

Conventional web applications do not support this behavior. This is because the model state needed to complete the page flow for the different use cases is typically stored in session scope. When the user switches from one tab to another in their browser, any form data that is submitted effectively overwrites the previous form data associated with the other tab. Therefore, the observable behavior of this type of user activity is a loss of session state or inconsistent results when switching between browser tabs.

Web browsers have evolved considerably over the past few years. Tabbed browsing is just one of these improvements. The Seam framework enables JSF applications to support user interaction across multiple browser tabs within the same session, significantly improving support for concurrency in Java web applications.

Let's look at how Seam supports concurrent conversations by simulating a scenario where the user opens two browser tabs and performs the same workflow in each tab. The following screenshot shows a second tab opened in the browser to the introductory page of our order processing page flow. Notice once again in the status bar of the browser window that the conversation ID is now six.

When we click on this hyperlink, we will be directed to the customer registration screen in our page flow, and the backing bean used for this form will be a new instance of the OrderBean class stored in a new long-running conversation.

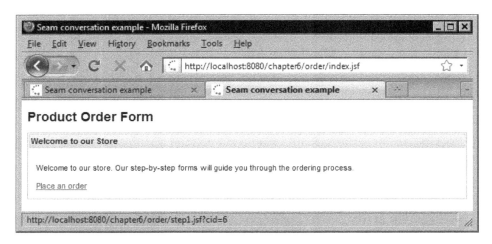

In the next screenshot, the user enters customer registration information for a new customer and clicks on the **Next Step** button. Note that we have not closed the original browser tab. That conversation is still active and we will be returning to it momentarily.

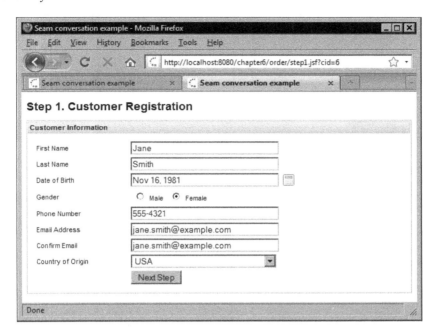

In the next screenshot, the user selects the product and shipping destination, and then clicks **Next Step**. The activity in the current browser tab is completely independent from the activity in the other browser tab. Remember that there are now two instances of our OrderBean class handling requests for this particular user.

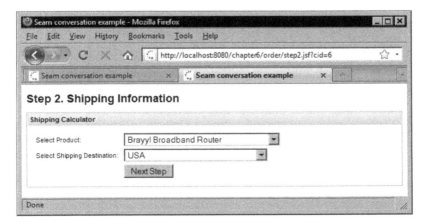

Finally, we arrive at the order details confirmation step once again. The next screenshot shows your information in the second browser tab just before it is submitted for processing.

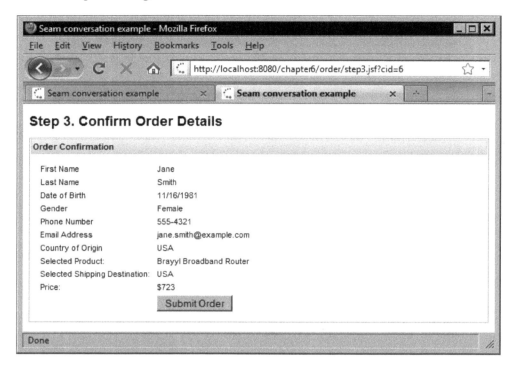

In a conventional web application, if we were to switch back to the original browser tab and refresh the page, we would see the state that is now shown in the second browser tab. In other words, the user would have overwritten the state of their original order by opening a new tab and completing the order forms in a new online ordering page flow.

Fortunately, the Seam framework was designed to support this type of concurrency, so when we switch back to the first tab and refresh the page, we see what the user expects to see: the original ordering page flow has not been modified and is in the same state as it was in, when we opened the second browser tab.

The next screenshot displays the first browser tab after we have refreshed the page. The view state is the same as it was before we started the second page flow.

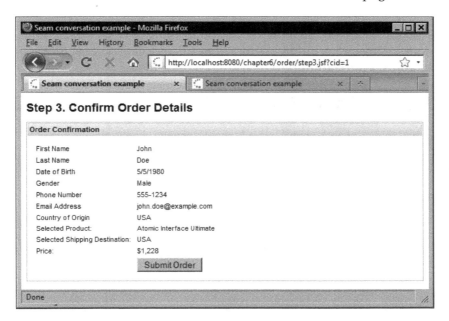

To conclude our concurrent conversations, we can now submit the orders. First, we submit the order in the first tab, as shown in the following screenshot. The backing bean receives the order information, creates a success message, and redirects to the success page. When the method returns, the first long-running conversation is concluded, at which point Seam downgrades it to a temporary conversation. When the view is rendered the stateful session bean instance is destroyed along with any state it was holding for the user.

When we switch to the second tab and submit the order, our second conversation is also concluded and the order information takes a minute for processing as shown in the following screenshot.

The JBoss Seam framework enables us to support multiple concurrent requests within the same browser window without any side effects. In Seam terminology, our application supports multiple concurrent workspaces.

Debugging Seam applications

The previous long-running conversation example gives us a good overview of how to use several features of the Seam framework together in a real-world scenario. Just like the Facelets framework provides a debug page that can be used to look "under the hood" to make sure that our JSF application is working as expected, Seam also provides a debug page that provides insightful information for developers. To enable the Seam debug page, first we must ensure that the JAR file names `jboss-seam-debug.jar` is located only in the `WEB-INF/lib` folder, and not in the EAR file lib directory. Next, we need to set the `debug` attribute to true in our `components.xml` file as follows:

META-INF/components.xml

```
<?xml version="1.0" encoding="UTF-8"?>
<components xmlns="http://jboss.com/products/seam/components"
   xmlns:core="http://jboss.com/products/seam/core"
   xmlns:persistence="http://jboss.com/products/seam/persistence"
   xmlns:security="http://jboss.com/products/seam/security"
   xmlns:drools="http://jboss.com/products/seam/drools"
```

```
xmlns:web="http://jboss.com/products/seam/web"
xmlns:mail="http://jboss.com/products/seam/mail"
xmlns:ui="http://jboss.com/products/seam/ui"
xmlns:transaction="http://jboss.com/products/seam/transaction"
xmlns:xsi="http://www.w3.org/2001/XMLSchema-instance"
xsi:schemaLocation="http://jboss.com/products/seam/core
                    http://jboss.com/products/seam/core-2.1.xsd
           http://jboss.com/products/seam/persistence
           http://jboss.com/products/seam/persistence-2.1.xsd
           http://jboss.com/products/seam/security
           http://jboss.com/products/seam/security-2.1.xsd
           http://jboss.com/products/seam/web
           http://jboss.com/products/seam/web-2.1.xsd
           http://jboss.com/products/seam/ui
           http://jboss.com/products/seam/ui-2.1.xsd
           http://jboss.com/products/seam/drools
           http://jboss.com/products/seam/drools-2.1.xsd
           http://jboss.com/products/seam/mail
           http://jboss.com/products/seam/mail-2.1.xsd
           http://jboss.com/products/seam/transaction
           http://jboss.com/products/seam/transaction-2.1.xsd
           http://jboss.com/products/seam/components
           http://jboss.com/products/seam/components-2.1.xsd">

<core:init debug="true"
    jndi-pattern="7627_06_Application/#{ejbName}/local" />

<core:manager conversation-id-parameter="cid" />

<transaction:ejb-transaction />

<persistence:managed-persistence-context
    name="em" auto-create="true" persistence-unit-jndi-name="java:/
    EntityManagerFactories/jsfbookData" />

<web:redirect-filter url-pattern="*.jsf" />

<ui:jpa-entity-loader entity-manager="#{em}" />

</components>
```

Now we can access the debug page in our browser by visiting `http://localhost:8080/chapter6/debug.jsf`. The following screenshot displays the output of the Seam debug page. We can see the activity of the two concurrent conversations in progress, conversations #1 and #6, from our order processing demonstration. We can use the Seam debug page to examine the state of our managed beans and other Seam components.

Summary

In this chapter, we explored how the JBoss Seam framework can be used to create powerful JSF applications using the full Java EE technology stack, including EJB3 session beans, JPA entities, and more. We also saw how to use Seam JSF controls and Hibernate Validator annotations to implement JSF validation for our application efficiently by applying the "DRY" principle. By adding Hibernate Validator annotations to our JPA domain model, we gain a twofold advantage: (a) we can use Hibernate Validator to implement declarative data integrity constraints in our JPA persistence layer, and (b) we can reuse the Hibernate Validator annotations in our domain model to declare user interface validation constraints for our JSF-based presentation layer.

Next, we looked at ways to decorate components in the user interface to enhance JSF validation. We saw how to use the `<s:decorate>` tag to reference an external validation template that provides decorations for invalid and required fields. We also explored a technique for adding Ajax capabilities to our JSF form and highlighting invalid fields using Seam JSF controls when validation fails. The Seam framework also provides a built-in component named "messages" that exposes our application's message bundle to any JSF page. We also examined how the Seam framework solves the concurrency problem associated with multiple browser tabs for JSF applications by introducing the new conversation scope. We studied how to implement a multistep page flow using long-running conversations.

The JBoss Seam framework greatly simplifies JSF application development by providing a set of user interface controls that solve a number of common problems in JSF, such as form validation, converting JPA entities, and preparing JSF-specific data structures for selection components. In the next chapter, we will see how Seam can be combined with the JBoss RichFaces and Ajax4jsf component libraries to create truly stunning next generation web user interfaces.

7
JBoss RichFaces and Ajax4jsf Components

The JBoss RichFaces and Ajax4jsf component libraries represent some of the most exciting technologies available today for JSF developers. This powerful set of components significantly enhances web development on the Java EE platform. In this chapter, we will explore how to use JBoss RichFaces and Ajax4jsf components together with the Seam framework to create next generation Java web applications based on JSF.

Introducing JBoss RichFaces and Ajax4jsf

JBoss RichFaces and Ajax4jsf are two of the most advanced JSF component libraries available today. RichFaces includes around 75 rich user interface components that can greatly enhance the visual appeal and interactivity of a Web 2.0 application. Ajax4jsf includes around 25 mostly non-visual tags that provide the Ajax infrastructure on which RichFaces components are based.

The JBoss RichFaces component library

JBoss RichFaces is one of the most advanced JSF component libraries available today. It provides a stunning set of full featured Ajax-enabled UI components to bring new levels of Web 2.0 usability and interactivity to the Java platform.

RichFaces provides rich input components, such as in-place editable text and selection controls, a color chooser control, a calendar control, and a suggestion box that supports autocompletion using Ajax. Additionally, RichFaces includes sophisticated panel and menu components for rendering advanced user interface layouts and menu structures. One of the most impressive features of the RichFaces component library is its support for working with dynamic data. RichFaces makes it very simple to implement a sortable, scrollable data table that renders dynamic data retrieved from a database by a backing bean.

The Ajax4jsf component library

The Ajax4jsf component library is a popular Ajax solution for the JSF framework. It was developed initially by Exadel and contributed as an open source project to JBoss in 2008. Since then, Ajax4jsf and RichFaces have become integrated and are now distributed as a single JSF component library.

One of the most interesting features of the Ajax4jsf library is that it can add a sophisticated level of Ajax support to existing JSF components that have no built-in Ajax capabilities. Ajax4jsf is the Ajax engine that powers RichFaces, and Seam includes built-in support for Ajax4jsf.

Some of the benefits of the Ajax4jsf library include:

- Automatically adding Ajax support to other non-Ajax JSF components
- Adding drag-and-drop capabilities to JSF user interfaces
- Synchronizing (queueing) Ajax requests on the client side to optimize and control bandwidth usage and communication between the browser and the server
- Limiting the number of components on the screen that will be refreshed after an Ajax request to improve performance
- Polling the server periodically using Ajax to display ongoing changes to a web page
- Persisting request-scoped backing beans between requests to support Ajax functionality

In this chapter, we will examine advanced topics in JSF web application development and will explore how to use the JBoss RichFaces and Ajax4jsf component libraries effectively. We will look at several examples of how to develop next generation web user interfaces using JBoss RichFaces, Ajax4jsf, and Seam. Conceptually, RichFaces provides many interesting visual UI components, while Ajax4jsf provides mostly non-visual Ajax-specific infrastructure support for the JSF presentation layer.

The tasks we will cover include:

- Accepting user input
- Using Ajax effectively
- Working with panel components
- Displaying data
- Using special components

Accepting user input

The JBoss RichFaces and Ajax4jsf component libraries contain a wealth of UI components that can be used to accept user input in new and interesting ways. By combining these components together effectively, we can significantly enhance the visual appeal and interactivity of our JSF pages. We will look at a number of examples of these components; such as the RichFaces in-place input text field, number spinbox, slider, calendar, color picker, combo box, pick list, and rich text editor components.

Rendering editable text

Let's begin by looking at the RichFaces `<rich:inplaceInput>` tag. This tag renders as an editable text control that enables users to click to edit the value of the component directly on the screen. This component allows us to control how the text becomes editable by defining the mouse event that activates the component using the `editEvent` attribute. It could be set to `ondoubleclick` for example. The default edit event is `onclick`.

```
<rich:panel style="width:220px;">
    <f:facet name="header">
        <h:outputText value="Contact Info"></h:outputText>
    </f:facet>
    <h:panelGrid columns="2">
        <h:outputText value="Name: " />
        <rich:inplaceInput defaultLabel="enter your name" />
        <h:outputText value="Email:" />
```

```
        <rich:inplaceInput defaultLabel="enter your email" />
      </h:panelGrid>
</rich:panel>
```

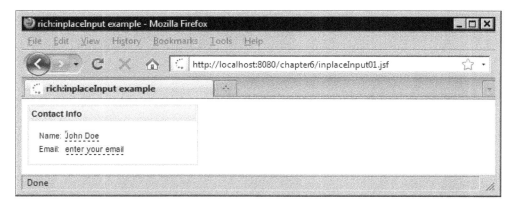

Rendering an in-place select component

The RichFaces library includes a similar in-place editing component that provides
a list of available options. The `<rich:inplaceSelect>` tag renders this component
and is useful for situations where a backing bean property is bound to a predefined
list of values, such as a list of countries.

Notice that in this example we are populating the list of items using a nested
`<s:selectItems>` tag, a Seam framework component tag that automatically
converts a list of objects to a list of `SelectItem` instances. We also use the Seam
`<s:convertEntity>` tag to provide automatic conversion of the `Country` type from
our JPA domain model.

This is a significant improvement because we no longer have to write custom
converters for our domain model classes or special backing bean methods to produce
lists of `SelectItem` objects.

```
<h:form>
<rich:panel style="width:320px;">
    <f:facet name="header">
        <h:outputText value="Countries" />
    </f:facet>
    <h:panelGrid columns="2">
        <h:outputText value="Selected Country: " />
        <rich:inplaceSelect
            value="#{shippingCalculator.country}"
            defaultLabel="Double click to edit" openOnEdit="true"
            showControls="true" editEvent="ondblclick" layout="block"
            viewClass="inplace" changedClass="inplace"
            changedHoverClass="hover" viewHoverClass="hover">
```

```
        <s:selectItems value="#{customerBean.countries}"
            var="country" label="#{country.name}" />
      <s:convertEntity />
      </rich:inplaceSelect>
    </h:panelGrid>
  </rich:panel>
</h:form>
```

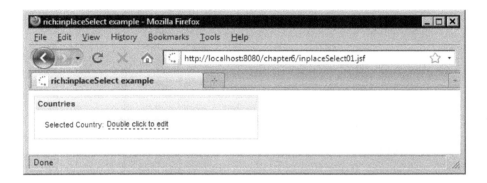

When the in-place select component is activated, a drop-down list of countries is presented to the user. The component also displays a green checkmark icon and a red cancel icon beside the list. Once the user selects a value from the list, clicking on the checkmark applies the selection while clicking on the cancel icon resets the component's value back to the previous state.

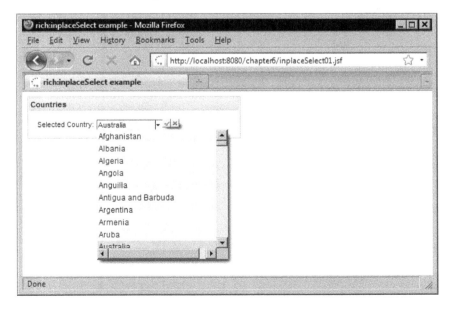

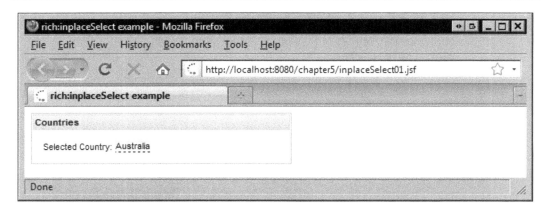

Combining in-place input and select components

The RichFaces in-place input and in-place select components can be combined to create a highly intuitive user interface. In this example, we render a list of products in an editable data table.

```
<h:form>
    <rich:dataTable value="#{productBean.products}" var="product"
        rows="5" columnClasses="left-aligned,left-aligned,
        right-aligned,centered">
        <rich:column>
            <f:facet name="header">
                <h:outputText value="Product Name" />
            </f:facet>
            <rich:inplaceInput value="#{product.name}" />
        </rich:column>
        <rich:column>
            <f:facet name="header">
                <h:outputText value="Category" />
            </f:facet>
            <rich:inplaceSelect value="#{product.category}">
                <s:selectItems value="#{productBean.productCategories}"
                    var="category" label="#{category.name}" />
            </rich:inplaceSelect>
        </rich:column>
        <rich:column>
            <f:facet name="header">
                <h:outputText value="Price" />
            </f:facet>
```

```
      <rich:inplaceInput value="#{product.price}">
        <f:convertNumber type="currency" currencySymbol="$"
          maxFractionDigits="0" />
      </rich:inplaceInput>
    </rich:column>
    <rich:column>
      <f:facet name="header">
        <h:outputText value="Quantity in Stock" />
      </f:facet>
      <rich:inplaceInput value="#{product.quantityInStock}" />
    </rich:column>
  </rich:dataTable>
</h:form>
```

The next screenshot demonstrates the use of the `<rich:inplaceInput>` component in a RichFaces data table. Notice how seamlessly the component fits into the user interface. This creates a very interesting visual effect that goes beyond the capabilities of the basic HTML widget library.

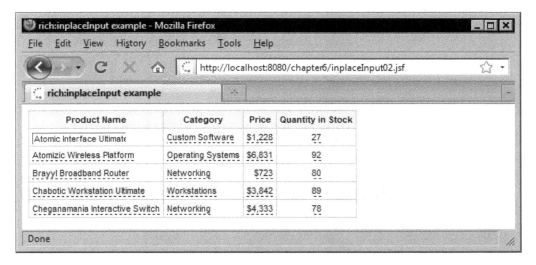

Similarly, when the user tabs to the next field in the data table, we can see another visually interesting RichFaces component in use. The `<rich:inplaceSelect>` renders a sophisticated drop-down list that appears when the user activates the component.

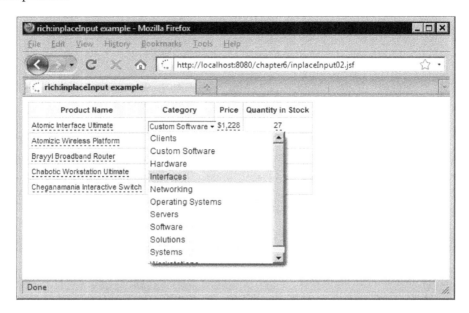

Once an in-place editing component's value has changed, RichFaces renders a small red decoration in the top-left corner of the field to provide a visual cue to the user that the original value has been modified. Once the form is submitted, the value is changed and the red decoration is cleared.

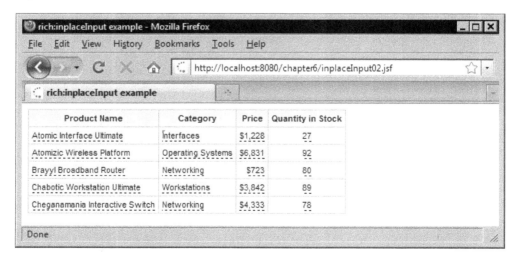

Rendering a slider component

One of the nice things about desktop software GUI toolkits is the presence of rich UI components that enhance user interaction. The Swing GUI toolkit, for example, includes a slider component that enables the user to adjust a numeric value gradually by clicking and dragging a control to the desired position.

The RichFaces library introduces a slider component that can be used to give JSF applications a more intuitive feel similar to desktop application behavior. The slider component supports horizontal and vertical orientations and can be bound to any numeric backing bean property.

This component is well suited to situations where the user wants to make more coarse-grained or imprecise adjustments to a numeric value, such as adjusting a volume, brightness, contrast, or zoom level. Adjusting the value using precise increments with this component can be challenging for the user (especially if the numeric range of the slider is fairly wide). For more precise numeric input, the `<rich:inputNumberSpinbox>` tag is recommended.

```
<rich:panel style="width:320px;">
    <f:facet name="header">
        <h:outputText value="Number Selector">
        </h:outputText>
    </f:facet>
    <h:panelGrid columns="2">
        <h:outputText value="Select Number: " />
        <rich:inputNumberSlider orientation="horizontal" />
    </h:panelGrid>
</rich:panel>
```

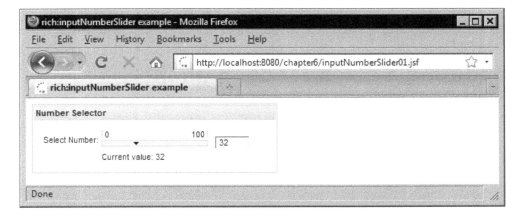

Rendering a number spinner component

While the RichFaces slider component provides a sophisticated type of control for selecting a numeric value, RichFaces also includes another numeric value component. The `<rich:inputNumberSpinner>` tag renders a text field with a pair of image buttons beside it that allow the user to adjust the numeric value incrementally. This component is useful in situations where the user wants to make more precise adjustments.

```
<rich:panel style="width:320px;">
    <f:facet name="header">
        <h:outputText value="Number Spinner">
        </h:outputText>
    </f:facet>
    <h:panelGrid columns="2">
        <h:outputText value="Select Number: " />
        <rich:inputNumberSpinner />
    </h:panelGrid>
</rich:panel>
```

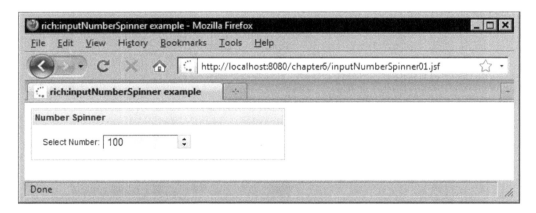

Rendering a calendar component

The RichFaces calendar component renders an elegant date selection control that allows the user to easily navigate between months, years, and dates.

```
<rich:panel style="width:320px;">
    <f:facet name="header">
        <h:outputText value="Calendar" />
    </f:facet>
    <h:panelGrid columns="2">
        <h:outputText value="Select Date: " />
```

```
        <rich:calendar popup="#{true}" />
    </h:panelGrid>
</rich:panel>
```

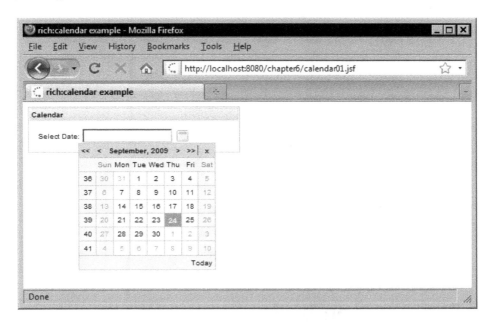

Rendering a color picker component

The RichFaces color picker component is rendered by the `<rich:colorPicker>` tag as a full featured color selection control on the screen similar to the controls provided by advanced photo editing software, such as Adobe Photoshop.

This component enables the user to select a color intuitively by dragging the mouse inside a rich color gradient area, by adjusting a slider on a color strip, or by entering **Red-Green-Blue (RGB)** and **Hue-Saturation-Brightness (HSB)** values. Optionally, the user can enter a hexadecimal color code often used in cascading style sheets. The component also provides an **Apply** and **Cancel** button that close the color picker component with or without applying the selection. The component can be bound to a backing bean property of type `java.awt.Color` or of type `java.lang.String`.

```
<h:form>
<rich:colorPicker
    value="#{customerBean.customer.favoriteColor}" />
</h:form>
```

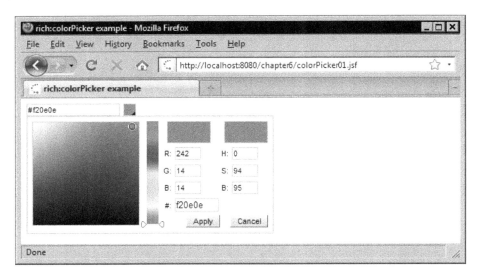

Rendering a combo box component

The RichFaces `HtmlComboBox` component is rendered by the `<rich:comboBox>` tag as a drop-down list that supports text entry. In this example, we bind the component to a list of countries. As the user types in a country name, the list of options is limited automatically to any elements that start with the string entered by the user.

This component is a simplified version of the `<rich:suggestionbox>` component, a more full-featured text selection component that supports Ajax-enabled dynamic autocompletion. We use the Seam `<s:selectItems>` tag in the following example to convert a list of `String` objects to a list of `SelectItem` objects. The `<s:selectItems>` tag will be covered later in this chapter.

The `<rich:comboBox>` tag is basically a more powerful version of the `<h:inputText>` tag that facilitates data entry by providing a drop-down list of possible values. The user is not constrained by the list of values; they can enter whatever free-form text they wish.

```
<rich:panel style="width:420px;">
    <f:facet name="header">
        <h:outputText value="Countries" />
    </f:facet>
    <h:panelGrid columns="2">
        <h:outputText value="Select an Interest: " />
```

```
        <rich:comboBox defaultLabel="Select" width="300">
            <s:selectItems value="#{customerBean.interestList}"
                label="#{item}" var="item" />
        </rich:comboBox>
    </h:panelGrid>
</rich:panel>
```

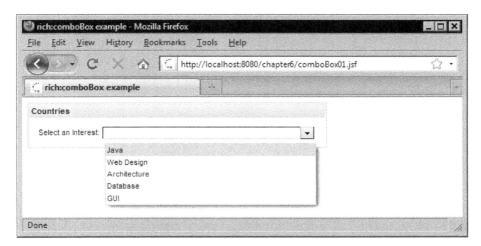

Rendering a suggestion box component with auto-complete

One of the coolest components in the RichFaces library list the suggestion box component. This component is rendered by the <rich:suggestionbox> tag and is associated with a text field in the view. This suggestion box component can communicate with the server using Ajax to provide an incrementally updating dynamic list of suggestions based on user input.

The following JSF markup demonstrates how to add the component to our JSF page. Notice in this example that we combine the Tomahawk <t:inputTextHelp> tag with the RichFaces <rich:suggestionbox> tag to implement a text box that shows help text and has auto-complete behavior. We also nest the <a4j:support> tag inside the Tomahawk <t:inputTextHelp> tag to add Ajax capabilities to the Tomahawk component. In our reRender attribute, we specify that the "selection" panel grid component that displays the selected suggestion should be updated after an Ajax request triggered by an onblur event.

```
<h:form>
    <t:inputTextHelp id="text"
        value="#{shippingCalculatorBeanSeam.country.name}"
        helpText="Enter a Country">
```

```
                    <a4j:support event="onblur" reRender="selection" />
        </t:inputTextHelp>
        <rich:suggestionbox id="suggestionBoxId" for="text"
              tokens=", []" rules="true"
              suggestionAction="#{customerBean.countryAutocomplete}"
              var="result" fetchValue="#{result}" rows="10"
              columnClasses="center" usingSuggestObjects="true">
                    <h:column>
                        <h:outputText value="#{result.name}" />
                    </h:column>
        </rich:suggestionbox>
    <h:panelGrid id="selection">
        <h:outputText
          value="You selected: #{shippingCalculatorBeanSeam.country.name}"
          rendered="#{shippingCalculatorBeanSeam.country.name ne null}" />
    </h:panelGrid>
    </h:form>
```

Notice in the preceding source code that we set the suggestionAction attribute of the <rich:suggestionbox> tag to a method expression that references a special method in our CustomerBean class named countryAutocomplete() that takes an Object and returns a List of Country objects. This method is implemented as follows. First we cast the suggestion object to a String, then if the value is not null or an empty String, we create a JPA named query, pass the suggestion String as the country name "like" argument for the where clause in our JPQL select statement, execute the query, and return a List of Country objects.

```
        @SuppressWarnings("unchecked")
        public List<Country> countryAutocomplete(Object suggestion) {
                List<Country> list = null;
                String text = (String) suggestion;
                if (text != null && text.length() > 0) {
                    Query query = em.createNamedQuery(Queries.
                                                   COUNTRIES_LIKE);
                    query.setParameter(1, text + "%");
                    list = query.getResultList();
                }
                return list;
        }
```

The named query is shown below:

```
        <query name="Country.findByNameLike">
                <![CDATA[
                select country
                from Country country
```

```
              where country.name like ?
              order by country.name
              ]]>
      </query>
```

The following screenshot demonstrates the Tomahawk `<t:inputTextHelp>` tag rendering a text field with help text:

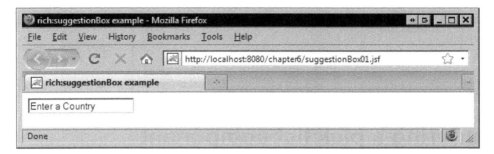

Next, we enter some text to trigger the suggestion box auto-complete behavior. The RichFaces suggestion box component uses Ajax to send the user's input to the server. The text is passed to our `CustomerBean.countryAutocomplete()` backing bean method where the text is included in a JPA query that fetches a list of countries from our database. The list of countries is sent back to the browser in the Ajax response and a list of countries is displayed below the text field.

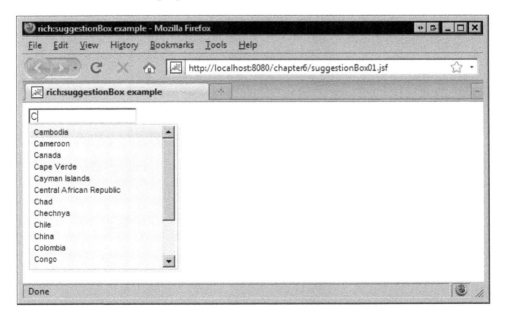

Once we tab out of the text field, the `onblur` event is fired and the text message is updated to reveal our selection:

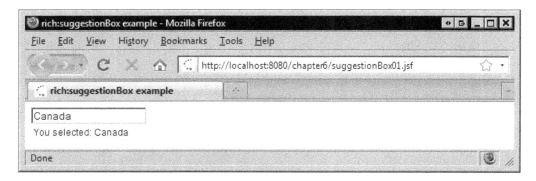

Rendering a pick list component

The RichFaces pick list component is inserted using the `<rich:pickList>` tag and is rendered on the screen as a pair of selection list boxes that support transferring items from one box to the other. This component supports moving items individually or in bulk between the two selection boxes. It can be used to managed more complex user interface tasks such as removing a subset of items from a master list.

The component renders a button for each of the four supported operations (moving one item, moving all items, removing one item, removing all items) and the labels for these buttons can be customized by the developer.

```
<f:facet name="header">
    <h:outputText value="Select Countries " />
</f:facet>
<h:panelGrid columns="2">
    <rich:pickList copyAllControlLabel="copy all label"
        copyControlLabel="copy label"
        removeAllControlLabel="remove all label"
        removeControlLabel="remove label">
      <f:selectItems value="#{customerBean.countrySelectItems}" />
    </rich:pickList>
</h:panelGrid>
```

This screenshot displays the `<rich:pickList>` component. It contains two list boxes and a set of controls for moving items from one list to another.

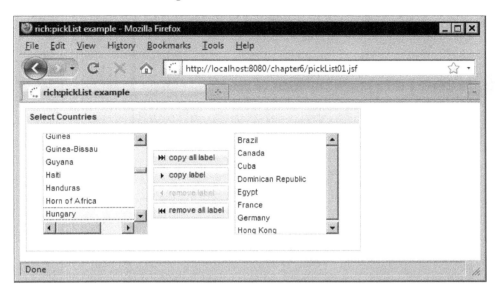

Rendering a rich text editor component

Often, users will be asked to input textual information such as a long description requiring several paragraphs of text. In this situation, the default HTML `<textarea>` element falls short of the functionality provided by desktop word processing software that many users are accustomed to. Fortunately, the RichFaces library includes a component that renders a rich text editor on the screen.

The `<rich:editor>` tag displays the TinyMCE rich text editor in the browser, enabling users to enter text using a powerful and full featured WYSIWYG editor. This component supports a wide range of customizations, such as which menu buttons to display, automatic text area resizing, width, height, and much more.

```
<rich:panel style="width:320px;">
   <f:facet name="header">
      <h:outputText value="Text Editor " />
   </f:facet>
   <rich:editor theme="advanced">
      <f:param name="theme_advanced_buttons1"
         value="bold,italic,underline,cut,copy,paste,pasteword" />
```

```
        <f:param name="theme_advanced_buttons2"
          value="strikethrough,bullist,numlist,outdent,indent" />
        <f:param name="theme_advanced_buttons3"
          value="hr,removeformat,visualaid,sub,sup,charmap" />
    </rich:editor>
</rich:panel>
```

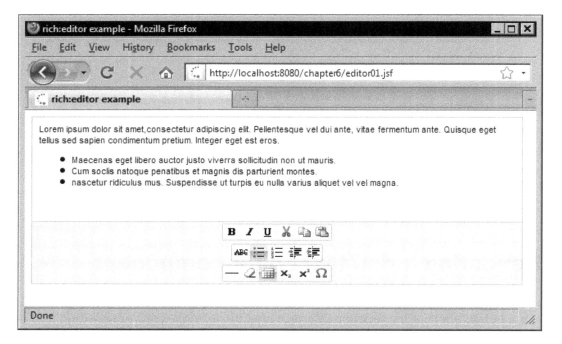

Using Ajax effectively

The Ajax4jsf tag library provides a number of powerful Ajax components that can significantly enhance the interactivity and performance of the user interface for a JSF application. One of the goals of Ajax is to enable more fine-grained communication between the browser and the web server, allowing the application to make incremental view updates without the overhead of a full-page reload for each minor change.

As Ajax-based interactivity can increase the "chattiness" of a web page, the developers of the Ajax4jsf library made sure to include some performance-tuning features in the component library. Let's examine some of the key features of Ajax4jsf and discuss how we can use Ajax effectively in combination with RichFaces and Seam to improve the end user experience for our application.

Understanding how Ajax4jsf works

Ajax4jsf is a powerful Ajax implementation for JSF that includes a number of advanced features. Before diving into the details, let's review the Ajax concept as a background for further discussion.

Ajax is an acronym for Asynchronous JavaScript and XML. It is a Rich Internet Application (RIA) development approach that involves submitting an HTTP request from a web page to the web server, waiting for a response, and then updating the HTML Document Object Model (DOM) dynamically. The browser's JavaScript engine provides the XMLHTTPRequest object that allows a script to marshal an HTTP request and response asynchronously while the page remains in an interactive state. The effect of this approach is that a web page can communicate with the web server and update itself incrementally, independent of the user's control and without interrupting the user's work with a full-page refresh.

One of the value propositions of a component-based web framework like JSF is that advanced capabilities such as Ajax can be encapsulated by the component library and delivered to the client without the developer needing to learn an Ajax scripting API. Effectively this means we can use advanced Ajax techniques without having to write a single line of JavaScript.

Ajax-enabled form submission

The Ajax4jsf component library includes the `<a4j:form>` tag that provides an Ajax-aware replacement for the standard JSF `<h:form>` tag. This tag is functionally identical to the standard `<h:form>`, in that it renders an HTML `<form>` element, but it also supports an Ajax-based form submission mode.

By setting the `ajaxSubmit` attribute to true, we indicate that the form should be submitted asynchronously using Ajax. Any command components inside the form will now trigger an Ajax request instead of the usual HTTP form submission.

The following example demonstrates five possibilities when using the standard JSF `<h:form>` and the Ajax4jsf `<a4j:form>` tag in combination with the standard JSF command button and the Ajax4jsf command button components.

```
<h:form>
   <h:commandButton value="Submit (No Ajax)" />
</h:form>
<a4j:form>
   <h:commandButton value="Submit (No Ajax)" />
</a4j:form>
<h:form>
   <a4j:commandButton value="Submit (Ajax)" />
```

```
    </h:form>
    <a4j:form ajaxSubmit="true">
        <h:commandButton value="Submit (Ajax)" />
    </a4j:form>
    <a4j:form>
        <a4j:commandButton value="Submit (Ajax)" />
    </a4j:form>
```

In this example, only the first two forms are not submitted using Ajax. The
`<a4j:commandButton>` component always performs an Ajax request instead of
the usual form submission. When the `<h:commandButton>` tag is nested in an
`<a4j:form>` tag with the `ajaxSubmit` attribute set to true, the `<h:commandButton>`
also fires an Ajax request when invoked.

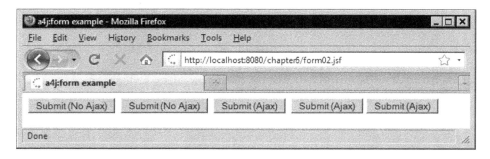

The following example demonstrates that the `ajaxSubmit` attribute of the
`<a4j:form>` tag must be set to true for `<h:commandButton>` tags to use Ajax. If this
attribute is not set, the `<h:commandButton>` tag's behavior is unchanged and results
in non-Ajax form submission.

```
    <h:panelGrid columns="2" columnClasses="align-top">
        <rich:panel>
            <f:facet name="header">
                <h:outputText value="Form with ajaxSubmit=true" />
            </f:facet>
            <a4j:form ajaxSubmit="true" reRender="name">
             <h:panelGrid id="grid">
                <h:outputLabel value="Enter a greeting:" />
                    <h:inputText value="#{backingBean.name1}" />
                    <h:commandButton value="Submit (Ajax)" />
             </h:panelGrid>
            <h:outputText id="name" value="#{backingBean.name1}" />
            </a4j:form>
        </rich:panel>
        <rich:panel>
```

```
        <f:facet name="header">
          <h:outputText value="Form with ajaxSubmit=false" />
        </f:facet>
        <a4j:form reRender="name">
         <h:panelGrid id="grid">
           <h:outputLabel value="Enter a greeting:" />
             <h:inputText value="#{backingBean.name2}" />
             <h:commandButton value="Submit (Non-Ajax)" />
         </h:panelGrid>
        <h:outputText id="name" value="#{backingBean.name2}" />
        </a4j:form>
    </rich:panel>
</h:panelGrid>
```

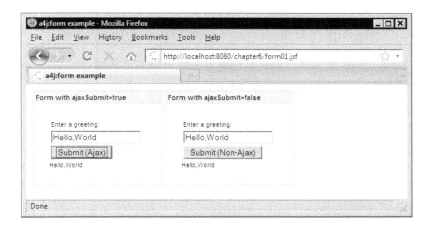

Invoking an Ajax-enabled command link

The `<a4j:commandLink>` tag is identical to the `<h:commandLink>` tag except that it submits a form using Ajax. It also has a `reRender` attribute that indicates a comma-separated list of identifiers for components to be re-rendered when the Ajax request is complete. This allows the page to update itself incrementally in response to user interaction.

```
<a4j:form><h:panelGrid columns="3" styleClass="gridhello"
          columnClasses="gridhellocolumn">
     <h:outputText value="Name:" />
     <h:inputText value="#{backingBean.name}" />
     <a4j:commandLink reRender="out">
     <h:outputText value="Say Hello" />
     </a4j:commandLink>
   </h:panelGrid>
</a4j:form>
<br />
<h:panelGroup id="out">
```

```
    <h:outputText value="Hello "
      rendered="#{not empty backingBean.name}" styleClass="outhello" />
    <h:outputText value="#{backingBean.name}" styleClass="outhello" />
    <h:outputText value="!" rendered="#{not empty backingBean.name}"
      styleClass="outhello" />
  </h:panelGroup>
```

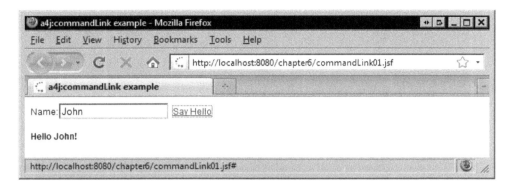

Polling the server asynchronously

The Ajax4jsf library includes a component that can be used to poll the server on a regular interval. This can be useful in situations where a backing bean is waiting on some long running background work to be completed.

An important consideration when using the `<a4j:poll>` is when to stop polling. Typically, we want to stop polling the server when a server-side process has finished. We can use the `enabled` attribute of the `<a4j:poll>` tag to control when polling should stop. Note that when combining the RichFaces/Ajax4jsf libraries with the JBoss Seam framework, conversation propagation can directly affect the expected polling behavior.

Let's look at two examples of how to use the `<a4j:poll>`. Both examples call a conversation-scoped backing bean for each Ajax poll request. Remember that by default Seam places conversation-scoped backing beans into a temporary conversation that is created and destroyed with each request. Therefore, the next example does not work as we might think. Polling continues indefinitely because the backing bean is created and destroyed for each poll request, so the polling state is reset each time.

```
    <h:form>
      <a4j:poll interval="1000" reRender="grid"
          enabled="#{backingBean.pollEnabled}" />
      <h:panelGrid id="grid">
      <h:outputText id="date" value="#{backingBean.today}">
          <f:convertDateTime type="both" timeZone="EST" />
```

```
    </h:outputText>
  <h:outputText id="count"
    value="Poll count: #{backingBean.pollCount}" />
  <h:outputText id="enabled"
    value="Polling enabled: #{backingBean.pollEnabled}" />
  <h:outputText value="Conversation: #{conversation.id}" />
  </h:panelGrid>
</h:form>
```

The following screenshot shows the result of the Ajax4jsf `<a4j:poll>` tag. The JSF page sends an Ajax request to the server once every second, and re-renders the panel grid to display the current time, the poll count, whether polling is enabled, and the current Seam conversation ID. The poll count never increases and polling is always enabled because the page and the backing bean are not associated with a long-running conversation, so a new conversation and a new instance of the backing bean are created for each request.

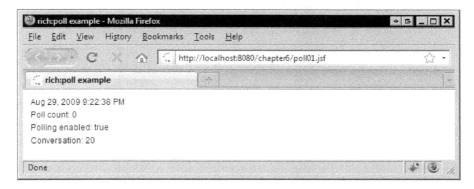

Let's look at an example of using the `<a4j:poll>` tag with a long-running Seam conversation. By nesting the `<s:conversationPropagation>` tag inside the `<a4j:poll>` tag we can control how Seam handles the conversation on the server side. In this case, we set the `type` attribute to `join` to indicate that Seam should begin a new long-running conversation if one is not already in progress, otherwise the request should join the existing long-running conversation.

Effectively we make sure the backing bean that is handling our polling requests is part of a long-running conversation, instead of a temporary one. The result is that our backing bean is created once and reused for each poll request, making it possible for us to reuse the polling state and the behavior of our view is as expected; after five polling requests, the `pollEnabled` property is set to false on the server side.

```
<h:form>
  <a4j:poll interval="1000" reRender="grid"
      enabled="#{backingBean.pollEnabled}">
    <s:conversationPropagation type="join" />
  </a4j:poll>
  <h:panelGrid id="grid">
  <h:outputText id="date" value="#{backingBean.today}">
      <f:convertDateTime type="both" timeZone="EST" />
   </h:outputText>
  <h:outputText id="count"
    value="Poll count: #{backingBean.pollCount}" />
  <h:outputText id="enabled"
     value="Polling enabled: #{backingBean.pollEnabled}" />
  <h:outputText value="Conversation: #{conversation.id}" />
  </h:panelGrid>
</h:form>
```

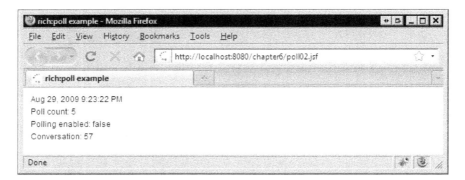

Panel components

The JBoss RichFaces library includes a number of useful components for rendering panels in our views. Using panels is a nice way to organize visual elements in our user interface.

Creating a basic panel

The RichFaces `<rich:panel>` tag renders a basic panel component that can be used to group related controls or information together with a descriptive header. The `<rich:panel>` tag supports a `header` facet that defines the text to be rendered in the panel header.

```
<rich:panel>
  <f:facet name="header">
    <h:outputText value="Panel Header" />
```

```
        </f:facet>
        <h:outputText value="Panel content here." />
    </rich:panel>
```

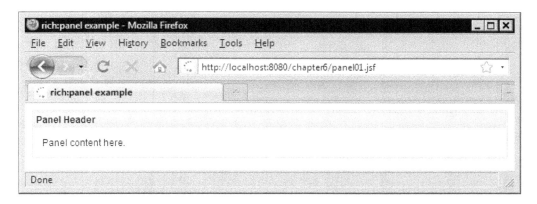

Rendering a panel bar

RichFaces also provides the `<rich:panelBar>` tag that renders a panel bar component as a group of panels organized into a vertical layout. Each panel in the panel bar arrangement has a clickable header that toggles the panel between an expanded and collapsed state. The `<rich:panelBar>` tag renders nested `<rich:panelBarItem>` tags as individual panels. The `label` attribute of the `<rich:panelBarItem>` tag defines the text to be displayed in the header of the panel.

```
<rich:panelBar width="300px">
  <rich:panelBarItem label="Recommended">
  ...
  </rich:panelBarItem>
  <rich:panelBarItem label="Most Popular">
    <rich:dataTable width="100%"
        value="#{productBean.randomProducts}"
        var="product" rows="3">
      <rich:column colspan="3">
        <h:graphicImage url="/images/#{product.icon}"
          style="text-align:left; vertical-align:middle;
          padding-right:5px" />
        <h:outputText value="#{product.name}" />
      </rich:column>
      <rich:columnGroup>
        <rich:column>
```

```
                    <h:outputText value="#{product.category.name}" />
            </rich:column>
            <rich:column>
              <h:outputText value="#{product.price}">
                <f:convertNumber type="currency" currencySymbol="$"
                  maxFractionDigits="0" />
              </h:outputText>
            </rich:column>
            <rich:column>
              <h:outputText value="In stock: #{product.quantityInStock}"
               />
            </rich:column>
          </rich:columnGroup>
        </rich:dataTable>
      </rich:panelBarItem>
      <rich:panelBarItem label="Favorites">
      ...
      </rich:panelBarItem>
      <rich:panelBarItem label="Purchased">
      ...
      </rich:panelBarItem>.
    </rich:panelBar>
```

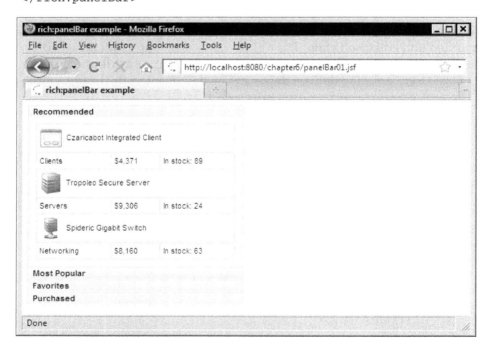

Rendering a panel menu

The `<rich:panelMenu>` and `<rich:panelMenuItem>` tags provide an alternative to
the `<rich:panelBar>` and `<rich:panelBarItem>` tags. This combination of tags
renders a set of Ajax-enabled menu items that support active, inactive, and rollover
states. In this example, clicking on a menu item triggers an Ajax request that invokes
an action listener method in our backing bean to select a set of products..

When the Ajax request is complete, we re-render another panel in the view to display
the selected products. Notice that the menu item icon can also be customized.
The following enumerated icon values are supported: `triangle`, `triangleUp`,
`triangleDown`, `disc`, `chevron`, `chevronUp`, `chevronDown`, and `grid`.

```
<h:panelGrid columns="2" columnClasses="align-top" cellpadding="10">
  <rich:panelMenu selectedChild="item2">
    <rich:panelMenuItem id="item1" label="Recommended"
        icon="triangle"
        actionListener="#{productBean.selectRecommendedProducts}" />
    <rich:panelMenuItem id="item2" label="Most Popular"
        actionListener="#{productBean.selectPopularProducts}" />
    <rich:panelMenuItem id="item3" label="Favorites"
        actionListener="#{productBean.selectFavoriteProducts}" />
    <rich:panelMenuItem id="item4" label="Purchased"
        actionListener="#{productBean.selectPurchasedProducts}" />
  </rich:panelMenu>.
  <rich:panel>
    <f:facet name="header">
      <h:outputText value="Selected Products" />
    </f:facet>
    <h:outputText value="Select a category"
      rendered="#{empty productBean.selectedProducts}" />
    <rich:dataTable id="selectedProducts" width="100%"
        value="#{productBean.selectedProducts}"
        var="product" rows="3">
      <rich:column colspan="3">
        <h:graphicImage url="/images/#{product.icon}"
          style="text-align:left; vertical-align:middle;
          padding-right:5px" />
        <h:outputText value="#{product.name}" />
      </rich:column>
      <rich:columnGroup>
        <rich:column>
          <h:outputText value="#{product.category.name}" />
        </rich:column>
        <rich:column>
          <h:outputText value="#{product.price}">
```

```
            <f:convertNumber type="currency" currencySymbol="$"
               maxFractionDigits="0" />
          </h:outputText>
        </rich:column>
        <rich:column>
          <h:outputText value="In stock: #{product.quantityInStock}"
            />
        </rich:column>
      </rich:columnGroup>
    </rich:dataTable>
  </rich:panel>
</h:panelGrid>
```

In the following screenshot, we can see the `<rich:panelMenu>` displayed as a vertical series of menu items in the left column of our two-column panel grid. The first `<rich:panelMenuItem>` has the `icon` attribute set to `triangle`, so it looks different from the remaining three menu items. The second menu item is selected, so the label is rendered using an italic font. The mouse is hovering over the second menu item, and it is shown in a highlighted state.

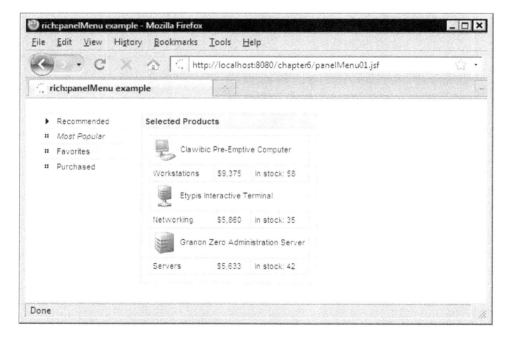

Rendering groups of menu items

The <rich:panelMenuGroup> tag can also be nested inside a <rich:panelMenu> tag to create a group of menu items. In this example, we render a panel menu with four panel menu groups. The first panel menu group is expanded, disclosing three panel menu items. When the user clicks on a panel menu item, an action listener method is invoked using Ajax, and the list of selected products is re-rendered.

In the following example, only the first <rich:panelMenuGroup> tag has any child <rich:panelMenuItem> tags. The remaining three <rich:panelMenuGroup> tags are simply there for illustration purposes. (When an empty <rich:panelMenuGroup> is included in the view, only the label is rendered and since there are no child menu items to display, the menu does not expand when clicked by the user.)

```
<h:panelGrid columns="2" columnClasses="align-top" cellpadding="10">
    <rich:panelMenu selectedChild="item2">
        <rich:panelMenuGroup label="Recommended">
        <rich:panelMenuItem label="Top Sellers"
            actionListener="#{productBean.selectPopularProducts}" />
        <rich:panelMenuItem label="Best Value"
            actionListener="#{productBean.selectPopularProducts}" />
        <rich:panelMenuItem label="Back to School"
            actionListener="#{productBean.selectPopularProducts}" />
    </rich:panelMenuGroup>
    <rich:panelMenuGroup id="item2" label="Most Popular"
        actionListener="#{productBean.selectPopularProducts}" />
    <rich:panelMenuGroup id="item3" label="Favorites"
        actionListener="#{productBean.selectFavoriteProducts}"
        reRender="" />
    <rich:panelMenuGroup id="item4" label="Purchased"
        actionListener="#{productBean.selectPurchasedProducts}" />
    </rich:panelMenu>
    <rich:panel>
    <f:facet name="header">
      <h:outputText value="Selected Products" />
    </f:facet>
    <h:outputText value="Select a category"
      rendered="#{empty productBean.selectedProducts}" />
    <rich:dataTable id="selectedProducts" width="100%"
        value="#{productBean.selectedProducts}"
        var="product" rows="3">
      <rich:column colspan="3">
        <h:graphicImage url="/images/#{product.icon}"
          style="text-align:left; vertical-align:middle;
          padding-right:5px" />
        <h:outputText value="#{product.name}" />
```

```
        </rich:column>
        <rich:columnGroup>
          <rich:column>
            <h:outputText value="#{product.category.name}" />
          </rich:column>
          <rich:column>
            <h:outputText value="#{product.price}">
              <f:convertNumber type="currency" currencySymbol="$"
                maxFractionDigits="0" />
            </h:outputText>
          </rich:column>
          <rich:column>
            <h:outputText value="In stock: #{product.quantityInStock}"
              />
          </rich:column>
        </rich:columnGroup>
      </rich:dataTable>
    </rich:panel>
  </h:panelGrid>
```

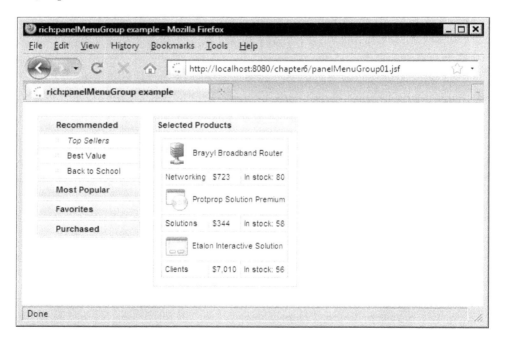

Rendering a tabbed user interface

Using tabs to subdivide a user interface is an effective way to maximize the use of screen real estate for web application. The RichFaces library includes useful components for rendering a tabbed user interface. The `<rich:tabPanel>` tag provides the parent container to which tab components can be added individually. The `<rich:tab>` tag can be nested inside the `<rich:tabPanel>` tag to create an individual tab. The text that is displayed in the tab header is defined using the `label` attribute of this tag. The following example demonstrates how to create a simple tab panel that groups related products together an interesting way.

```
<rich:tabPanel>
  <rich:tab label="Recommended">
  ...
  </rich:tab>
  <rich:tab label="Most Popular">
<rich:dataGrid width="100%" value="#{productBean.randomProducts}"
    var="product" columns="3" elements="6" cellpadding="5"
    cellspacing="5">
      <rich:panel>
        <f:facet name="header">
          <h:outputText value="#{product.name}" />
        </f:facet>
        <h:panelGrid columns="2" width="100%"
          columnClasses="align-top">
          <h:outputText value="Category:" />
          <h:outputText value="#{product.category.name}" />
          <h:outputText value="Price:" />
          <h:outputText value="#{product.price}">
            <f:convertNumber type="currency"
              currencySymbol="$" maxFractionDigits="0" />
          </h:outputText>
          <h:outputText value="In Stock:" />
          <h:panelGroup>
            <h:outputText value="#{product.quantityInStock}"
             />
            <h:graphicImage url="/images/#{product.icon}"
              style="float:right;" />
          </h:panelGroup>
        </h:panelGrid>
      </rich:panel>
</rich:dataGrid>
</rich:tab>
  <rich:tab label="Favorites">
  ...
```

```
      </rich:tab>
      <rich:tab label="Purchased">
      ...
      </rich:tab>
</rich:tabPanel>
```

In the next example, the contents of the tab are displayed using the
`<rich:dataGrid>` tag. The six selected products are arranged into a series of three
columns by two rows. The `<rich:dataGrid>` tag is covered in more detail later on in
this chapter.

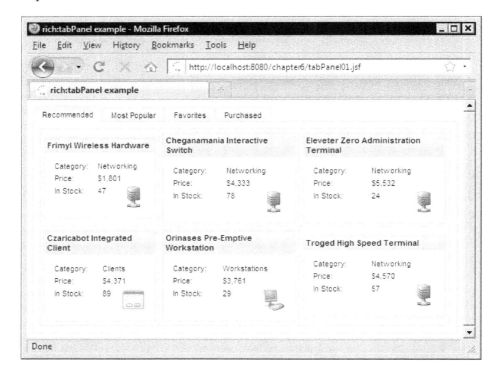

Rendering a toggle panel

Another type of panel provided by the RichFaces component library is the toggle
panel. This component is rendered as a clickable link or icon that displays one or
more panels in a navigable sequence. The `<rich:togglePanel>` tag supports three
switching modes: client-side, server-side, and Ajax. The `stateOrder` attribute accepts
a comma-separated list of facet names that defines the order in which the panels are
displayed. The component expects a named facet for each of the user defined toggle
states. In this example, we have a `closed` facet, a `tip1` facet, and a `tip2` facet for three
possible states. We also define the initial state of the toggle panel as the `tip1` facet.

The <rich:toggleControl> tag is closely related to the <rich:togglePanel> tag. The <rich:toggleControl> tag provides a state-switching control that enables the user to click on a link or an icon in order to switch the toggle panel to a different state. When the user clicks on the info.gif image or on the **Information** label, the toggle panel component is activated and the next panel in the sequence is displayed. Notice that each tip facet has two <rich:toggleControl> tags (one for the image and one for the text label) that enable the user to toggle the state of the toggle panel component. The facet rendered by clicking on the toggle control is determined by the switchToState attribute.

```
<h:form>
    <rich:togglePanel switchType="client"
        stateOrder="closed,tip1,tip2" initialState="tip1">
      <f:facet name="closed">
       <h:panelGroup>
        <rich:toggleControl style="padding-right:3px">
          <h:graphicImage url="/images/info.gif" style="border:0;
            vertical-align:middle;" />
        </rich:toggleControl>
        <rich:toggleControl>
          <h:outputText value="Information" />
        </rich:toggleControl>
       </h:panelGroup>
      </f:facet>
      <f:facet name="tip1">
        <h:panelGrid cellpadding="0" cellspacing="0" border="0"
          columns="1">
          <h:outputText value="Did you know you can reserve items
                              from our store for up to 48 hours?" />
          <rich:separator height="1" />
          <h:panelGrid columns="3">
             <rich:toggleControl switchToState="closed">
               <h:graphicImage url="/images/close.gif"
                 style="border:0;" />
             </rich:toggleControl>
             <rich:toggleControl switchToState="tip2"
                 value="Next Tip &gt;" />
          </h:panelGrid>
        </h:panelGrid>
      </f:facet>
      <f:facet name="tip2">
        <h:panelGrid cellpadding="0" cellspacing="0" border="0"
          columns="1">
        <h:outputText value="Our sales staff is always ready to
                            assist. Please call 1-800-555-1234." />
```

```
                    <rich:separator height="1" />
                    <h:panelGrid columns="3">
                        <rich:toggleControl switchToState="closed">
                            <h:graphicImage url="/images/close.gif"
                               style="border:0;" />
                         </rich:toggleControl>
                        <rich:toggleControl switchToState="tip1"
                               value="&lt; Previous Tip" />
                    </h:panelGrid>
                </h:panelGrid>
            </f:facet>
        </rich:togglePanel>
    </h:form>
```

The facet named in the `initialState` attribute of the `<rich:togglePanel>` tag is shown by default, as seen in the following screenshot:

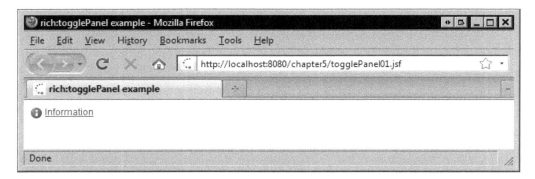

When the user clicks on the image or the text label in the first screenshot, the toggle control component displays the facet named in the `<rich:toggleControl>` tag's `switchToState` attribute.

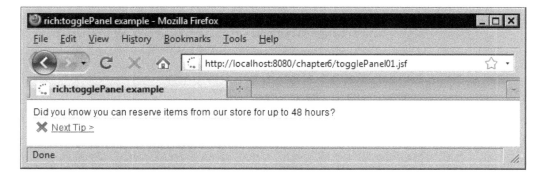

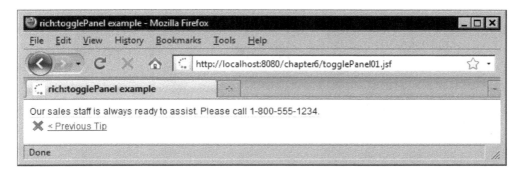

Displaying data

The combination of the JBoss Seam framework, the RichFaces component library, and the Ajax4jsf component library is an excellent set of technologies for implementing dynamic data-driven JSF applications. RichFaces provides a number of components that support a range of data-oriented tasks, such as rendering a data table, sorting data, pagination, complex data tables, and more.

Rendering a data table

One of the most important data components in the RichFaces component library is the RichFaces data table component rendered by the `<rich:dataTable>` tag. This component is an extended version of the standard JSF data table component, so the two components have many of the same attributes. RichFaces also provides the `<rich:column>` tag that renders an extended version of the standard JSF HTML column component and provides rich behavior such as the ability to sort in ascending or descending order, the ability to filter the data in the column, column and row span attributes, custom sort icons, and more. In the next example, we render a simple RichFaces data table displaying the customers in our database.

```
<rich:dataTable value="#{customerBean.customers}" var="customer"
rows="5" columnClasses="left-aligned,centered,centered,centered">
    <rich:column>
        <f:facet name="header">
            <h:outputText value="Customer Name" />
        </f:facet>
        <h:outputText value="#{customer.fullName}" />
    </rich:column>
    <rich:column>
        <f:facet name="header">
            <h:outputText value="Gender" />
        </f:facet>
```

```
            <h:outputText value="#{customer.male ? 'Male' : 'Female'}" />
        </rich:column>
        <rich:column>
            <f:facet name="header">
                <h:outputText value="Date of Birth" />
            </f:facet>
            <h:outputText value="#{customer.birthDate}">
                <f:convertDateTime type="date" />
            </h:outputText>
        </rich:column>
        <rich:column>
            <f:facet name="header">
                <h:outputText value="Country of Origin" />
            </f:facet>
            <h:outputText value="#{customer.countryOfOrigin.name}" />
        </rich:column>
    </rich:dataTable>
```

The following screenshot shows the rendered RichFaces `<rich:dataTable>` tag containing `<rich:column>` tags. The RichFaces data table component provides a more stylized presentation of a data table than the standard JSF HTML data table component.

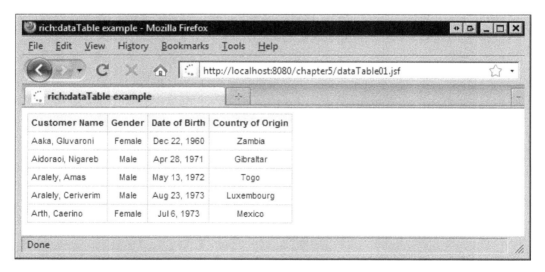

Rendering a data table with a header, footer, and caption

In this example, we render the RichFaces data table component using a table header, footer, and caption to display additional information about the data in the table. This time our data table is rendering product information from our database.

```
<rich:dataTable value="#{productBean.products}" var="product" rows="5"
columnsWidth="200, 150, 50, 10" columnClasses="left-aligned,left-
aligned,right-aligned,centered" footerClass="centered">
    <f:facet name="caption">
        <h:outputText value="Company XYZ Product List" />
    </f:facet>
    <f:facet name="header">
        <h:outputText value="Available Products" />
    </f:facet>
    <rich:column>
        <f:facet name="header">
            <h:outputText value="Product Name" />
        </f:facet>
        <h:outputText value="#{product.name}" />
    </rich:column>
    <rich:column>
        <f:facet name="header">
            <h:outputText value="Category" />
        </f:facet>
        <h:outputText value="#{product.category.name}" />
    </rich:column>
    <rich:column>
        <f:facet name="header">
            <h:outputText value="Price" />
        </f:facet>
        <h:outputText value="#{product.price}">
            <f:convertNumber type="currency" currencySymbol="$"
              maxFractionDigits="0" />
        </h:outputText>
    </rich:column>
    <rich:column>
        <f:facet name="header">
            <h:outputText value="Quantity in Stock" />
        </f:facet>
        <h:outputText value="#{product.quantityInStock}" />
    </rich:column>
    <f:facet name="footer">
```

```
                    <h:outputText value="New Products Available Next Week" />
            </f:facet>
     </rich:dataTable>
```

The following screenshot demonstrates the `<rich:dataTable>` tag used in combination with table and column headers and footers, as well as a table caption facet.

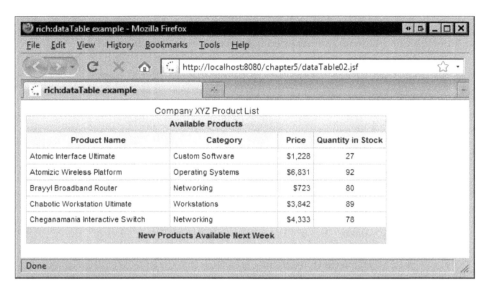

Implementing sortable data table column headers

The RichFaces component library makes it trivially easy to render a sortable data table. The `<rich:column>` tag has a number of attributes that control sorting behavior. In this example, we enable sorting on each column simply by setting the `sortBy` attribute of the `<rich:column>` tag. This attribute expects an EL expression that references the property of the row object that should be used for sorting the data in that column. No additional work is required. The RichFaces data table component also tracks the sort order and toggles from ascending to descending whenever the user clicks a column header.

```
<rich:dataTable value="#{productBean.products}" var="product"
     rows="5" columnsWidth="200, 150, 50, 10"
     columnClasses="left-aligned,left-aligned,right-aligned,centered"
     footerClass="centered">
  <f:facet name="caption">
     <h:outputText value="Company XYZ Product List" />
```

```
        </f:facet>
        <f:facet name="header">
            <h:outputText value="Available Products" />
        </f:facet>
        <rich:column sortBy="#{product.name}">
            <f:facet name="header">
                <h:outputText value="Product Name" />
            </f:facet>
            <h:outputText value="#{product.name}" />
        </rich:column>
        <rich:column sortBy="#{product.category.name}">
            <f:facet name="header">
                <h:outputText value="Category" />
            </f:facet>
            <h:outputText value="#{product.category.name}" />
        </rich:column>
        <rich:column sortBy="#{product.price}">
            <f:facet name="header">
                <h:outputText value="Price" />
            </f:facet>
            <h:outputText value="#{product.price}">
                <f:convertNumber type="currency" currencySymbol="$"
                    maxFractionDigits="0" />
            </h:outputText>
        </rich:column>
        <rich:column sortBy="#{product.quantityInStock}">
            <f:facet name="header">
                <h:outputText value="Quantity in Stock" />
            </f:facet>
            <h:outputText value="#{product.quantityInStock}" />
        </rich:column>
        <f:facet name="footer">
            <h:outputText value="New Products Available Next Week" />
        </f:facet>
    </rich:dataTable>
```

The next screenshot demonstrates one of the most powerful features of the RichFaces data table component: the built-in support for column sorting behavior.

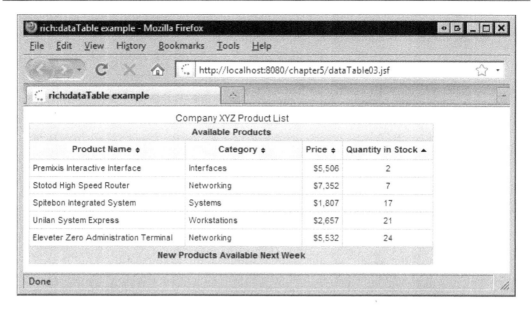

Filtering rows in a data table

Another nice feature of the RichFaces data table is the component's ability to filter rows using a slider component. We can use the `<rich:dataFilterSlider>` tag to add a slider to the page that the user can interact with to filter out rows that have an arbitrary value above the numeric limit set by the component.

In this example, we use the `<rich:dataFilterSlider>` tag to enable the user to filter out products that have a price above a certain price limit. The user can now browse products that fit within their price range. To implement this, we use the `for` attribute of the `<rich:dataFilterSlider>` tag to specify the ID of the data table that we are filtering. The `forValRef` attribute specifies a non-EL value that represents the expression used to obtain the original data set. The component needs this information so it can construct an EL expression to obtain data needed to restore the list when the slider changes.

The `filterBy` attribute specifies a getter method name that will be invoked on each row object to determine if the return value of this method is within the range specified by the slider component. If the getter methods return a value which is greater than the current value of the slider component, that row will be filtered out of the data table. Note that we also specify the numeric range and increment value of the slider component by setting the `startRange`, `endRange`, and `increment` attributes.

The `manualInput` attribute determines whether the value of the slider component can be set by entering text into a text field. This attribute is true by default. If the attribute is set to false, the text field is hidden and the value of slider component cannot be set by manual input into the text field, but only through the slider control.

The `storeResults` attribute determines if a UIData object containing the row data is stored in session scope. Setting this to true can improve rendering performance, but since UI components are not thread-safe, care must be taken to ensure that only one Ajax request at a time is modifying the UIData object. Therefore, using the `storeResults` attribute in conjunction with the `eventsQueue` attribute to ensure that any Ajax requests generated by this component are queued on the client side is recommended.

The `trailer` attribute specifies whether a trailer is rendered to the left of the slider handle. If this attribute is set to false (the default), the background behind the slider handle shows a consistent shadow gradient. If the attribute is set to true, the space to the left of the slider handle has a white background. The style of the trailer can be specified using the `trailerStyleClass` attribute. For example, the background color could be changed to green or red.

The `handleValue` attribute specifies the initial slider handle value.

```
<h:form>
    <h:outputLabel for="slider" value="Filter by Price" />
    <rich:dataFilterSlider id="slider" for="productTable"
        forValRef="productBean.products" filterBy="getPrice"
        manualInput="true" storeResults="true" width="400px"
        startRange="0" endRange="9999" increment="100" trailer="true"
        eventsQueue="sliderQueue" handleValue="2500" />
    <rich:dataTable id="productTable"
        value="#{productBean.products}" var="product"  rows="5"
        columnsWidth="200, 150, 50, 10"
        columnClasses="left-aligned,left-aligned,
        right-aligned,centered" footerClass="centered">
    <f:facet name="caption">
        <h:outputText value="Company XYZ Product List" />
    </f:facet>
    <f:facet name="header">
        <h:outputText value="Available Products" />
    </f:facet>
    <rich:column sortBy="#{product.name}">
        <f:facet name="header">
            <h:outputText value="Product Name" />
        </f:facet>
        <h:outputText value="#{product.name}" />
    </rich:column>
    <rich:column sortBy="#{product.category.name}">
        <f:facet name="header">
```

```
                    <h:outputText value="Category" />
                </f:facet>
                <h:outputText value="#{product.category.name}" />
            </rich:column>
            <rich:column sortBy="#{product.price}">
                <f:facet name="header">
                    <h:outputText value="Price" />
                </f:facet>
                <h:outputText value="#{product.price}">
                    <f:convertNumber type="currency" currencySymbol="$"
                      maxFractionDigits="0" />
                </h:outputText>
            </rich:column>
            <rich:column sortBy="#{product.quantityInStock}">
                <f:facet name="header">
                    <h:outputText value="Quantity in Stock" />
                </f:facet>
                <h:outputText value="#{product.quantityInStock}" />
            </rich:column>
            <f:facet name="footer">
                <h:outputText value="New Products Available Next Week" />
            </f:facet>
        </rich:dataTable>
    </h:form>
```

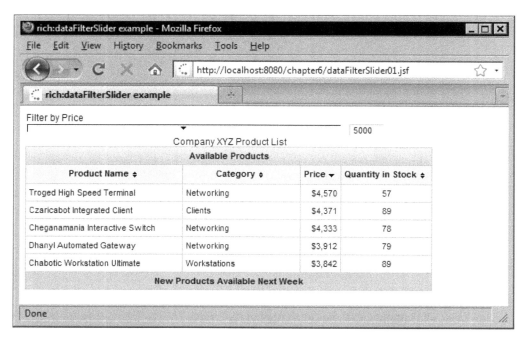

Rendering a data grid

One of the more powerful data components in the RichFaces library is the `HtmlDataGrid` component. This component has similar behavior to a data table, except it renders any arbitrary child components for each item in the data set. The `<rich:dataGrid>` tag has a number of attributes that can control the appearance of the data grid.

We can specify the number of columns in the grid by setting the `columns` attribute. The `elements` attribute specifies how many items should be rendered in the grid. So, for example, if we set the `columns` attribute to three and the `elements` attribute to five, a 2 x 3 grid will be rendered on screen with elements in the first five cells and nothing in the sixth cell.

In this example, we render six random products in a 2 x 3 grid. Each product is rendered as a panel with the product title in the panel header and some information about the product in the body of the panel.

```
<rich:dataGrid width="100%" value="#{productBean.randomProducts}"
    var="product" columns="3" elements="6" cellpadding="5"
    cellspacing="5">
        <rich:panel>
            <f:facet name="header">
                <h:outputText value="#{product.name}" />
            </f:facet>
            <h:panelGrid columns="2" width="100%"
              columnClasses="align-top">
                <h:outputText value="Category:" />
                <h:outputText value="#{product.category.name}" />
                <h:outputText value="Price:" />
                <h:outputText value="#{product.price}">
                    <f:convertNumber type="currency"
                      currencySymbol="$" maxFractionDigits="0" />
                </h:outputText>
                <h:outputText value="In Stock:" />
                <h:panelGroup>
                    <h:outputText value="#{product.quantityInStock}"
                      />
                    <h:graphicImage url="/images/#{product.icon}"
                      style="float:right;" />
                </h:panelGroup>
            </h:panelGrid>
        </rich:panel>
</rich:dataGrid>
```

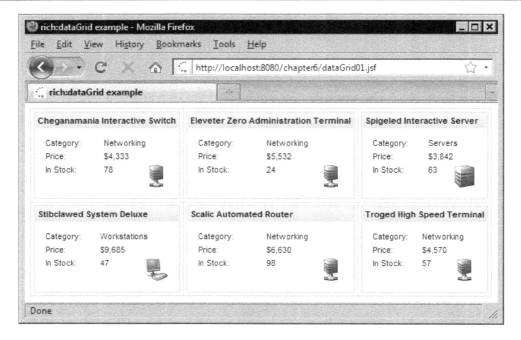

Adding a data scroller

The RichFaces component library includes a powerful component that can be used to add data scrolling behavior to any RichFaces data component. The `<rich:datascroller>` tag has a number of attributes that can affect the behavior and appearance of the data scroller. The most important attribute is the `for` attribute. This attribute specifies which data component the scroller is associated with. The `maxPages` attribute determines the maximum number of pages that can be scrolled. Each page is rendered as a separate numbered cell in the data scroller component.

The `boundaryControls` attribute specifies whether the first and last page navigation controls are rendered, the `fastControls` attribute specifies whether the fast navigation controls are rendered, and the `stepControls` attribute specifies whether the next and previous navigation controls are rendered. Fast navigation controls enable the component to navigate by an arbitrary number of pages across the data set. The fast navigation button is displayed between the step button and the boundary button. The `fastStep` attribute determines how many pages are skipped when scrolling the data set using the fast navigation buttons. The default value is zero, so we set the `fastStep` attribute to 2 to enable the user to skip two pages at a time when scrolling in either direction.

The `boundaryControls`, `fastControls`, and `stepControls` attributes each expect
enumerated values: `show` indicates the controls are always visible, `hide` indicates
the controls are always hidden, and `auto` indicates that unnecessary controls are
automatically hidden.

```
<h:form>
    <rich:dataGrid id="productGrid" value="#{productBean.products}"
        align="center" var="product" columns="3" elements="6"
        border="4" cellpadding="5" cellspacing="3"
        footerClass="centered">
    <f:facet name="caption">
        <h:outputText value="Company XYZ Product List" />
    </f:facet>
    <f:facet name="header">
        <h:outputText value="New Products" />
    </f:facet>
    <f:facet name="footer">
        <h:outputText value="Review Latest Products Every Week" />
    </f:facet>
    <rich:panel>
            <f:facet name="header">
                <h:outputText value="#{product.name}" />
            </f:facet>
            <h:panelGrid columns="2" width="100%"
              columnClasses="align-top">
              <h:outputText value="Category:" />
              <h:outputText value="#{product.category.name}" />
              <h:outputText value="Price:" />
              <h:outputText value="#{product.price}">
                  <f:convertNumber type="currency"
                      currencySymbol="$" maxFractionDigits="0" />
              </h:outputText>
              <h:outputText value="In Stock:" />
              <h:panelGroup>
                  <h:outputText value="#{product.quantityInStock}"
                      />
                  <h:graphicImage url="/images/#{product.icon}"
                      style="float:right;" />
              </h:panelGroup>
            </h:panelGrid>
        </rich:panel>
    </rich:dataGrid>
</h:form>
```

```
<rich:datascroller for="productGrid" maxPages="5" align="center"
    boundaryControls="show" fastControls="show" fastStep="2"
    stepControls="show" page="3" />
</h:form>
```

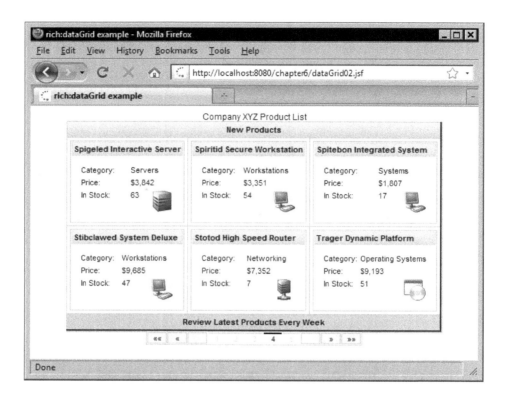

Customizing the data scroller

The RichFaces `<rich:datascroller>` tag allows customization of the appearance of this component. We can control the number of pages scrolled by setting the `maxPages` attribute. We can also specify what is rendered in the page region of the component. The `pageIndexVar` and `pagesVar` attributes specified the names of the component-scoped variables for the current page index and the number of pages. In this example, we use these variables to render information about the current page and the total number of pages within a facet named `pages`.

```
<rich:datascroller align="center" for="productTable" maxPages="3"
    pageIndexVar="pageNumber" pagesVar="numberOfPages">
    <f:facet name="pages">
        <h:outputText value="Page #{pageNumber} / #{numberOfPages}"
        />
```

```
        </f:facet>
    </rich:datascroller>
```

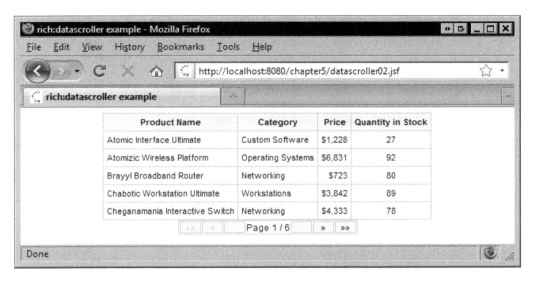

Rendering an ordered list

In the Facelets chapter, we saw how to render a dynamic list using the `<ui:repeat>` tag. In the chapter that covers Apache MyFaces Tomahawk, we saw how to render dynamic data as an ordered list using the Tomahawk `<t:dataList>` tag. The RichFaces library also includes two dynamic list tags: the `<a4j:repeat>` tag and the `<rich:dataOrderedList>` tag. The `<a4j:repeat>` tag is very similar to the `<ui:repeat>` and `<t:dataList>`, except it includes additional behavior to simplify updating individual list items after an Ajax request. The `<rich:dataOrderedList>` tag produces an HTML ordered list from a `List` or `DataModel`. This tag also supports customization through CSS. In this example, we render a list of products as an ordered list. Notice that we set the `value` attribute to a List of objects, and the `var` attribute to the name of the iteration variable for our component. The `<rich:dataOrderedList>` tag also supports a `rows` attribute that can be used to limit the number of items to be displayed. This could be useful in a situation where we are rendering the Top 5 most popular items, for example.

Notice the use of the `type` attribute. This attribute expects an enumerated value defined by the HTML `<ol>` element's `type` attribute specification. The HTML `<ol>` element's `type` attribute accepts an enumerated value from the set "1, A, a, I, i". These values determine which type of list numbering to use:

- **1** indicates an ordered list (1, 2, 3, and so on)

- **A** indicates an uppercase alphabetical list (A, B, C, and so on)

- **a** indicates a lowercase alphabetical list (a, b, c, and so on)

- **I** indicates an uppercase Roman numeral list (I, II, III, and so on)

- **i** indicates a lowercase Roman numeral list (i, ii, iii, and so on)

```
<rich:dataOrderedList value="#{productBean.products}"
    var="product" rows="5" type="1">
    <h:outputText value="#{product.name}" />
    <br />
    <h:outputText value="Price: " />
    <h:outputText value="#{product.price}">
        <f:convertNumber type="currency" currencySymbol="$"
         maxFractionDigits="0" />
    </h:outputText>
    <br />
    <h:outputText value="Quantity: " styleClass="label" />
    <h:outputText value="#{product.quantityInStock} " />
    <br />
    <br />
</rich:dataOrderedList>
```

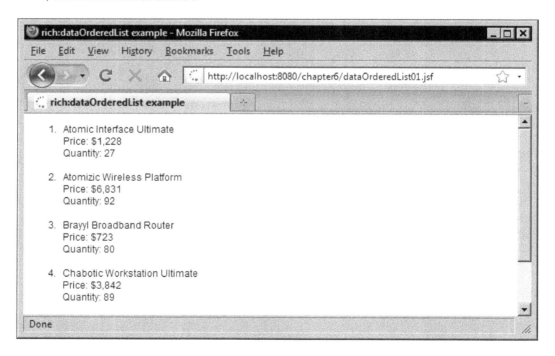

Customizing an ordered list

In this example, we set the type attribute of the <rich:dataOrderedList> tag to the value I. The list now renders its items using uppercase Roman numerals.

```
<rich:dataOrderedList value="#{productBean.products}" var="product"
    rows="5" type="I">
        <h:outputText value="#{product.name}" />
        <br />
        <h:outputText value="Price: " />
        <h:outputText value="#{product.price}">
        <f:convertNumber type="currency" currencySymbol="$"
          maxFractionDigits="0" />
      </h:outputText>
      <br />
      <h:outputText value="Quantity: " styleClass="label" />
      <h:outputText value="#{product.quantityInStock} " />
      <br />
      <br />
</rich:dataOrderedList>
```

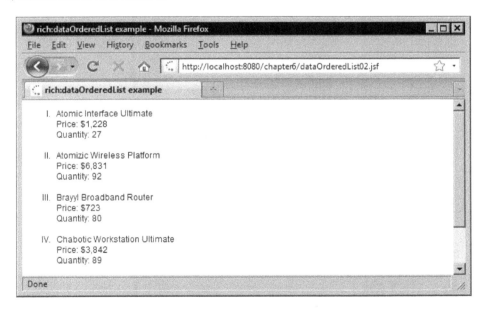

Rendering a data definition list

To render an HTML definition list, we can use the RichFaces
`<rich:dataDefinitionList>` tag. This tag is similar to the
`<rich:dataOrderedList>` tag, except it renders an HTML `<dd>` element instead
of the `<ol>` element. This tag can also be bound to a List or `DataModel` using the
`value` attribute. The `var` attribute specifies the name of the iterator variable to use
while rendering the data. To define the definition term, we declare a `term` facet that
specifies the content to render for the HTML `<dt>` element. The child content of this
tag will be rendered within the HTML `<dd>` element for each item in the list.

```
<rich:dataDefinitionList value="#{productBean.products}" var="product"
    rows="5" columnClasses="left-aligned,left-aligned">
    <f:facet name="term">
        <h:outputText value="#{product.name}" />
    </f:facet>
    <h:outputText value="Price : " styleClass="label" />
    <h:outputText value="#{product.price}">
        <f:convertNumber type="currency" currencySymbol="$"
            maxFractionDigits="0" />
    </h:outputText>
    <br />
    <h:outputText value="Quantity : " styleClass="label" />
    <h:outputText value="#{product.quantityInStock}" />
    <br />
    <br />
</rich:dataDefinitionList>
```

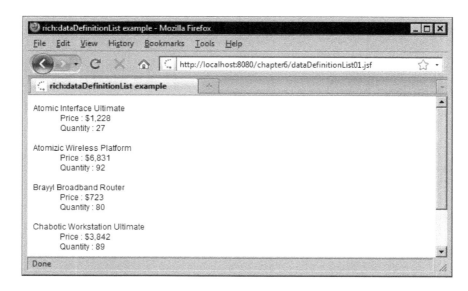

Using special components

The RichFaces component library includes a number of special-purpose components that can be used to enhance the functionality of an existing JSF application. Some examples of these include the RichFaces `HtmlGmap` and `HtmlVirtualEarth` components, which render a Google Maps object and a Microsoft Virtual Earth object respectively.

Rendering a Google Maps object

The `<rich:gmap>` tag can be used to render a Google Maps object on our JSF page. This tag can be combined with Ajax4jsf tags to integrate the Google map with custom JavaScript functions and JSF backing bean data.

In this example, we will be using the JavaScript Object Notation (JSON) to transfer data between our JSF application and web browser. Ajax4jsf supports this data transfer format and automatically serializes our Java objects into JSON data structures.

To begin, we write a new Java class named `Location` that will encapsulate the geographic information needed to display different locations on the map, ensuring the best Ajax performance by limiting the size of our JSON data structures.

```java
package chapter5.model;

import java.io.Serializable;
import java.util.UUID;
/**
 * Simple POJO class for RichFaces JSON data transfer.
 *
 * @author Ian
 *
 */
public class Location implements Serializable {
    /**
     *
     */
    private static final long serialVersionUID = 1L;
    private String id = UUID.randomUUID().toString();
    private double latitude;
    private double longitude;
    private String name;
    private int zoom;

    public Location() {
```

```
    }
    public Location(String name, double latitude, double longitude, int
zoom) {
        super();
        this.latitude = latitude;
        this.longitude = longitude;
        this.name = name;
        this.zoom = zoom; The
    }
    public String getId() {
        return id;
    }
    public double getLatitude() {
        return latitude;
    }
    public double getLongitude() {
        return longitude;
    }
    public String getName() {
        return name;
    }
    public int getZoom() {
        return zoom;
    }
    public void setId(String id) {
        this.id = id;
    }
    public void setLatitude(double latitude) {
        this.latitude = latitude;
    }
    public void setLongitude(double longitude) {
        this.longitude = longitude;
    }
    public void setName(String name) {
        this.name = name;
    }
    public void setZoom(int zoom) {
        this.zoom = zoom;
    }
}
```

Next, we add a backing bean named `MapBean` to work with map-related data and events. Notice that we've added Seam annotations to this class to declare it as a conversation-scoped managed bean. The `getLocations` method prepares and list of `Location` objects that contain the geographic information (the latitude and longitude) needed to display the location in the map.

```
package chapter5.bean;

import java.util.ArrayList;
import java.util.List;

import org.jboss.seam.ScopeType;
import org.jboss.seam.annotations.Name;
import org.jboss.seam.annotations.Scope;

import chapter5.model.Location;

@Name("mapBean")
@Scope(ScopeType.CONVERSATION)
public class MapBean {

    private List<Location> locations;

    private Location selectedLocation;

    private int zoom = 15;

    public Location findLocation(String id) {
        Location found = null;
        for (Location location : getLocations()) {
            if (location.getId().equals(id)) {
                found = location;
                break;
            }
        }
        return found;
    }

    public List<Location> getLocations() {
        if (locations == null) {
            locations = new ArrayList<Location>();
            locations.add(new Location("Eiffel Tower (Paris)", 48.858333,
2.294444, zoom));
            locations.add(new Location("Parthenon (Greece)", 37.971389,
23.726389, zoom));
            locations.add(new Location("Colosseum (Rome)", 41.89,
12.49222, zoom));
        }
        return locations;
    }
```

```
public Location getSelectedLocation() {
   return selectedLocation;
}

public int getZoom() {
   return zoom;
}

public void setSelectedLocation(Location location) {
   this.selectedLocation = location;
}

public void setZoom(int zoom) {
   this.zoom = zoom;
}
}
```

Our next step is to write the JSF markup needed to render a Google map in the view. In this example, we render a simple Google map along with the RichFaces `HtmlInputNumberSlider` component and the standard JSF `HtmlSelectOneMenu` component. The slider component demonstrates how to interact with the Google map using JavaScript to control the zoom level of the map. The drop-down menu component demonstrates how to interact with the Google map using JavaScript to control the location displayed on the map.

Facelets, JSF 1.2, and Google Maps XHTML compatibility

The markup produced by Google Maps is not compatible with strict XHTML, but our document is using the XHTML Transitional DTD which allows for some flexibility so there are no compatibility issues. If were using the XHTML Strict DTD, then we would have to surround our markup with the `<f:view contentType="text/html">` ... `<f:view>` tags.

Also note from the markup that we are using the `<a4j:jsFunction>` tag to render a dynamically generated JavaScript function. This is an example of the technique known as **Runtime Code Generation (RTCG)**. The Ajax4jsf tag enables us to define a JavaScript function declaratively that will be generated when the view is rendered. This function is named `showLocation` and when it is invoked, it calls the Google Maps API to center the map on a new location of our choice.

The data attribute defines a reference to a JSON object named data that will be used within the function. In this case, we use the data object to provide the latitude, longitude, and zoom level information needed to construct a new GLatLng object from the Google Maps API, which we then pass to the setCenter function of the Google map object. Notice that we reference the Google map object by the name map. This variable name is defined using the gmapVar attribute of the <rich:gmap> tag.

The showGScaleControl attribute is set to false to hide the Google Maps scale control. The default value of this attribute is true. To support our use of the <h:selectOneMenu> tag, we specify a custom converter named locationConverter using the converter attribute. We use a custom JavaBean class named Location to encapsulate the location data. As this class is not a JPA entity, we could not use Seam's <s:convertEntity> tag. Therefore, a custom converter was needed. Notice that we use the Seam API Component.getInstance() method to obtain a reference to our "mapBean" Seam-enabled JSF managed bean. The converter class source code is as follows:

```
package chapter6.converter;
import javax.faces.component.UIComponent;
import javax.faces.context.FacesContext;
import javax.faces.convert.Converter;
import org.jboss.seam.Component;
import chapter6.bean.MapBean;
import chapter6.model.Location;
/**
 * This converter class handles Location object conversion. Because
the Location
 * class is not a JPA entity, we are using a custom converter instead
of Seam's
 * built-in JPA entity converter.
 *
 * @author Ian
 *
 */
public class LocationConverter implements Converter {
    public Object getAsObject(FacesContext context, UIComponent
                              component, String value) {
        Object result = null;
        if (value != null) {
            MapBean bean = (MapBean) Component.getInstance("mapBean");
            result = bean.findLocation(value);
        }
        return result;
    }
    public String getAsString(FacesContext context, UIComponent
                              component, Object value) {
```

```
        String result = null;
        if (value instanceof Location) {
           result = ((Location) value).getId();
        } else {
           result = String.valueOf(value);
        }
        return result;
   }
}
```

The following markup demonstrates how to use the `<rich:gmap>` tag on a JSF page. Notice that we use the Google Map JavaScript API in the `oncomplete` attribute of our `<a4j:jsFunction>` tag to control the map location and zoom.

```
<!DOCTYPE html PUBLIC "-//W3C//DTD XHTML 1.0 Transitional//EN"
"http://www.w3.org/TR/xhtml1/DTD/xhtml1-transitional.dtd">
<html xmlns="http://www.w3.org/1999/xhtml" xmlns:h="http://
java.sun.com/jsf/html" xmlns:rich="http://richfaces.org/rich"
xmlns:a4j="http://richfaces.org/a4j" xmlns:f="http://java.sun.com/jsf/
core" xmlns:s="http://jboss.com/products/seam/taglib">
<head>
<meta http-equiv="Content-Type" content="text/html; charset=utf-8" />
<title>rich:gmap example</title>
<a4j:loadStyle src="./css/style.css" /></head>
<body>
    <h:form id="mapForm">
          <a4j:jsFunction name="showLocation"
              data="#{mapBean.selectedLocation}" reRender="zoom"
              oncomplete="map.setCenter(new GLatLng(data.latitude,
                                  data.longitude),data.zoom)" />
     <h:panelGrid columns="2">
       <rich:inputNumberSlider id="zoom" showInput="false" minValue="1"
           maxValue="18" onchange="map.setZoom(this.value)" />
       <h:selectOneMenu value="#{mapBean.selectedLocation}"
         converter="locationConverter">
         <s:selectItems noSelectionLabel="Select Location"
           value="#{mapBean.locations}"
           var="item" label="#{item.name}" />
         <a4j:support event="onchange" oncomplete="showLocation()" />
       </h:selectOneMenu>
     </h:panelGrid>
       <rich:gmap id="gmap" gmapVar="map" mapType="G_NORMAL_MAP"
           showGScaleControl="#{false}" />
    </h:form>
</body>
</html>
```

In the previous example, when the user selects one of the locations from the drop-down menu, the selected location is instantly displayed in the Google map. How does this work? Notice that we have added a child `<a4j:support>` tag to our `<h:selectOneMenu>` tag. We set the `event` attribute to `onchange` to indicate that Ajax4jsf should fire an Ajax request to submit the form data to the server when the component's value changes. When the Ajax request is complete, the `oncomplete` attribute informs Ajax4jsf to invoke the custom JavaScript function named `showLocation()`. Ajax4jsf obtains the selected `Location` object from our managed bean, serializes it as a JSON data structure, invokes our custom `showLocation` JavaScript function and the Google map is updated.

The following screenshot shows a hybrid map view of the Parthenon in Greece that results from the user selecting the second item in the list.

Rendering a Microsoft Virtual Earth object

The RichFaces component library includes another special-purpose component that can render a Microsoft Virtual Earth object, or a Microsoft Bing Map as it is now called. We can use the same backing bean and model object for this example as we used in the Google Maps example. In fact, the only difference between this example and the Google Maps example is the use of the `<rich:virtualEarth>` tag and the implementation of the `setLocation` JavaScript function, as shown in the following markup. Notice in the `oncomplete` attribute of our `<a4j:jsFunction>` tag that we use the Microsoft Virtual Earth JavaScript API to control the map location and zoom level.

```
<html xmlns:rich="http://richfaces.org/rich" xmlns:a4j="http://
richfaces.org/a4j" xmlns:h="http://java.sun.com/jsf/html"
xmlns:s="http://jboss.com/products/seam/taglib" xmlns:f="http://java.
sun.com/jsf/core">
<head>
<meta http-equiv="Content-Type" content="text/html; charset=utf-8" />
<title>rich:virtualEarth example</title>
<a4j:loadStyle src="./css/style.css" />
</head>
<body>
<h:form>
    <a4j:jsFunction name="showLocation"
        data="#{mapBean.selectedLocation}" reRender="zoom"
        oncomplete="map.SetCenterAndZoom(new VELatLong(data.latitude,
                                  data.longitude), data.zoom)" />
    <rich:virtualEarth id="gm" style="width:500px"
        dashboardSize="Normal" mapStyle="Birdseye" var="map" />
    <h:panelGrid columns="2">
        <rich:inputNumberSlider id="zoom" value="#{mapBean.zoom}"
            showInput="false" minValue="1" maxValue="19"
            onchange="map.SetZoomLevel(this.value)" />
        <h:selectOneMenu value="#{mapBean.selectedLocation}"
            converter="locationConverter">
          <s:selectItems noSelectionLabel="Select Location"
            value="#{mapBean.locations}" var="item"
            label="#{item.name}" />
            <a4j:support event="onchange" oncomplete="showLocation()" />
        </h:selectOneMenu>
    </h:panelGrid>
</h:form>
</body>
</html>
```

The following screenshot shows the Eiffel Tower displayed in a birdseye view using the Microsoft Virtual Earth API.

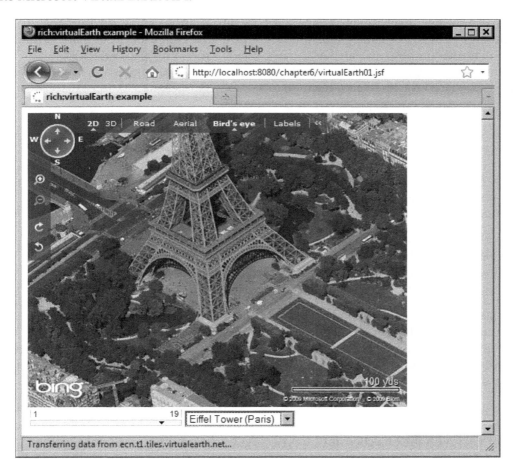

Summary

In this chapter, we explored how the RichFaces and Ajax4jsf component libraries can be combined to create next generation JSF applications using the full Java EE technology stack. We looked at examples of how to accept user input using a range of advanced components, such as the in-place input and in-place select, number slider, number spinbox, calendar, color picker, combo box, suggestion box, pick list, and rich text editor RichFaces components.

The JBoss RichFaces and Ajax4jsf component libraries add a wealth of Ajax capabilities to existing JSF applications. To use Ajax effectively, we learned how to invoke an Ajax request using the Ajax4jsf `<a4j:commandButton>` and `<a4j:commandLink>` tags, how to add Ajax capabilities to other JSF components using the `<a4j:support>` tag, and how to poll the server using the `<a4j:poll>` tag. We also examined a number of ways to minimize client/server communication, reduce the size of JSON data structures, and optimize Ajax performance.

The RichFaces component library includes a number of useful components for laying out elements on the screen using panels. We looked at the basic RichFaces panel component, panel bar component, the panel menu component, the tabbed panel component, and the toggle panel component.

We also looked at how to render dynamic data using RichFaces components. We examined the RichFaces data table component, and we learn how to add sorting, filtering, and scrolling behavior to a data table. The RichFaces data grid component can also be used to render dynamic data, and is also compatible with the RichFaces data scroller component.

Finally, we examined some special-purpose RichFaces components. We learn how to render an interactive Google Maps object or Microsoft Virtual Earth object, and how to interact with the objects using Ajax4jsf tags and a custom JavaScript function.

Learning JSF: Next Steps

This book explored a number of popular JSF component libraries with the goal of providing the most useful information possible to help JSF developers get up to speed quickly with the many excellent JSF UI components available today.

The JSF ecosystem is in constant evolution, and new JSF technologies are being released at a rapid pace. It is not possible (or sensible) to try to cover everything in one book, so this appendix serves as a guidepost for further study on JSF topics that could not be covered here.

We will take a quick look at some new and upcoming JSF developments that are worth noting:

- JSF 2.0: The next generation of the JSF framework
- PrimeFaces: An outstanding UI component library

JSF 2.0

Perhaps the most important change in the history of JSF is the release of JSF 2.0. JSF 1.0 was the initial release of the framework, and it was a bit rough around the edges. Therefore, JSF 1.1 and JSF 1.2 were subsequently released to address some of the minor shortcomings of the framework and to provide enhancements to support developers.

JSF 2.0, however, is a significant step forward in the evolution of the JSF framework, with several important new features and improvements, including:

- New JSF annotations added to ease configuration
- A simplified navigation mapping convention
- A web resource loading mechanism for images, stylesheets, JavaScript files, and so on
- Facelets is now integrated into the core JSF framework

- The new "composite" JSF tag library for creating composite components
- Built-in support for adding Ajax capabilities to UI components with `<f:ajax>`

Let's look at how each of these features work. This is not intended to provide complete coverage, but rather a brief introduction to JSF 2.0.

New JSF annotations added to ease configuration

Before JSF 2.0, and without the benefit of the Seam framework, JSF developers needed to declare each managed bean in `faces-config.xml`. Maintaining two separate files for one application artifact (the managed bean) adds overhead to the JSF development cycle. Therefore, a number of new annotations were added to simplify and centralize JSF configuration metadata into managed bean classes themselves:

- `@ManagedBean`: This annotation must be applied before the managed bean Java class declaration and replaces the `<managed-bean>` element in `faces-config.xml`.

- `@ManagedProperty`: This annotation must be applied before the instance variable of a JSF managed bean property and replaces the `<managed-property>` element in `faces-config.xml`.

- `@RequestScoped`, `@SessionScoped`, `@ApplicationScoped`, `@NoneScoped`, `@ViewScoped`, and `@CustomScoped`: One of these annotations may be applied before the managed bean Java class declaration. These annotations replace the `<managed-bean-scope>` element and enable applications to define custom bean scopes.

These new annotations eliminate the need to use XML to declare managed beans. Therefore, our `faces-config.xml` file now looks like so. Notice that the `<faces-config>` XML element now has the version "2.0" and references a different XSD file. Also notice the absence of any managed bean declarations.

faces-config.xml (JSF 2.0)

```
<?xml version="1.0" encoding="UTF-8"?>
<faces-config xmlns="http://java.sun.com/xml/ns/javaee"
    xmlns:xsi="http://www.w3.org/2001/XMLSchema-instance"
    xsi:schemaLocation="http://java.sun.com/xml/ns/javaee
    http://java.sun.com/xml/ns/javaee/web-facesconfig_2_0.xsd"
    version="2.0">
```

```
<application>
        <resource-bundle>
                <base-name>messages</base-name>
                <var>bundle</var>
        </resource-bundle>
        <locale-config>
                <default-locale>en</default-locale>
                <supported-locale>fr</supported-locale>
                <supported-locale>es</supported-locale>
        </locale-config>
</application>
<converter>
        <description>This converter handles conversion between
        String and Country objects.</description>
        <display-name>Country Converter</display-name>
        <converter-id>countryConverter</converter-id>
    <converter-class>jsf2.converter.CountryConverter
    </converter-class>
</converter>
<validator>
        <description>This birthdate validator checks a date to make
        sure it is within the last 120 years.</description>
        <display-name>Custom Date Validator</display-name>
        <validator-id>customDateValidator</validator-id>
        <validator-class>jsf2.validator.CustomDateValidator
    </validator-class>
</validator>
</faces-config>
```

Our managed bean classes are now annotated as follows:

BackingBean.java

```
package jsf2.bean;

import javax.faces.bean.ManagedBean;
import javax.faces.bean.RequestScoped;

@ManagedBean
@RequestScoped
public class BackingBean {

    ...

}
```

CustomerBean.java

```
package jsf2.bean;
import javax.faces.bean.ManagedBean;
import javax.faces.bean.SessionScoped;
@ManagedBean
@SessionScoped
public class CustomerBean {

    ...

}
```

Simplified navigation mapping convention

The JSF 2.0 release introduces a simplified navigation mapping convention that can also reduce XML configuration. Instead of declaring navigation rules and outcomes in `faces-config.xml` and then referencing these outcomes in the `action` attributes of the JSF tags for command buttons and links, we can now simply specify the view ID (the file name without the file extension) and the JSF framework will infer the correct view from the `action` attribute.

JSF 1.x Navigation Mapping

The more verbose style of navigation mapping from JSF 1.x is demonstrated below.

shoppingCart.jsf

```
<h:commandButton value="Checkout" action="checkout" />
```

faces-config.xml

```
<navigation-rule>
  <navigation-case>
    <from-view-id>/shoppingCart.jsf</from-view-id>
    <outcome>checkout</outcome>
    <to-view-id>/checkout.jsf</to-view-id>
  </navigation-case>
</navigation-rule>
```

JSF 2.0 Navigation Mapping

The simpler, convention-based navigation mapping style from JSF 2.0 is demonstrated next. It is functionally equivalent to the previous example, but does not require any navigation rules to be declared in `faces-config.xml`.

shoppingCart.jsf

```
<h:commandButton value="Checkout" action="checkout" />
```

When the **Checkout** button is pressed, the JSF framework looks for a view in the same directory as `shoppingCart.jsf` named `checkout.jsf` (or whatever file extension is used for the `javax.faces.FACELETS_VIEW_MAPPINGS` context parameter in `web.xml`) and navigates to that view after processing the event.

If the destination view is in another directory, we can use a leading slash / character to specify an absolute path to the view.

We can also indicate that a redirect is required like so:

```
<h:commandButton value="Checkout"
  action="checkout?faces-redirect=true" />
```

A Web resource loading mechanism for images, stylesheets, JavaScript files, and so on

One of the enhancements to JSF 2.0 is a resource loading mechanism for web page artifacts, such as images, cascading style sheets, and JavaScript files; resources such as these can be packaged inside a web application's root directory or a JAR file.

To include resources in a web application, we must create a folder named `resources` below the Web root folder. To include resources in a JAR file, we must create a folder named `resources` below the `META-INF` folder of the JAR file. Any files under the resources directory can be loaded by JSF at request time. The organization of files below the resources directory is up to the developer. A good practice is to create the following directory structure for static resources:

- /resources/css: Cascading stylesheets (`*.css`)
- /resources/images: Image files (`*.gif`, `*.jpg`, `*.png`,and so on)
- /resources/javascript: JavaScript files (`*.js`)
- /resources/media: Flash files and other multimedia (`*.swf`, `*.mp3`, and so on)
- /resources/components: Composite JSF components (`*.xhtml` - covered in next section)

One of the advantages of this feature is the ability to reference classpath resources using EL expressions. JSF 2.0 introduces a new implicit object to the JSF EL, the "resource" map. This map can be used to obtain resources for rendering at request time, as shown in the following example:

```
<h:graphicImage value="#{resource['images:icon.gif']}" />
```

The map argument in the EL expression is a String literal specifying the resource library followed by a colon character followed by the resource name. The resource library is the directory below the `resources` directory. The resource name is the filename of the resource.

An alternative to using the `resources` implicit EL object is to use the new `library` and `name` attributes of the `<h:graphicImage>`, `<h:outputScript>`, and `<h:outputStylesheet>` JSF tags. Therefore, the following example is functionally equivalent to the previous one:

```
<h:graphicImage library="images" name="icon.gif" />
```

The HTML produced by this example is as follows. Notice that the `src` attribute value is identical for both images.

```
<!DOCTYPE html PUBLIC "-//W3C//DTD XHTML 1.0 Transitional//EN"
"http://www.w3.org/TR/xhtml1/DTD/xhtml1-transitional.dtd">
<html xmlns="http://www.w3.org/1999/xhtml">
<head>
<meta http-equiv="Content-Type" content="text/html; charset=utf-8" />
<title>JSF 2.0 Example</title>
</head>
<body>
<img src="/jsf2/javax.faces.resource/icon.gif.jsf?ln=images" />
<img src="/jsf2/javax.faces.resource/icon.gif.jsf?ln=images" />
</body>
</html>
```

Facelets is now integrated in JSF 2.0

Another great feature of JSF 2.0 is that the Facelets view definition framework that we know and love, is now integrated into the core JSF framework. This means that a separate `jsf-facelets.jar` file is no longer needed when deploying a JSF 2.0 application, and specifying the `FaceletViewHandler` in the `<view-handler>` element in `faces-config.xml` is also no longer necessary provided that the `version` attribute of the `faces-config` element in `faces-config.xml` is set to "2.0".

The new "composite" JSF tag library for creating composite components

One of the coolest features of JSF 2.0 is the ability to create composite components using declarative markup. We can now create advanced UI components that are composed of other UI components without writing any Java code.

One of the principles emphasized in JSF 2.0 is convention over configuration. This means that we can spend more time actually building JSF applications, and less time writing configuration files. This is especially apparent with the new JSF 2.0 composite components feature.

JSF 2.0 introduces a new tag library named "composite" for declaring composite components. A **composite component** can be a typical Facelets XHTML document that uses special tags to declare a component interface and a component implementation. The following "Hello World" example demonstrates the key concepts behind how to create a composite UI component.

/resources/components/helloworld/hello.xhtml

```
<!DOCTYPE html PUBLIC "-//W3C//DTD XHTML 1.0 Transitional//EN"
"http://www.w3.org/TR/xhtml1/DTD/xhtml1-transitional.dtd">
<html xmlns="http://www.w3.org/1999/xhtml" xmlns:h="http://java.sun.
com/jsf/html" xmlns:composite="http://java.sun.com/jsf/composite">
<head>
<meta http-equiv="Content-Type" content="text/html; charset=utf-8" />
<title>JSF 2.0 Example</title>
</head>
<body>

  <!-- Component interface -->
  <composite:interface>
    <composite:attribute name="name" />
    <composite:attribute name="actionListener"
         method-signature="void sayHello(javax.faces.event.
                                         ActionEvent)"
       />
  </composite:interface>

  <!-- Component implementation -->
  <composite:implementation>
    <h:form>
      <h:panelGrid>
        <h:panelGroup>
          <h:outputLabel value="Enter your name: " />
          <h:inputText value="#{cc.attrs.name}" />
```

```
        <h:commandButton value="Say Hello"
            actionListener="#{cc.attrs.actionListener}" />
        </h:panelGroup>
        <h:outputText value="Hello, #{cc.attrs.name}!"
          rendered="#{cc.attrs.name ne null}" />
      </h:panelGrid>
    </h:form>
  </composite:implementation>
</body>
</html>
```

Let's discuss the previous example in detail. First, notice the path of the filename. The file for our composite component is named `/resources/components/helloworld/hello.xhtml`. The `helloworld` directory of the file defines the tag library, and the file name (without the file extension) defines our tag name. Simply by creating the file we are effectively declaring a new tag named "hello" in our "helloworld" custom tag library.

Next, notice the declaration of the "composite" XML namespace to import the new composite components tag library. This tag library provides JSF infrastructural support that enable developers to declare composite components.

Next, notice that the `<body>` tag contains two child tags, a `<composite:interface>` tag and a `<composite:implementation>` tag. The code outside these tags will not be used, but by defining our component in a complete XHTML document we can edit the document more easily with typical web authoring tools.

The `<composite:interface>` tag is responsible for specifying the composite component's interface. Think of the attribute names and values that will be accepted by our custom tag. In our example, the "hello" tag has two attributes, a `name` attribute and an `actionListener` attribute. Also notice that the `actionListener` attribute expects a JSF EL method expression that resolves to a Java method with the signature `void sayHello(javax.faces.event.ActionEvent)`. This signature is interpreted by the JSF framework to mean "any void method that accepts a `javax.faces.event.ActionEvent parameter`". The name of the method is not important, and the parameter variable is not specified.

The `<composite:implementation>` tag is responsible for defining the implementation details of our composite component. Here we can see that the component will render an `<h:form>` tag that contains an `<h:panelGrid>` tag with a label, text field, command button, and text message. Notice that we are using a new implicit EL object named "cc" for "composite component". The `attrs` property of the `cc` object is a map that has as its keys the names of the attributes we specified in our `<composite:interface>` declaration. The values of the map are the values assigned to the attributes (if any) when our composite component is used in a JSF view. Essentially, we are "passing through" any literal values or EL expressions specified by the page author to the components used in our composite component implementation.

Now that we understand how to define composite components, let's look at how to use them in a JSF view. In the following example, we render a simple Facelets page that includes a new namespace we have not seen before. Notice the declaration of the "helloworld" namespace. The URL for this namespace is `http://java.sun.com/jsf/composite/components/helloworld`. The important part of this URL is `http://java.sun.com/jsf/composite`. JSF will simply try to resolve the URL by looking for a composite component library below our `/resources` directory that has a folder structure that matches the part of the URL that remains when the "composite" namespace URL is removed.

So our "helloworld" namespace declaration instructs the framework to look for a folder named `/resources/components/helloworld` in the root of our web application. All composite component libraries follow this naming convention. As long as the directory structure and the namespace declaration are consistent, JSF will be able to locate our composite components.

Next we declare our `<helloworld:hello>` tag and set some of its attributes. Here we can use the typical JSF EL value expressions and method expressions that we are accustomed to using. Remember that the JSF composite component infrastructure will pass along the EL expressions to the actual underlying UI components (the text field and command button).

index.jsf

```
<!DOCTYPE html PUBLIC "-//W3C//DTD XHTML 1.0 Transitional//EN"
"http://www.w3.org/TR/xhtml1/DTD/xhtml1-transitional.dtd">
<html xmlns="http://www.w3.org/1999/xhtml" xmlns:h="http://java.
sun.com/jsf/html" xmlns:ui="http://java.sun.com/jsf/facelets"
xmlns:helloworld=
     "http://java.sun.com/jsf/composite/components/helloworld">
<head>
<meta http-equiv="Content-Type" content="text/html; charset=utf-8" />
<title>JSF 2.0 Example</title>
```

```
</head>
<body>
  <helloworld:hello name="#{backingBean.name}"
            actionListener="#{backingBean.sayHello}" />
</body>
</html>
```

The result of requesting this page in the browser is shown in the next screenshot. Thanks to JSF 2.0 composite components, we are now able to reuse and combine UI components in new and interesting ways to create new components, without writing a single line of Java code.

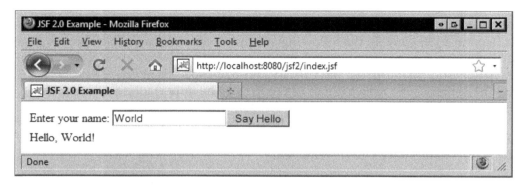

Built-in support for adding Ajax capabilities to UI components with <f:ajax>

Solving the Ajax problem is one of the crowning achievements of JSF 2.0. One of the problems with the numerous Ajax-enabled JSF component libraries available today is that they cannot be combined together, due to conflicts between their respective Ajax JavaScript libraries. The JSF Expert Group recognized this problem and spent considerable effort to find a working solution.

After consultations with the OpenAjax Alliance—an independent organization made up of vendors and open source software developers that is committed to the standardization and interoperability of Ajax solutions—the JSF framework now has its own Ajax JavaScript namespace. What this means is that JSF component developers can now use a single Ajax JavaScript API to ensure the compatibility of their components with those from other developers.

In addition to standardizing Ajax for the JSF framework, JSF 2.0 introduces another cool feature: the `<f:ajax>` tag. This new tag has been added to the JSF Core tag library and provides behavior similar to the `<a4j:support>` tag from the Ajax4jsf tag library. Like the `<a4j:support>` tag, the `<f:ajax>` tag can also add Ajax capabilities to other JSF components, even those that have no built-in Ajax behavior.

The `<f:ajax>` tag has a number of attributes, but we will focus on three of them to get a better understanding of how this tag can be used. Let's enhance our "Hello World" composite component example by adding Ajax behavior to our form. Notice that we have created a new composite component file for this example named `helloAjax.xhtml`. With minor exceptions, it is identical to the previous example.

/resources/components/helloworld/helloAjax.xhtml

```
<!DOCTYPE html PUBLIC "-//W3C//DTD XHTML 1.0 Transitional//EN"
"http://www.w3.org/TR/xhtml1/DTD/xhtml1-transitional.dtd">
<html xmlns="http://www.w3.org/1999/xhtml" xmlns:f="http://java.sun.
com/jsf/core" xmlns:h="http://java.sun.com/jsf/html" xmlns:ui="http://
java.sun.com/jsf/facelets" xmlns:composite="http://java.sun.com/jsf/
composite">
<head>
<meta http-equiv="Content-Type" content="text/html; charset=utf-8" />
<title>JSF 2.0 Example</title>
</head>
<body>
  <!-- Component interface -->
  <composite:interface>
    <composite:attribute name="name" />
    <composite:attribute name="actionListener"
         method-signature="void sayHello(javax.faces.event.
                                         ActionEvent)"
      />
  </composite:interface>
  <!-- Component implementation -->
  <composite:implementation>
    <h:form>
      <h:panelGrid>
        <h:panelGroup>
          <h:outputLabel value="Enter your name: " />
          <h:inputText id="input" value="#{cc.attrs.name}" />
          <h:commandButton value="Say Hello"
            actionListener="#{cc.attrs.actionListener}">
            <f:ajax execute="@this input" render="text" />
```

```
            </h:commandButton>
          </h:panelGroup>
            <h:panelGroup id="text">
            <h:outputText value="Hello, #{cc.attrs.name}!"
              rendered="#{cc.attrs.name ne null}" />
            </h:panelGroup>
        </h:panelGrid>
      </h:form>
    </composite:implementation>
  </body>
</html>
```

Notice the `<f:ajax>` tag nested inside the `<h:commandButton>` tag. As we know, using Ajax is a two-step process; the first step is to define which components should be included in the request, and the second step is to define which components should be updated in the view when the Ajax request is complete. The `<f:ajax>` tag in the previous example has an `execute` attribute that specifies which components should be included in the Ajax request. In this way it is similar to the `process` attribute of the `<a4j:support>` tag. Here we specify the value `@this input` for the `execute` attribute. The keyword "@this" is part of a small set of reserved keywords which are new in JSF 2.0, and implies the parent UI component (the command button in this case). The "input" value is the ID of the text field component.

As we can see, the `execute` attribute accepts a space-separated list of keywords and/or component identifiers and indicates which components should be processed in the request. In this scenario, the text field's value will be submitted to the server, and the command button's `actionListener` method will be invoked on the server during the JSF request processing lifecycle. We could have simply specified `@form` in the `execute` attribute to indicate that the form all its child components are to be included in the Ajax request, but this example takes a more fine-grained approach to Ajax communication which also gives us the opportunity to learn more about the new `<f:ajax>` tag.

Next, notice the render attribute on the `<f:ajax>` tag. This attribute is similar to the `reRender` attribute of the `<a4j:support>` tag. Like the `execute` attribute, the `render` attribute accepts a space-separated list of keywords and/or component identifiers to indicate which component(s) should be updated in the view when the Ajax request is completed. In this example, we specify that the `<h:panelGroup>` tag containing the text message should be rendered.

Note that we had to move the component identifier from the `<h:outputText>` tag to the `<h:panelGroup>` tag because the `<h:outputText>` tag is not rendered unless the user enters a value, therefore when the user clicks the button for the first time, an Ajax request is sent and the view is only partially updated, but as the text message was not rendered the first time, JSF is unable to update that component in the view. By specifying the parent component, we are able to dynamically update the text message in the view and work around this issue.

The JSF page that uses our new and improved Ajaxified "Hello World" composite component is very similar to the previous example. As we can see from the source code below, the only difference is the use of the `<helloworld:helloAjax>` tag instead of the `<helloworld:hello>` tag. Once again, convention over configuration is the rule here, and JSF knows where to look to find our newly defined composite component. It will search for a file named `helloAjax.xhtml` in the `/resources/components/helloworld` directory at the root of our web application.

```
<!DOCTYPE html PUBLIC "-//W3C//DTD XHTML 1.0 Transitional//EN"
"http://www.w3.org/TR/xhtml1/DTD/xhtml1-transitional.dtd">
<html xmlns="http://www.w3.org/1999/xhtml" xmlns:h="http://java.
sun.com/jsf/html" xmlns:ui="http://java.sun.com/jsf/facelets"
xmlns:helloworld="http://java.sun.com/jsf/composite/components/
helloworld">
<h:head>
<meta http-equiv="Content-Type" content="text/html; charset=utf-8" />
<title>JSF 2.0 Example</title>
</h:head>
<body>
  <helloworld:helloAjax name="#{backingBean.name}"
            actionListener="#{backingBean.sayHello}" />
</body>
</html>
```

To summarize, JSF 2.0 introduces a number of excellent new features that significantly enhance JSF development, such as new JSF annotations added to ease configuration, simpler navigation mapping, a Web resource loading mechanism, direct integration of the Facelets framework, composite components, and built-in Ajax support. Now that we have covered what's new in JSF 2.0, let's look at another exciting development in the JSF ecosystem: the PrimeFaces component library.

The PrimeFaces component library

While titans such as ICEfaces, Apache MyFaces Trinidad, JBoss RichFaces, and Ajax4jsf have dominated the Ajax-enabled JSF component landscape, another open source project has quietly been building momentum and is set to raise the bar for professional grade Ajax-based JSF component libraries. That project is PrimeFaces (`http://primefaces.prime.com.tr`), and with more than 70 high quality UI components, this library is definitely worth checking out. Some of the more interesting components in the PrimeFaces library include:

- An accordion component (renders vertically expanding panels)
- A breadcrumb component (includes icons and automatically stretches to reveal text)
- An autocomplete component (supports skinning and animation)
- A CAPTCHA component (to add security features to JSF pages)
- A carousel component (supports horizontal scrolling for image collections)
- A number of chart components (pie, line, column, stacked column, bar, and so on)
- A collector component (simplifies working with Java collections)
- A color picker component (RGB, HSV, hexadecimal modes)
- A data exporter component (supports Excel, PDF, CSV, and XML)
- A dock component (similar to the dock on the Mac OS X desktop)
- An effect component (supports multiple effects, for example, blind, clip, drop, fold, and so on)
- A growl component (renders JSF FacesMessages as floating panels similar to Mac OS X)
- An idle monitor component (renders a pop-up message if no user activity)
- A layout component (supports a resizable split pane orientation)
- A light box component (for image slideshows)
- A password strength component (measures password strength, displays a bar)
- A terminal component (renders an interactive console)
- A wizard component (supports multistep screen navigation)
- Many more!

Next steps

Our journey into JSF has just begun. Learning to use existing JSF components is just the beginning. Our next challenge is to learn how to write custom JSF components.

Index

Thank you for buying
JSF 1.2 Components

About Packt Publishing

Packt, pronounced 'packed', published its first book "*Mastering phpMyAdmin for Effective MySQL Management*" in April 2004 and subsequently continued to specialize in publishing highly focused books on specific technologies and solutions.

Our books and publications share the experiences of your fellow IT professionals in adapting and customizing today's systems, applications, and frameworks. Our solution based books give you the knowledge and power to customize the software and technologies you're using to get the job done. Packt books are more specific and less general than the IT books you have seen in the past. Our unique business model allows us to bring you more focused information, giving you more of what you need to know, and less of what you don't.

Packt is a modern, yet unique publishing company, which focuses on producing quality, cutting-edge books for communities of developers, administrators, and newbies alike. For more information, please visit our website: www.packtpub.com.

Writing for Packt

We welcome all inquiries from people who are interested in authoring. Book proposals should be sent to author@packtpub.com. If your book idea is still at an early stage and you would like to discuss it first before writing a formal book proposal, contact us; one of our commissioning editors will get in touch with you.

We're not just looking for published authors; if you have strong technical skills but no writing experience, our experienced editors can help you develop a writing career, or simply get some additional reward for your expertise.

Apache MyFaces Trinidad 1.2: A Practical Guide

ISBN: 978-1-847196-08-8   Paperback: 292 pages

Develop JSF web applications with Trinidad and Seam

1. Develop rich client web applications using the most powerful integration of modern web technologies

2. Covers working with Seam security, internationalization using Seam, and more

3. Get well-versed in developing key areas of web applications

4. A step-by-step approach that will help you strengthen your understanding of all the major concepts

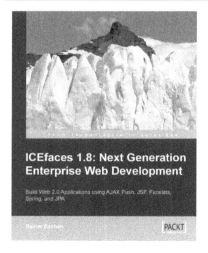

ICEfaces 1.8: Next Generation Enterprise Web Development

ISBN: 978-1-847197-24-5   Paperback: 292 pages

Build Web 2.0 Applications using AJAX Push, JSF, Facelets, Spring and JPA

1. Develop a full-blown Web application using ICEfaces

2. Design and use self-developed components using Facelets technology

3. Integrate AJAX into a JEE stack for Web 2.0 developers using JSF, Facelets, Spring, JPA

Please check **www.PacktPub.com** for information on our titles

Seam 2.x Web Development

ISBN: 978-1-847195-92-0   Paperback: 300 pages

Build robust web applications with Seam, Facelets, and RichFaces using the JBoss application server

1. Develop rich web applications using Seam 2.x, Facelets, and RichFaces and deploy them on the JBoss Application Server

2. Integrate standard technologies like JSF, Facelets, EJB, and JPA with Seam and build on them using additional Seam components

3. Informative and practical approach to development with fully working examples and source code for each chapter of the book

Tomcat 6 Developer's Guide

ISBN: 978-1-847197-28-3   Paperback: 416 pages

Build better web applications by learning how a servlet container actually works.

1. Take your Java EE web programming skills to the next level by getting an expert's level understanding of the servlet specification and its reference implementation, Apache Tomcat.

2. Build a Tomcat distribution from its source code, and explore the components, classes, and technologies that make up this container.

3. Use standard development tools such as Eclipse, Ant, and Subversion to dissect a Tomcat distribution.

www.ingramcontent.com/pod-product-compliance
Lightning Source LLC
Chambersburg PA
CBHW081505050326
40690CB00015B/2932